MAKERS OF THE TWENTIETH CENTURY

General editor Alan Bullock

ARTUS

Self-portrait by Pablo Picasso, 1906

Illustrations on previous page:
ABOVE LEFT *Edmund Hillary with Sherpa Tenzing (left) near the summit of Everest;* ABOVE RIGHT *Pele playing for the USA in 1976;* BELOW LEFT *Violinist Yehudi Menuhin* BELOW RIGHT *Paul Ehrlich at work in his laboratory*

Copyright © Weidenfeld and Nicolson 1981

First published in 1981 by Artus Publishing Co. Ltd
91 Clapham High Street, London SW4 7TA

All rights reserved

Designed by Martin Richards

Picture research by Lucy Shankleman and Janey Beamish

Colour separations by Newsele Litho Ltd
Filmset by Keyspools Ltd, Golborne, Lancashire
Printed and bound by LEGO, Vicenza, Italy

Contributors

RC	–	Richard Cavendish
D de V	–	Dirk de Villiers
CD	–	Craig Dodd
RE	–	Roger Eglin
BG	–	Benny Green
PG	–	Peter Gillman
GH	–	Georgina Howell
IJ	–	Ian Jarvey
NM	–	Nicholas Mason
SM	–	Sheridan Morley
GN	–	Graham Norton
TO	–	Tony Osman
CO	–	Charles Osborne
GP	–	George Perry
RT	–	Robert Taylor
AW	–	Alan Wilkinson
SW	–	Stephen Wood

Chairman Mao of Communist China

Contents

Introduction

The most interesting part of editing this book has been the argument about who should be included and who should be left out. And now that the list has been settled the argument is likely to be renewed by the readers, for this is a matter on which no two people are likely to agree. Of course there are some names that have to be in: Churchill, Roosevelt, Lenin, Stalin and Mao Tse-tung among political leaders; Picasso and Matisse among painters; Einstein, Max Planck and Rutherford among scientists; Freud and Keynes among thinkers; Toscanini and Casals among musicians; the playwright Bertolt Brecht; the poet W.B. Yeats, and the greatest of clowns, Charlie Chaplin.

But once you have drawn up this core list, there are a thousand or more names that have to be weighed and balanced against each other, and then personal preferences begin to tell. How *many* scientists, for example – some of whom may have changed all our lives but whose names are barely known outside the scientific world? How *many* performers and entertainers – names acclaimed by and familiar to one generation, forgotten by the next, sometimes (although rarely) to be rediscovered by a third? How do you balance the claims of writers and philosophers against inventors, film producers and dress designers? If a lot of readers dislike modern art, do you leave out the artists who have revolutionized painting and sculpture in this century? How much attention do you pay to publicity, the ballyhoo which several times a year greets 'The Play – or the Book, or the Film – of the Century', only to see it superseded by yet another 'instant masterpiece' before the year is out? How long should you wait to let time sift the names that will really be remembered?

Even more controversial, how far ought we to have weighted our selection to make sure that more women or more names from outside Europe and the United States were included, even if this meant leaving out men or Europeans or Americans with greater claims?

These are the sort of questions that putting together such a book raises. And this is half its fascination, trying to pick the names by which later generations will characterize the times in which we have lived, in the same way that we talk about the nineteenth century as the age of Gladstone and Disraeli, of Turner and Constable, Dickens and George Eliot, Darwin and Marx – names that conjure up a vanished world, as the names in this book will one day bring to life again the world in which you and I once lived.

These questions lead on to another and more difficult one. In what sense can we say that any individual has been a 'maker' of the twentieth century? Perhaps you can say this of earlier centuries, when there were fewer people in the world, life was far less complicated, and a Luther, a Napoleon or a Newton could really change the course of history and stamp his ideas or his personality upon an age. But is that still possible in this tumultuous, crowded century of ours, when the population of the world has increased from 2000 million to 4200 million in the last fifty years and could well increase by half again before the year 2000? Can men any longer make history? Some people would argue that this has always been an illusion, that what determines the character of an age and the course of events is the interplay of impersonal economic and social forces – the growth of population, for example, the movement of people from the countryside to the cities, inflation, technological change, and so on.

Who can deny the importance of such forces? And yet, as an historian of the twentieth century, I can point to occasions when the appearance of a man with particular qualities has not quite reversed the tide of history but rather made the difference between its flowing into one channel instead of another. I believe this was true of Lenin and the Russian Revolution of 1917; of Roosevelt and the United States in the Great Depression; of Churchill in 1940. I also believe it was true of Hitler. If he had been killed in a car crash before he became Chancellor, it seems very likely to me that the course of history would have been changed. To take an example: would the terrible extermination of six million Jews, the Holocaust, then have taken place? Very likely not, would be my answer.

Of course these are not everyday situations, but there have been enough such occasions in this century, with its long record of upheaval, of wars and revolutions, to justify saying that some men have continued to make history.

Let me take another kind of example. No doubt someone at some time was going to challenge the view of the universe which had been held by every scientist since the seventeenth century and formulate the Theory of Relativity. But the man who actually did it was a young Jewish scientist aged twenty-six, working, of all places, in the Swiss Patent Office at Berne, and no one can take away from him the role he played. *There* was a man who set his mark on the twentieth century and made history, and there are others whose contribution was equally decisive in shaping men's ideas – the way they look at the world – or in extending their capacities in ways unknown before: artists such as Mondrian, Henry Moore and Stravinsky; scientists such as Paul Ehrlich and the Curies; inventors such as Marconi and the Wright brothers. (Look them up if you want to know what they accomplished.)

Finally, there's that much larger group who, if they have not shaped the history of the twentieth century in the way I've just illustrated, nonetheless are recognized by the rest of us as *embodying* some special characteristic of the century: men like Pope John XXIII, for instance, or – very differently – Bernard Shaw or the Marx Brothers, Greta Garbo or Louis Armstrong. Each has left an individual and representative mark on the age.

But of course there's no reason why you should bother yourself with such questions at all. I said that, for me, they make up half the fascination of this book – but only half. The other half is just to turn the pages and marvel at the extraordinary range of talent, temperament and genius which the twentieth century has thrown up. The random alphabetical arrangement makes it all the more vivid: take any letter and look at the strange bedfellows it brings together.

Some people who write about the twentieth century can see only the horrors and the violence. But there is another side to it, which this book reflects, and that is its creativity. Certainly I would not have wanted to live in any other age, and one of my reasons for saying that is the remarkable and gifted men and women who have been active in my own lifetime, your contemporaries as well as mine, the most remarkable of whom have been caught by the camera and the biographer and brought together within the covers of this book.

Alan Bullock

A

Konrad Adenauer (1876–1967) German
Political leader

'Der Alte' ('the old one') they called him. In a Germany crushed and demoralized in defeat in the Second World War, with the Nazis' brutality exposed, this old man brought Germany back to a sense of self-respect. The nation that had lost its soul following Hitler (*q.v.*) finally found a politician of stern and unbending rectitude.

A lawyer by training, Adenauer was from an old Rhineland family, staunchly Catholic, which embodied the traditions of a Germany older than the Prussian-dominated empire that came into existence with the forging of a German state only six years before Adenauer was born.

Adenauer played a part in party politics in the late 1920s and early 1930s, but withdrew from public life when Hitler came to power in 1933. In 1945, his native city of Cologne was occupied by allied forces; Adenauer was appointed Lord Mayor for a second term (the first had been in 1917), as he was entirely without Nazi associations. But in October of that year, at the age of sixty-nine, he was dismissed by the British military governor overseeing Cologne. He immediately turned to politics and, from his strong Catholic belief, helped to found the Christian Democratic Union, which emerged as one of the two major parties in post-war West Germany.

As the Western Allies gradually restored democracy to a now federal West Germany, a national Parliament and Government was needed. The CDU chose Adenauer as its candidate for Chancellor (Prime Minister) and in 1949, by a single vote (his own) and at the age of seventy-three, he became the first head of

Dr Konrad Adenauer, Federal Chancellor of West Germany 1949–63

Government of a new democratic Federal German Republic. He brought to this post his immense respectability and integrity and restored his country, step by step, to a place in Europe and then in the world. He did this as a convinced European – his Germany played a full part in NATO, the Western European Union and the European Common Market. In 1958 De Gaulle (*q.v.*) came to power in France and the two men found much in common, De Gaulle seeing Adenauer as the only other ruling statesman in Europe. Germany's re-entry into international affairs now had the solid backing of France, and Adenauer laid to rest a hundred years of hatred between the two peoples. He resigned as Chancellor in 1963.

Giovanni Agnelli (b. 1921) Italian
Car manufacturer

Agnelli, famous in his youth for his tanned good looks and charm and his super-rich playboy life, took over the family firm of Fiat (Fabbrica Italiana Automobile Torino) in 1966. Founded in 1899 by Agnelli's grandfather, a Piedmontese cavalry officer, Fiat flourished under Mussolini (*q.v.*) and later, when its technocrat manager, Vittorio Valletta, stepped down in 1966 at the age of eighty-two, a similar managerial successor was needed. 'I decided I was the best person and I took over', says Agnelli. With the family holding control of the company, there was no argument. Swiftly, Agnelli had managers retiring at sixty-five, brought in a team of young men and pushed decision-making down the line. Fiat's excessive dependence on sales of the tiny, bug-like Topolino was ended as he instituted a vigorous expansion programme that took Fiat into bigger and more expensive cars.

By the late 1970s Fiat was Europe's largest car-maker (although it has since been overtaken) and as a result of Agnelli's energetic diversification policy, apart from cars Fiat is in steel, buses, tractors, trucks, car components, aero engines and civil engineering; it also owns *La Stampa*, one of Italy's largest newspapers. In a country in which privately owned industry has largely been crushed by debt, Agnelli is the voice of capitalism, almost of Italy itself. He is far from

The 'Robogate', part of Fiat's fully automated production line (see Giovanni Agnelli)

conventional. Until a few years ago Fiat used to sack communists; now Agnelli has won the respect of some of the party's leaders. He has also put Fiat's dealings with unions on a more professional basis. He shocked the establishment by selling a slice of Fiat to Libya and building car plants for communist countries. Through the family holding company the Agnellis control Juventus football club, Cinzano, skiing resorts, retailing chains, cement companies, a publisher and vast chunks of American real estate.

Rarely has one family and its head had so much impact on a country. Thanks to Agnelli, the north west of Italy, centring on Turin, has come to enjoy a level of prosperity that is the envy of the still impoverished, rural south. Strangled by an erratic bureaucracy and unstable political structure, Italy has found it hard to achieve the broadly based prosperity of its fellow Common Market members, but Agnelli has become symbolic of an alternative Italy that can align its institutions to twentieth-century capitalism.

Muhammad Ali (b. 1942) American
Boxer

He called himself 'the Greatest' long before anyone was prepared to believe it. He went on calling himself 'the Greatest' long after the world had accepted the fact, forgotten it, and reluctantly handed over the accolade to other men. But for fifteen years or so – from the early 1960s to the mid-1970s – the Greatest he undoubtedly was.

He was born Cassius Clay in Louisville, Kentucky, won the Olympic light-heavyweight gold medal as a teenager in 1960, and soon afterwards turned professional. Then came the love-hate years with his public, a shouting, bragging, self-opinionated, self-exaggerating super-bore outside the ring and a genius inside it: a heavyweight with a lightweight's footwork, an

artist's skill and a sledgehammer punch. In 1964, against nearly all prediction, he took Sonny Liston's world heavyweight title, and knocked out the fearsome ex-champion in a single round in their return fight the following year. In the mid-1960s he disposed of challengers as if he were swatting flies, until in 1967, now a converted Black Muslim and renamed Muhammad Ali, he refused to fight in Vietnam, was stripped of his title and consigned to the boxing wilderness.

His rehabilitation in the 1970s was a drama in itself. Perhaps his victories weren't quite so easy, but his bragging had blossomed into an engaging elegance and he was idolized from the cities of America to the depths of the underprivileged Third World. He won back his title in one of the century's greatest sporting spectaculars – the fight with George Foreman in Zaire. He lost it in 1978 to the young Leon Spinks and astonished everyone by winning it back in the rematch. And only in 1980 when he was ill-advised enough to return from the fat life – and lost sadly and sluggishly to the new title-holder Larry Holmes – did the fairy tale seem finally at an end.

Ali's personality bolstered the appeal of professional boxing for nearly two decades. It is some measure of his greatness that there are serious doubts as to whether the sport can survive a further two decades after his retirement.

Roald Amundsen (1872–1928)
Norwegian
Explorer

By beating Captain Scott to the South Pole by a month, Amundsen won the enduring enmity of the British. Yet his success was gained through those attributes in which Scott was weakest: decisiveness, single-mindedness, and a gift for meticulous preparation.

Amundsen had established his reputation by sailing the North-West passage and then started preparing an expedition to the North Pole. But when the Americans reached it first in 1909, Amundsen turned south, to Scott's dismay. Scott had set himself an elaborate programme of scientific research to justify his venture, but Amundsen had only one goal: the Pole. His party, unlike Scott's sailors, were expert skiers, and his choice of transport proved crucial. Scott could not decide between dogs, ponies or tractors, and in the end employed all three, with poor results; Amundsen took only dogs, and then ruthlessly slaughtered half of them en route to provide food for men and surviving dogs.

After a steady eight-week trek across the ice in mostly good weather, Amundsen planted the Norwegian flag at the South Pole on 16 December 1911. He left a note for Scott and then followed his line of well-stocked supply depots to reach the sea on 25 January 1912, sailing for

LEFT *Muhammad Ali*

Captain Roald Amundsen, who beat Scott to the South Pole in 1911

BELOW *Louis Armstrong*

Norway a week later. Scott's party was still struggling on the ice-cap, doomed. Amundsen was hailed as a hero by all except the British; they, Amundsen wrote, were 'very bad losers'. Amundsen became a rich man through shipping, and then turned to flight. In 1928 he took off in a sea-plane to search for an Italian explorer lost in the Arctic, and never returned.

Louis Armstrong (1900–71) American
Trumpeter and singer

Born in New Orleans, Armstrong learned the rudiments of trumpet-playing as a teenager in reform school. By 1922 he had joined the band of Joe 'King' Oliver and began to enjoy a wider fame.

The series of recordings made under his own name between 1925 and 1927, known to jazz history as the 'Hot Fives and Sevens', are now seen to be a dramatic turning-point in the development of the music, for such extraordinary virtuosity as he possessed meant that the days of the old New Orleans school – in which any solo instrumentals were subordinated to the demands of the band – were numbered. Throughout the 1930s Armstrong led a large orchestra and toured the world, becoming an international star famed for his gravel-voiced singing and broad comedy effects as well as his playing. Concurrently, 'Satchmo' (a corruption of 'Satchelmouth'), as he was popularly known, enjoyed an intermittent career in films, where a succession of ridiculous roles as a groom, stableboy, servant or tramp did nothing to repress his overwhelming impact. His eminence continued to grow throughout his life.

Armstrong's achievement was that virtually single-handed he evolved a new musical language whose vocabulary consists of sweeping phrases imbued with a romantic vivacity which has appealed to all tastes, and whose grammar is simple enough for any student to digest, though to produce from such simple rules effects as profound as Satchmo's has proved impossible for others. A number of compositions, including 'Struttin' with Some Barbecue' and 'Dipper-mouth Blues', bear his name, but they are little more than notated versions of his improvising style.

Neil Armstrong (b. 1930) American
Astronaut

As commander of the American spacerocket Apollo 11, Armstrong achieved the greatest 'first' in the history of exploration when, at 3.56 a.m. BST on 21 July 1969, he set foot on planet Earth's single moon.

From the small town of Wapakoneta, Ohio, Armstrong developed an early passion for flying,

and made seventy-eight combat missions as a pilot while serving in Korea, being shot down once but parachuting to safety. He joined the National Aeronautics and Space Administration (NASA) as a research pilot in 1955 and flew the X-15 rocket plane to the edge of space, reaching 4,000 m.p.h. and an altitude of forty miles.

When NASA developed its Gemini and Apollo programmes, Armstrong grabbed his chance to go the step beyond into deep space. His first venture came in 1966 when, as command pilot of Gemini 8, he and his co-pilot performed the first successful docking of two vehicles in space, and then survived a disconcerting mechanical fault that caused the craft to spin wildly, before returning to Earth.

Shy, unflappable, and from a clean middle-America mould, his cool professionalism won him the coveted place at the command of Apollo 11; his aphorism, 'one small step for man but one giant leap for mankind' when he stepped on to the cratered surface of the Sea of Tranquillity, was hardly inspired, but it signalled a moment of human and technological triumph for a divided America and a troubled world. Armstrong later became Professor of Aerospace Engineering at the University of Cincinnati, but his spare-time recreation betrays the irresistible lure of the skies: he goes gliding.

Fred Astaire (b. 1899) American
Dancer, singer and actor

Born in Omaha, Nebraska, on 10 May 1899, Astaire was a child performer in vaudeville from the age of four. For several years he was regarded by many, including himself, as an extension of the talents of his elder sister, Adele, with whom he worked constantly until her marriage and retirement in 1932. So marked did this dependence appear that there were many judges who doubted his ability to sustain his career alone, although Adele herself strongly disagreed,

insisting that it was Fred who masterminded their partnership. During the 1920s the pair of them became recognized as the most original dance team in the American musical theatre, starring in a succession of hit musicals including Gershwin's (q.v.) *Lady Be Good* and *Funny Face*, both of which were staged in London starring the Astaires, who became the most popular American artists ever to appear in the West End.

After Adele's retirement, Astaire went to Hollywood and, in a series of nine films with the actress Ginger Rogers, became one of the most powerful of all box-office figures. A number of composers dashed west to write for the team, including George Gershwin. After Ginger

ABOVE LEFT *Neil Armstrong, commander of Apollo 11*
ABOVE *the lunar module rejoins the command ship after lunar landing, 21 July 1969*

The dazzling Fred Astaire

Rogers' retirement in favour of more dramatic roles, Astaire continued to make musical pictures with a variety of partners. Although never quite establishing the rapport he had enjoyed with Rogers, he continued to choreograph and execute routines of startling brilliance and originality. In 1949 he was awarded a special Oscar for services to the musical film. At the end of the 1950s he drifted gently into semi-retirement, publishing an autobiography, *Steps in Time*. A dapper, slightly built man with a natural grace, Astaire's best films include *Top Hat* (1935) and *The Bandwagon* (1953), a musical romance with considerable autobiographical overtones. He is a talented amateur pianist and has published several songs, one of which, 'I'm Building Up to an Awful Let-Down', reached the hit parade in 1935.

W.H. Auden

W. H. Auden (1907–73) American, ex-British
Poet and playwright

Wystan Hugh Auden was one of the most important poets of his generation. He began to write poetry at the age of fifteen, apparently at the suggestion of a school friend who casually proposed that he try his hand at it. By the time he arrived at Oxford University, Auden had acquired the basis of a sound poetic technique and was already known as a poet. At Oxford he soon became the intellectual leader of a group of fellow poets, among them Stephen Spender, C. Day Lewis and John Betjeman. Auden's first volume of verse was privately printed by his friend Spender, but he was quickly taken up by the publishers Faber and Faber on the advice of T.S. Eliot (*q.v.*), and soon began to make a name for himself as a poet of assured technical ability. Like many writers and artists who emerged in the early 1930s, Auden's sympathies were broadly socialist and working-class, though he was never a poet of propaganda.

The most successful of Auden's early volumes of verse were *The Orators* (1932) and *Look, Stranger!* (1936). In collaboration with the novelist Christopher Isherwood he wrote a series of plays, *The Dog Beneath the Skin, The Ascent of F6* and *On the Frontier*, which combined experimental poetic technique with popular song in presenting themes of social and political concern.

In 1936 Auden married Thomas Mann's (*q.v.*) daughter Erika in order to help her escape from Nazi Germany, but in 1939 he and Isherwood left England to live in the United States, their departure considered by some as a gesture of betrayal of their native country. Auden himself always maintained that he had left England not to escape an imminent war but because he found the family atmosphere claustrophobic and felt he could more easily write in the United States with its open society. He later became an American citizen.

Auden's verse of the 1930s is generally thought to be his best work, though the poet himself came to disown much of it. His post-war volumes, among them *The Age of Anxiety* (1947), are, however, considerably more complex, until they give way to the domestic poems of his last years. He was the co-author of two entertaining books of travel, *Letters from Iceland* (with Louis MacNeice, 1937) and *Journey to a War* (with Isherwood, 1939), and, in collaboration with his friend Chester Kallman, was also the librettist of a number of operas, most notably Stravinsky's (*q.v.*) *The Rake's Progress* (1951).

B

Francis Bacon (b. 1909) Irish
Painter

Bacon, a self-taught painter, was born in Dublin of English parents. He settled in London in 1925, then travelled to Berlin and Paris, returning to London in 1929. It was late in that year that he began painting in oils, and in 1933 he exhibited in a group exhibition at the Mayor Gallery. During the next ten years he worked very little and it was not until 1944 that he began seriously again. With his 1944 *Three Studies for Figures at the Base of the Crucifixion*, which was influenced by Picasso's (*q.v.*) savagely distorted 1927 drawings of female bathers, Bacon became one of the most controversial painters in England. This picture is an adaptation from memory of photographs of animals, and it anticipates much of Bacon's later work.

Head VI (1949) is one of the first of Bacon's paintings of popes, based on a photograph of

fellow dancers eventually decided to leave Russia while they were on a tour of Germany. From Berlin they made their way to London, and Balanchine eventually went to the United States. There he choreographed important musicals as well as a ballet for baby elephants to Stravinsky's (*q.v.*) *Circus Polka.*

His association with Stravinsky had begun after Balanchine had been given the post of Ballet Master with Diaghilev's (*q.v.*) Ballets Russes at the age of twenty. Though he had produced several ballets during this time it was the very last two, *Prodigal Son* and *Apollon Musagète* (music by Stravinsky), which have become modern masterpieces. The latter was the key work in his development as a neo-classical choreographer, the style which he developed into what is now for all practical purposes the American style of classical ballet.

After Diaghilev's death, Balanchine refused the post of Ballet Master at the Paris Opera,

Velasquez's portrait *Pope Innocent X*, which Bacon considered 'one of the greatest portraits that have ever been made'. Photographs and X-rays have been the source for a number of his paintings.

The subjects of the last twenty years include the Crucifixion, bullfights, portraits of friends done from memory or photographs, and a long series of self-portraits. These are ferocious and psychologically penetrating records of the human face, in which flesh is torn apart and gouged to expose layers beneath the skin. Bacon himself does not see these distortions as horrific or degrading, although the human condition represented in the 1963 *Lying Figure with Hypodermic Syringe* cannot fail to shock the viewer.

The space in which Bacon's tortured figures exist creates a sense of claustrophobia, of windowless prison cells from which there is no escape. His figures seem trapped, aware of the futility of life. More and more in recent years he has produced these images and portraits in series, often using the triptych format. Bacon is one of the greatest figurative painters since 1945, whose vision hides nothing of the character and actions of human existence.

George Balanchine (b. 1904) American, ex-Russian
Choreographer

Balanchine joined the Imperial Ballet School in St Petersburg in 1914 and graduated in 1921. His career spans the entire history of modern classical ballet, and he has played an influential part in most of the great changes. Soon after graduating he organized evenings of experimental ballet which did not please the Soviet authorities. Frustrated, Balanchine and some

Choreographer George Balanchine in rehearsal with a member of the New York City Ballet

preferring to form his own company and then to settle in America at the invitation of Lincoln Kirstein, who had a vision of an American national ballet. Together they opened the School of American Ballet, which still exists, in 1934, producing dancers for the company that developed from it in 1948, the New York City Ballet, and for other American and European companies. For the School Balanchine choreographed *Serenade* (the music was Tchaikovsky's) which has also become a modern classic, and in 1937 he organized a Stravinsky festival, foreshadowing the monumental festival of 1972 for which he and his fellow choreographers of the New York City Ballet created dances for almost every piece of music that Stravinsky ever wrote. Balanchine still directs the New York City Ballet; he creates new works every season, coaches dancers and ruthlessly looks afresh at his old ballets, constantly revising them. For him they are living works of art to be seen anew; he is a true revolutionary.

James Baldwin (b. 1924) American
Novelist and essayist

James Baldwin was born into a Negro family in the Harlem district of New York City. His first novel, *Go Tell It On the Mountain* (1953), written while he was in his early twenties, is a semi-autobiographical account of the religious awakening of a fourteen-year-old Negro youth in Harlem. Its author was immediately acclaimed as a new novelist of style, perception and great power, and his insights into the feelings of his people in particular and of urban Americans in general suggested that a new major novelist had arrived.

Baldwin's early experiences had been varied. After high school he took a number of odd jobs and then moved to Europe, living in Paris from 1948 to 1956. Later he was active in the Civil Rights movement in the United States, and began to publish non-fiction books on subjects of concern to him, especially the plight of the American Negro. The most notable of these are *Notes of a Native Son* (1955), *Nobody Knows My*

Name (1961) and *The Fire Next Time* (1963), the last-named an especially passionate and forceful indictment of American society. Baldwin's second novel, *Giovanni's Room* (1956), is set in Paris and deals with a homosexual relationship, while his third, *Another Country* (1961), is concerned with personal relationships between Negroes and whites.

Although he has continued to produce novels, among them *Tell Me How Long the Train's Been Gone* (1968) and *Little Man* (1975), and has also written plays, one of which, *Blues for Mr Charlie* (1964), was extremely successful, Baldwin's reputation in recent years has rested as firmly upon his impassioned essays about the problems encountered by Negroes in America as upon his fiction. He is an important and impressive spokesman for his race.

Cristobal Balenciaga (1895–1972)
Spanish
Fashion designer

Balenciaga was the king of *haute couture* during the 1950s and 1960s, and set standards of workmanship that have never been surpassed. Born at Guetaria, a tiny Spanish fishing-village,

RIGHT *James Baldwin*

FAR RIGHT *A Spanish-style evening dress by Balenciaga*

by the age of twenty he had opened his own dressmaking establishment in San Sebastian, where he himself chose the cloth for his customers and cut, sewed and fitted the clothes.

In 1937 he fled from the Spanish Civil War and went to Paris. Balenciaga had scarcely opened his premises at 10 Avenue George v when the whole of Europe was plunged into the Second World War. In occupied Paris he refused to keep within the authorized yardage of fabrics for models. When the Houses of Balenciaga and Grès were ordered to be closed for a fortnight as a result, other couturiers helped them to finish their collections so that the shows might all open on time.

Balenciaga was utterly uncompromising in his insistence on perfect work. Once when another couturier doubted whether a certain mohair fabric were workable, he was shown a buttonhole of the fabric made by Balenciaga himself. After gazing at it for some minutes, the couturier said 'Frame it!' Balenciaga cared nothing for public opinion and would turn down orders rather than rush them through, made no concessions to hard-worked staff or to clients, and always refused to show his collections to the press until a month after his private clients had placed their orders.

He revolutionized the way women dressed during the 1950s, making absolutely plain, soft, narrow suits with rounded shoulders and sleeves, concave fitted fronts, and long, curved backs. He was the first to put tweed suits with knee-high leather boots. His most famous dress was the sack of 1957, straight and narrow from the shoulders to the hem, but it is his amazingly sculptural and formal evening-dresses that will be remembered – stiff satin taffetas blown up like pumpkins and raised above the ankles in front, buoyant curving skirts, bows the size of umbrellas wrapping up the tightest sheaths. In 1968 Balenciaga decided that he could no longer keep alive the high standards on which he insisted, closed down his salon on impulse, and died in Valencia four years later.

Frederick Banting (1891–1941)
& Charles Best (1899–1978) Canadian
Physiologists

Before Banting and Best made their great discovery of insulin, people who suffered from diabetes invariably died of it; now they can lead full lives.

Frederick (later Sir Frederick) Banting was born in Alliston, Ontario, qualified as a doctor in 1916, and served in the First World War as a military doctor. He was awarded a Military Cross for heroism. After the war he turned to the study of diabetes (particularly diabetes mellitus) in which sugars accumulate in the blood and

LEFT *Frederick Banting and* BELOW LEFT *Charles Best, discoverers of insulin*

eventually in the urine, a disruption which caused death.

Experiments had shown several years earlier that removing the pancreas from experimental animals led them to develop symptoms that seemed very like those of diabetes, but it seemed unlikely that the whole pancreas was involved in dealing with sugars: its main function is to produce digestive juices. But there were little clumps of cells (called 'islets of Langerhans') in the pancreas, and Banting thought that these might produce a vital hormone that could be extracted and used to treat diabetics who, it was presumed, could not make enough of this hormone for themselves.

The problem was that if the pancreas is taken from an animal, the digestive juices in it destroy its contents, including the islets. Then Banting read an account of an experiment, using dogs, in which the tubes that carried the digestive juices from the pancreas were simply tied up, so that the juices stayed in. The pancreas withered, but Banting reckoned that the islets might survive.

John Macleod, Professor of Chemistry at the University of Toronto, gave Banting permission to work there in 1921 and provided him with an assistant, Charles Best, a medical student on vacation. Banting and Best's experiments were startlingly successful. They tied off the tubes from the pancreas, found that the islets did indeed survive, and extracted from them a chemical that would remove the symptoms of diabetes from dogs whose pancreas had been removed. In other words, for treating diabetes – it cannot be cured – the chemical in the islets was all that counted.

The chemical was eventually named insulin and it was tried on human diabetics in 1922 and 1923. It turned out that animal insulin works for humans, and it is still used to treat the disease.

Karl Barth (1886–1968) Swiss
Theologian

Born at Basle and educated in Germany, Barth was to become a commanding figure in Protestant theology of this century. He openly opposed the Nazis, despite being deprived of his professorship and expelled from Germany. He was Professor of Theology at Basle until his retirement in 1962. In the debates within Protestant Christianity about the status of the bible and the meaning of the life and death of Christ, Barth represented a bold and influential compromise between the liberal theologians, who could reconcile their views with lack of faith, and the fundamentalists, who wanted to stick to the letter of the biblical text.

Barth argued that the historical event of Jesus's life was a revelation of the word of God to man, and that, at best, the bible and theological commentary are human attempts to grasp and articulate that word. Such attempts, because they are human, are prone to error, and hence it is the job of theologians to describe the word of God as they understand it and to expose what they consider to be the errors of earlier interpretations. This work can take place only within a framework, namely the acceptance of and commitment to the word of God.

Karl Barth

The Beatles British
John Lennon (1940–80)
Paul McCartney (b. 1942)
George Harrison (b. 1943)
Ringo Starr (Richard Starkey) (b. 1940)
Musicians

Until the Beatles, rock'n'roll was essentially an American preserve, and those performers who flourished in England were imitators. When Beatlemania burst upon the British scene in 1963 it was quickly recognized that a courageous new rock sound had been found, and the charts were dominated not merely by the Beatles but by succeeding groups, many from their own home town of Liverpool. The hysterical Beatlemania phenomenon swept through the United States in 1964 as the group made its first tour, appearing on 9 February before the nation on the Ed Sullivan Show.

The Beatles represented more than the overturning of accepted musical conventions; they were their own cultural revolution. Their manager, Brian Epstein, cultivated for them a neat image of dark suits and well-brushed hair. Parents and even grandparents accepted them in their living-rooms approvingly, feeling that they had closed the gulf of understanding with the young but without realizing the burden of teenagers' complaints – often the sexual frustration of the bewildered adolescent, which was reflected in such early Beatles songs as 'Please, Please Me', 'I Want to Hold Your Hand', 'She Loves You' and 'Can't Buy Me Love'.

The Beatles never stood still; they developed and matured and, above all, in each of the four a distinctive personality emerged. Epstein said that he regarded John as the mind, Paul as the soul, George as the heart and Ringo as the body, and was at pains to assert that the sum of the Beatles was greater than the parts. The song-writing team of Lennon and McCartney is probably the most successful in the history of popular music. Album followed album and they quickly became millionaires. The hit film *A Hard Day's Night* (1964) was followed by *Help!* (1965).

In 1966 the age of flower children was upon the world, with drugs, love, peace and psychedelic hallucination rampant. The Beatles released in early 1967 the album that is their apotheosis during this period, *Sgt Pepper's Lonely Hearts Club Band*, in which vivid lyrics, glowing harmonies and unfettered imagination were let loose in perhaps the most remarkable best-selling record of all time. Epstein killed himself in the same year; and the Beatles embraced eastern mysticism, travelling to India to receive instruction from Maharishi Mahesh Yogi. Their business affairs became chaotic and their so-called *White Album* a puzzling mess. By 1970 the Beatles were formally dissolved, the impending break-up signposted in the film *Let It Be* (1970),

and each began a successful independent career. The assassination of John Lennon in December 1980 proved a traumatic reminder of the greatness of the group during their brief years of success, and of their legacy.

Samuel Beckett (b. 1906) Irish
Playwright and novelist

Born in Dublin of Anglo-Irish Protestants (as were Wilde, Yeats [*q.v.*] and Shaw [*q.v.*]), Beckett's earliest ambition was to play cricket for Ireland, and he is as a result the only Nobel prizewinning dramatist ever to achieve an entry in Wisden Cricketers' Almanac.

Soon after graduating from Trinity College, Dublin, he settled in Paris, where he has lived ever since, finding work first as a sort of secretary to James Joyce (*q.v.*) and later as a teacher. His first novel, *Murphy*, was published in England in 1938, but for the next twenty years he wrote (almost exclusively in French) novels of quite remarkable pessimism. Having nearly lost his life in 1938 – he was stabbed by a Frenchman – he later joined the French Resistance after escaping from the Nazis in Paris by a long and tortuous journey to the south of France, a journey that some critics suggested was to give him the origins of the play that made his name, *En Attendant Godot* (*Waiting for Godot*).

First performed in Paris in 1953 (in London in 1955), *Waiting for Godot* was an unexpected but almost immediate success all over the world – a curiously obscure and mysterious but still haunting tragi-comedy about a couple of tramps forever waiting for the unknown Godot who never appears. Its influence is as pervasive in the theatre as Salvador Dali's (*q.v.*) in modern painting, and Beckett's later plays – *Endgame* (1957), *Krapp's Last Tape* (1958) and *Happy Days* (1961) being perhaps the most important – have inspired universal critical reverence.

A play written in 1969 and entitled *Breath* had no actors, no dialogue and lasted all of half a minute, thereby causing some critics to speculate that Beckett had finally reached the end of the cul-de-sac he himself had created. Others took it more plausibly as a gesture of either self or critical mockery, and though there have always been those who reckon that Beckett is wilfully inclined to ignore the demands of an audience (*Happy Days* features a monologue by a woman buried up to her neck in sand that lasts the length of the entire play) there are many others who believe that he has freed playwrights from the constraints of the well-made play and taught audiences to think for themselves. Though never a commercial moneymaker at the box-office, Beckett remains unarguably among the most influential and resonant dramatists of the century.

David Ben-Gurion (1886–1973) Israeli, ex-Polish
Political leader

The first political leader of an independent Israel, Ben-Gurion was convinced of the rightness of Zionism – a national home for the Jews in Palestine – from the time he was a boy. He also became a socialist early in his life. He emigrated to Palestine in 1906, and in spite of poor health worked as a farm labourer. He also at that time helped to form one of the first Jewish armed defence groups to repel Arab raids. He entered politics in 1910 as a socialist and journalist, changing his name (originally David Gryn) to honour David Ben-Gurion, who died with the last defenders of Jerusalem against the Romans in AD 70.

After the First World War Palestine was entrusted to Britain, with the right of Jews to establish a national home there internationally recognized, due largely to the efforts of Chaim Weizmann (*q.v.*). In 1920 Ben-Gurion became General-Secretary of the Jewish Confederation of Labour, and later he formed the Mapai (Workers' United Party). Ben-Gurion encouraged the immigration of Jews from Europe,

LEFT *The Beatles: (from the top) John Lennon, George Harrison, Paul McCartney and Ringo Starr*

BELOW *Samuel Beckett, author of* Waiting for Godot, Endgame *and* Happy Days; *his influence has been universal*

socialist settlements in Israel, and the Haganah, a self-defence organization to cope with violence which had begun on a large scale between Arabs and Jews, urged on by one Arab slogan, 'Death to the Jews'. Ben-Gurion was often at variance with the more moderate leaders of world Zionism, and he defied British attempts to limit Jewish immigration, especially after the end of the Second World War.

He and other Jewish leaders accepted the United Nations plan for the partition of Palestine in 1947, but the Arabs did not. So while heading the Jewish Shadow Cabinet, Ben-Gurion took firm steps to secure the new state. He read the Proclamation of Independence and became the first Prime Minister, establishing the new army and driving the Arabs out of Jewish territory (and capturing some land designated Arab). In 1949 an armistice was signed. Ben-Gurion then oversaw the phenomenal development of his nation, integrating people drawn from all over the world. Helped by funds from Jews overseas, Israel came to have more schools, universities, art galleries, newspapers and symphony orchestras per capita than any other country in the world.

In the summer of 1956 Nasser, the Egyptian leader, announced the nationalization of the Suez Canal, at that time owned by an international company in which the British and French Governments were major shareholders. Anthony Eden, Britain's Prime Minister, saw Nasser as an Arab Hitler and the 'seizure' of the canal as the first of what would be many aggressions unless he were firmly resisted. After all diplomatic procedures to achieve this aim had apparently been exhausted (America seemed uncooperative), members of the British and French Governments made contact with the Israelis for joint secret military operations to remove the canal from Egyptian control. Ben-Gurion directed the Israeli effort, which was completely successful, but the other two powers, after great international pressure, withdrew.

In 1963 Ben-Gurion resigned and went to his kibbutz. However, in 1965 he was re-elected to the Knesset (Israel's Parliament) as the head of a small group of independents, a seat he held until he died in 1973.

Alban Berg (1885–1935) Austrian
Composer

Alban Berg lived his entire life in Vienna, and died there at the comparatively early age of fifty. His musical talent was recognized when he was fifteen, and on the death of his father a rich aunt helped him to continue his studies. Despite the fact that he was asthmatic from an early age and never in good health, he was a prolific composer, especially in his youth. In his late teens Berg became a pupil of Arnold Schoenberg (*q.v.*)

and his earliest works of any note were written under Schoenberg's influence, among them the *Altenberg Lieder* and the Piano Sonata Opus 1. In 1917 he began work on what was to prove his masterpiece, the opera *Wozzeck*, eventually performed in 1925 to great public acclaim, in spite of attacks on the work from the more conservative critics.

Berg's Chamber Concerto (1923–5), dedicated to his teacher on the occasion of Schoenberg's

David Ben-Gurion, first premier of an independent Israel

ABOVE *Alban Berg;* LEFT *the poster for Berg's* Lulu, *Covent Garden, 1981*

fiftieth birthday, was followed by one of his most powerful works, the *Lyric Suite* for string quartet; in two of its movements Berg made use of the twelve-note method of composition which had been recently developed by Schoenberg. After the rise to power of the Nazis in 1933 the growing popularity of Berg's music in Germany was brought to an abrupt halt; but in Austria his music was still performed, and in a cottage he had purchased on the Wörthersee he worked on a second opera, *Lulu*, which was not quite complete at the time of his death. In the spring of 1935 the violinist Louis Krasner commissioned a violin concerto from Berg; his most popular and accessible work, it was also his last.

Irving Berlin (b. 1888) American, ex-Russian
Songwriter

Berlin was born Israel Baline at Temun in Russia on 11 May 1888 and his family moved to New York in 1893, where he was raised in poverty. He left school at eight and became a singing waiter at sixteen. In 1907 he made his debut as a published

Irving Berlin: George Gershwin said he 'is American music'

songwriter with 'Marie from Sunny Italy'. Three years later he was writing words and music of best-selling songs, and by 1911 had established his own publishing house and marked the advent of the new songwriting age with 'Alexander's Ragtime Band'. His first Broadway show, a revue called *Watch Your Step*, opened in 1914, and by 1920 he was so well established in the musical theatre that he built his own house, The Music Box. His output remained prolific, and included a period in the 1920s when he turned his attention to the waltz, producing songs like 'Always' and 'What'll I Do?'. In 1935 he entered on an especially brilliant interlude by writing film scores. He later returned to the theatre with the musicals *Annie Get Your Gun* and *Call Me Madam*.

Never formally trained, Berlin's working methods have necessarily been eccentric: the limitation of his keyboard technique to the key of F sharp inspired his use of a piano with a manual gadget which shifted the keys into other tonalities. His freedom from convention has enabled him to deploy startling effects, including unprepared modulation and the use of two middle sections to the same song. Of all the great songwriters, he has been the most prone to writing indifferent material, but at his best he justifies the observation of George Gershwin (*q.v.*) who, when asked to define Berlin's place in American music, replied, 'Berlin *is* American music'. His most famous, although not his best song, 'White Christmas', has sold more than a hundred million records. When asked which type of songs he liked composing best, he is said to have replied, 'Hits'!

William Beveridge (1879–1963) British
Economist and social scientist

Born in Bengal, Beveridge taught law at Oxford and entered the civil service in the Board of Trade.

He was active in Liberal Party politics and became an expert on unemployment, publishing a notable report on the subject in 1909. He became director of the London School of Economics (1919–37) and later master of University College, Oxford (1937–44). His major scholarly work was a contribution to economic history, *Prices and Wages in England from the Twelfth to the Nineteenth Century* (1939).

Beveridge will perhaps be best remembered for his contributions to the construction of the British Welfare State, to which as much if not more was contributed by Liberal thinkers as by Labour. The famous Beveridge Report (*Social Insurance and Allied Services*) of 1942 was highly popular, but not with the Government, and its scheme of comprehensive and contributory social insurance for old age, ill-health and disablement was largely implemented after 1945

by a new Labour Government. His second great work, *Full Employment in a Free Society* (1944), was an attempt to diagnose and draw up a blueprint for a post-war society that would have full employment as a primary aim for the Government. His expectation was that, allowing for unavoidable unemployment, a figure of about three per cent unemployed of the work-force should be aimed at. The post-war Governments that accepted his ideas managed rates of more like one and a half per cent.

Beveridge was raised to the peerage in 1946.

Ernest Bevin (1881–1951) British
Political and labour leader

Bevin, one of the most influential figures in the British Labour movement, founded the country's largest union, the Transport and General Workers' Union, in 1922. During the inter-war years Bevin became the main driving force in the Trades Union Congress, helping to transform it into a powerful body that no Government could afford to ignore. In May 1940 Bevin joined Winston Churchill's (*q.v.*) wartime Coalition Government as Minister of Labour. He played a crucial part in the achievement of total victory in the war by successfully mobilizing the workers in the wartime economy; the productivity performance of British industry during the Second World War was the envy of Nazi Germany. Under Bevin's astute and sensitive direction manpower was organized without any need to resort to terror or coercion. Moreover, Bevin ensured that the Government did not impose wage and price controls. He was a passionate believer in free collective bargaining, and in the power of reason and common sense to convince workers of the rightness of his policies.

In July 1945 Bevin was made Foreign Secretary in the Labour Government after the Party's landslide victory, a post he held until shortly before his death on 14 April 1951. He played a vital part in the creation of the North Atlantic Treaty Organization in 1949. During the 1930s Bevin, unlike many of his Labour colleagues, had taken a realistic view of foreign affairs, believing it was necessary to rearm and oppose the spread of Fascism. He had no illusions about Soviet Communism, and although he was anxious to continue the wartime alliance with Stalin (*q.v.*) after the war, Bevin was determined to resist any further encroachments by the Soviet Union into the west after their military occupation of eastern and central Europe. He was a firm believer in Britain's special relationship with the United States and was unsympathetic to any moves towards a united Europe that might endanger Britain's wider world interests.

Bevin was born on 7 March 1881 in Winsford, Somerset. He never knew who his father was and his mother died when he was eight. Despite a deprived and poverty-stricken childhood, Bevin developed a massive self-sufficiency and confidence that lasted all his life. He had earthy common sense, a distrust of intellectuals, an intuitive grasp of fundamentals and an imaginative flair, qualities that made him a constructive influence on the development of the Labour movement. Bevin was often accused by his critics of being a dictator in his Union, but wrongly so. He believed in loyalty to decisions once they were reached. In Government he had no time for the intrigue and petty jealousies of some of his colleagues and he proved to be a faithful Cabinet member.

LEFT *Lord Beveridge at University College, Oxford*

Ernest Bevin by T.C. Dugdale (detail)

Humphrey Bogart in The African Queen, *1952*

Humphrey Bogart (1899–1957)
American
Actor

The most legendary of screen anti-heroes came, surprisingly, from a wealthy Manhattan background (his father was a surgeon) and spent his early acting years playing stage juveniles. In 1930 he made his film debut, and for the next ten years performed in literally dozens of films, usually typecast as a gangster following his success on Broadway in *The Petrified Forest*, a role he repeated on the screen.

The legend began in 1941 when Bogart played the fugitive in *High Sierra* as a thinking criminal. Its screenwriter, John Huston, made his directorial debut with Bogart's next film, casting him as the trench-coated, avenging private detective, Sam Spade, in *The Maltese Falcon*. In the following year Bogart appeared in *Casablanca*, in perhaps his most definitive role, as Rick, the bitter, sardonic café-owner working out the direction of his true allegiance from a neutral wartime port. Later, he was to play similar self-reliant characters in such films as *To Have and Have Not*, *The Big Sleep*, Huston's *The Treasure of Sierra Madre* and *The African Queen*. He was married four times, but it was his last wife, the youthful ingénue of *To Have and Have Not*, Lauren Bacall, who was his outstanding partner, and who nursed him through the illness that killed him a few days short of his fifty-eighth birthday.

In later years 'Bogey' became a totem for a new generation of young people, who found his image of lonely, world-weary scepticism an appealing symbol in the cynical 1960s. Bogart was his own man, in real life as in his films, and he exuded a screen presence at odds with his slight, stooping frame and characteristic lisp – the result, literally, of a stiff upper lip, a wound from navy service in the First World War. Today, Bogart seems the most indestructible of the great movie stars who emerged from the Hollywood machine of the 1930s.

Niels Bohr (1885–1962) Danish
Physicist

Bohr was awarded the Nobel Prize in 1922 for discovering why heated atoms give out light of only particular colours, colours that can be used like fingerprints to identify chemical elements. But his importance in twentieth-century science goes much further than his work in atomic structure. He attracted scientists from all over the world to his Institute of Theoretical Physics in Copenhagen, and as a result some of the most important developments in modern science were made there. Escaping from German-occupied Denmark in the Second World War, Bohr carried to America the news that the Germans understood how to make an atom bomb, and assisted American scientists in developing the bomb that ended the war in Japan. Later he was active in the Atoms of Peace movement.

Niels Bohr, the son of a professor of physiology, was born and died in Copenhagen. He studied at Copenhagen University, and then, as a postgraduate, went to the Cavendish Laboratory in Cambridge to work with Ernest Rutherford (*q.v.*). Rutherford had discovered that an atom is largely empty, with a dense, positively charged central nucleus surrounded by a cloud of electrons with negative charges. The problem was that this arrangement should not be stable: the electrons should fall into the nucleus, pulled by their electrical charge, and the energy released by their fall should appear as light of a range of colours.

Bohr recognized that Max Planck's (*q.v.*) discoveries, made at the turn of the century, could solve this apparent mystery. Planck had realized that energy is not given out or taken in continuously, but in 'packages' called quanta. The electrons, therefore, would continue to circle

FAR LEFT *Niels Bohr, Nobel laureate in physics, 1922;* LEFT *death cloud over Nagasaki: the atomic explosion of 9 August 1945*

Dietrich Bonhoeffer, leading theologian and courageous critic of the Nazis; he was hanged for plotting to kill Hitler

the atom until they gave out an exact quantum of energy and moved into the next available inner ring. This quantum would correspond to light of an exact frequency and colour unique for each atom.

In 1939, when Bohr went to the United States, he explained that two Germans had found that particles called neutrons could produce fission in atoms. This is the basis of the atom bomb and of atomic energy. He predicted the isotope of uranium that would be needed, and encouraged the Americans to make the atom bomb.

Dietrich Bonhoeffer (1906–45) German
Theologian

Born at Breslau in Prussia (now Wroclaw, Poland), Bonhoeffer was the son of a professor at Berlin University. He studied theology at the Universities of Tübingen and Berlin, was ordained a Lutheran minister, and spent a year at Union Theological Seminary in New York. He returned to an appointment at Berlin University in 1931.

In 1933 Adolf Hitler (*q.v.*) came to power in Germany. Bonhoeffer was an outspoken and courageous critic of Nazi policies, especially the treatment of the Jews, and became a leading figure in the Confessional Church, which was the centre of Protestant opposition to the Nazi regime. In 1939 he fled to New York, but returned home again within two weeks, feeling that it was his Christian duty to 'share the trials of this time with my people'. Employed in the Military Intelligence Department, which was a hotbed of anti-Nazi resistance, he was arrested in

1943 for plotting to kill Hitler, and tortured and imprisoned. In the following year the bomb-plot against Hitler's life failed and evidence was found linking Bonhoeffer with the conspiracy. He was hanged at Flössenberg in Bavaria, aged thirty-nine.

Bonhoeffer's writings, and his uncompromising courage, have given him considerable influence on liberal Christian theology since the war. His best-known book, *Letters and Papers from Prison*, was published in 1951. He believed that humanity had come of age and that the Christian emphasis on the weakness and littleness of man was no longer appropriate. He wanted the Churches to strip themselves of their traditional privileges and trappings, to become more up to date and involve themselves more effectively in the modern secular world. He spoke of 'Christian worldliness' and hoped for a Christianity with less emphasis on heaven and salvation and more on living in this world by Christian moral standards and in imitation of Christ.

Bjorn Borg (b. 1956) Swedish
Tennis player

In competitive sport there is no such thing as 'the best ever'. Records are made to be broken, and players are for ever breaking them. In lawn tennis, Tilden in the 1920s, Perry in the 1930s, Gonzales in the 1950s and, particularly, Laver in the 1960s, have all had claims to overall supremacy at the game. Even given the constant improvement in coaching, competition and technique, the undisputed champion of the latter half of the 1970s, Borg, could never be considered in a lower rank than these others.

With an on-court taciturnity that earned him the nickname 'Iceborg', and which was in marked contrast with the rows and antics of lesser players, Borg's concentration, his superhuman stamina, machine-like ground-stroke control and astonishing accuracy took him almost effortlessly from boy prodigy (at fifteen years of age he represented Sweden in a victorious Davis Cup match, the youngest ever to appear in the competition) to world domination by the age of twenty-four, with five French championships up to 1980, the first at the age of seventeen, fifty-five consecutive tournament match victories in 1978, and five Wimbledon championships in succession.

His self-taught style, with its two-handed backhand, its reliance on heavy topspin and a minimum of serve-and-volley net-rushing, was thought unsuitable for the modern game – until Borg proved that no modern technique could beat it. His style was held to be quite unsuited to grass-court play – until he mastered the unique courts of Wimbledon in his unprecedented five successive championships.

His rackets are strung to an unbelievable eighty pounds per square inch (most professionals find the ball hard enough to control at sixty to sixty-five pounds), his appetite for practice is almost obsessional, and Borg's will to win tournaments – big or small – is quite overpowering (despite a continuing inability to lift the US Championships).

By the start of the 1980s, Borg's belief in his own invincibility – so often proved correct – had transformed the game of his opponents, the attitude of the fans, almost the nature of tennis itself; and it had made Borg a multi-millionaire and a tennis legend.

BELOW *The great two-handed backhand of Bjorn Borg*

RIGHT *Don Bradman giving one of the many high-scoring performances of his career in the 1934 Test at Headingley*

Donald Bradman (b. 1908) Australian Cricketer

Bradman was the most prolific run-maker in the history of cricket. Born at Cootamundra, New South Wales, on 27 August 1908, he became a cricketer in his teens, joining the New South Wales state side in 1927 and scoring 118 on his debut. For many years his later innings of 452 not out stood as a world record, and he remains the only batsman to have scored six treble centuries and thirty-seven double centuries. In Test cricket he was just as dominant, scoring a record twenty-nine centuries in international matches, including 300 in a day against England

at Leeds in 1930. He returned to England again in 1934, 1938 and 1948, on the latter two occasions as Australian captain, in which capacity he showed a ruthless mastery of tactics almost as remarkable as his batting technique. After his retirement at the end of the 1948 tour he continued to dominate Australian cricket as a selector. He was knighted in 1949.

Technically Bradman was the most perfect high-scoring batsman of all time, able to make runs at a fast pace without ever seeming to hurry, or to give bowlers the slightest reason to hope for his dismissal; though purists have noted that his infallibility did not extend to pitches on which rain had expedited the task of the slower bowlers. Amazingly, he scored a century in every third innings, and could claim a Test batting average of 99·94. But his eminence tended to be a lonely one, and his popularity as a man among his fellow cricketers never quite matched the admiration they felt for his technical achievements.

William (1862–1942) & Lawrence Bragg (1890–1971) British
Physicists

Only once has a Nobel Prize been awarded to a father and son for their work together. It happened in 1915, when the Braggs won the prize for showing how X-rays could be used to discover how atoms were arranged in a crystal.

William Bragg was assured of fame in science even before he started on X-ray work. He was born in Cumberland, and studied first mathematics and then physics at Cambridge. In 1886 he became a professor at the University of Adelaide. While there he gave a semi-popular lecture on radioactivity, which aroused his own interest in the subject. Radium is one of the radioactive elements, and Bragg showed that the alpha rays that came from it did not all have the same range in air, which would have been expected, but a number of sharply limited ranges. Bragg decided that each batch of alpha rays came from a different substance, and that these substances were produced as radium decomposed step by step.

He returned to England in 1909 as a professor of physics at Leeds University, and heard there of Max von Laue's experiments with X-rays. Von Laue had shown that if a beam of X-rays were directed at a crystal, the atoms in the crystal, arranged in regular patterns, scattered the X-rays so that the beam emerged as a regular pattern of faint rays. Both William Bragg and his son Lawrence realized that they could use this discovery to find out in what patterns the atoms in the crystal were arranged. It was actually Lawrence who first took up this line of research. First they calculated the wavelength of various beams of X-rays, and then used it to work out the arrangement of the atoms in a crystal. The results were often startling. They discovered that the atoms of those chemicals that would conduct electricity when dissolved in water – common salt is one example – were not joined directly together: they are simply grouped in regular patterns and held together in bulk by electrical charges.

The technique the Braggs developed – it is called X-ray diffraction – is immensely important in modern science and has been used to find the

TOP *Sir Lawrence Bragg: Christmas Lectures 1961/2 on electricity at London's Royal Institution;* ABOVE *Sir William Bragg, President of the Royal Society 1935–40, by Harold Knight (detail)*

arrangement of atoms in an enormous range of crystals, both of minerals and of chemicals important to life. We now understand how muscles work and how a living cell divides to produce two identical cells through developments of the Braggs' research.

Constantin Brancusi (1876–1957)
Romanian
Sculptor

Brancusi graduated from the School of Fine Arts in Bucharest in 1902, and two years later he arrived in Paris (where he lived for the rest of his life) and enrolled at the Ecole des Beaux-Arts. For a brief period he worked in the studio of the great sculptor Rodin, whose *Balzac* Brancusi considered the 'starting-point of modern sculpture'. Several of his early portraits show Rodin's influence, but he soon realized that 'nothing can grow in the shadow of great trees'.

Brancusi's belief in direct carving, which was to have a profound influence on the development of early twentieth-century sculpture, was a reaction against bronze casting and the mechanical reproduction in stone of a clay or plaster model. In his early mature works, such as the first version of his famous block-like *The Kiss* (1907), he greatly simplifies form and eliminates the busy surface detail and modelling which characterize much of the sculpture of Rodin's generation. He was not interested in the external shape of objects but 'in the essence of things'. The naturalism of his early work became gradually replaced by smooth, refined surfaces, as he reduced and

The Kiss *by Constantin Brancusi, 1907*

simplified images in his quest for pure essence of form. In his sculptures of the human figure he concentrated not on the whole but on individual parts – the head, torso or buttocks, the subjects of much of Rodin's work.

Like many major twentieth-century artists, Brancusi was influenced by primitive art. The polished bronze head *First Cry* (1914) probably derives from an African carving, while the 1915 *Maistra* has its roots in Romanian folklore.

Birds and fish are the subject of many of his bronzes and carvings, of which *Bird in Space* (in several versions) is the best known. The form of a bird has been refined and simplified to an extraordinary degree and yet, as with almost all his work, the sculpture is not abstract but adapted from nature, its subtle, gentle curves suggesting movement. In 1937 he designed the steel 100-feet-high *Endless Column* for a garden in his native Romania; despite its height, the sculpture is reminiscent of the soaring movement of *Bird in Space*.

Brancusi's influence on sculptors such as Moore (*q.v.*) Barbara Hepworth and the Italian artist Amedeo Modigliani has been considerable. As Moore wrote, Brancusi's special mission was 'to make us once more shape-conscious', and like Cézanne in painting, his influence on modern sculpture has been enormous.

Marlon Brando (b. 1924) American
Actor

When the young Brando, after three years' stage experience, took Broadway by storm in 1947 with his portrayal of Tennessee Williams' (*q.v.*) uncouth Stanley Kowalski in *A Streetcar Named Desire*, he put the new style of naturalistic acting – The Method – firmly on the map, and became the prototype of a generation of mumbling, twitching, scratching actors, not one of whom could match him for intensity of purpose and magnetic presence. It was only a matter of time before the effects of the New York Actors' Studio, of which Brando was the prominent member, were felt in Hollywood movies, and he made his debut in Stanley Kramer's *The Men* as an embittered paraplegic war veteran. He followed this with the screen version of *A Streetcar Named Desire*, the title role in *Viva Zapata!* and Marc Antony in Mankiewicz's *Julius Caesar*, being nominated for an Academy Award in each part. He achieved the Best Actor Award in 1954 with his next film, Kazan's powerful exposé of corruption in New York's docks, *On the Waterfront*.

Brando's rebellious, brooding, explosive persona provided a focal point for the 1950s Beat Generation, and even traditionalists were forced to acknowledge the strength of his appeal. As a reaction to his stereotyped image he played in a number of unsuitable parts, ranging from

Napoleon to the hero in *Guys and Dolls*, then made an astonishing directing debut in a Western, *One-Eyed Jacks*, which proved to be the precursor of a tougher, more ruthless approach to the legend of the West. Brando's career faltered with poor films, but by the 1970s he was able to mount a spectacular resuscitation with his performance in *The Godfather*, for which he won a second Oscar, and in Bertolucci's controversial *Last Tango in Paris*. He is the only actor who can command two million dollars for barely appearing in a film, and his expensive services were minimally provided in *Superman* and *Apocalypse Now*.

Georges Braque (1882–1963) French
Painter

The son of a house-painter, Braque was born in Argenteuil, near Paris. In 1902 he settled in Montmartre and studied at the Académie Humbert and later at the Ecole des Beaux Arts.

The work of his compatriot Cézanne, which he saw in 1907, was a revelation for Braque and for the next two years was to profoundly influence his painting. Later that year he met Picasso (*q.v.*) who had recently completed *Les Demoiselles d'Avignon*, a picture which bewildered Braque as it did most of Picasso's contemporaries, but

Marlon Brando in the screen version of A Streetcar Named Desire, *1952*

form with an intricate network of fractured planes, describing the same object from different angles in a single image. To prevent his work becoming totally abstract, by 1912 Braque made several innovations: the use of lettering, imitation wood-graining, and an enriched surface texture made by mixing sand with the pigments. *The Fruit Dish* (1912) was the first *papier collé*, a form of collage, in which wallpaper was fixed to the surface.

In the 1920s, with a limited range of subjects, Braque produced superb still-life and figure compositions, but his crowning achievement was the group of eight studio paintings made between 1949 and 1955. He was above all a painter of still-life subjects and his work has none of the anguish and violence that characterizes the art of many of his contemporaries. At the end of his life he explored the harmonious relationships between objects with a richness of colour not used in his Cubist work of 1910–12. Quiet, poetic, serene, these are works of formal perfection.

Bertolt Brecht (1898–1956) German
Dramatist and poet

Playwright, poet and also director, Brecht was arguably the most influential European dramatist of the century, though ironically still perhaps best known for having written a musical play with Kurt Weill, *The Threepenny Opera*, in 1928.

After his first two plays (*Baal*, 1930 and *Man Is Man*, 1926) Brecht turned to Marxist musicals (*The Threepenny Opera*; *Rise and Fall of the City of Mahagonny*, 1930) and then to updated and politicized rewrites of accepted classics (*St Joan of the Stockyards*, 1930).

In 1933, after breaking with Weill and as a result of Hitler's rise to power, Brecht left Germany and began, in first Scandinavia and then America, to write the often epic-form

The Round Table (Le Guéridon) *by Georges Braque, 1929*

Braque's *Nude* of 1907–8 was an attempt to grapple with some of the pictorial problems suggested by this revolutionary work.

During the summer of 1908, under the continuing influence of Cézanne, Braque produced a series of landscapes and still-lifes, such as *Trees at L'Estaque*, in which there is no single, consistent viewpoint, and in which trees and buildings are composed of simplified planes that are tilted in various directions. A critic who saw these paintings described Braque as having reduced everything 'to geometric outlines, to cubes', and from this review the term Cubism was born. Throughout that summer Picasso's art was taking a similar course, and for the next six years they worked closely, 'like mountaineers roped together', as Braque described them; by 1910–11 their paintings had become almost indistinguishable. Only a few earth colours were used as they concentrated on defining space and

theatrical classics that have made his name. Most plays took two or three years to write, with several rewrites: *The Life of Galileo* (1937–9), *Mother Courage* (1936–9), *The Good Woman of Setzuan* (1935–41), *Puntila* (1940), *Arturo Ui* (1941), *Schweik in the Second World War* (1942–3), *The Caucasian Chalk Circle* (1943–5).

After the war his playwriting consisted mainly of adaptations and revisions, but in 1949 he returned with his actress wife Helene Weigel to Germany at the invitation of the East German Government to form a state theatre company, his legendary Berliner Ensemble. By now Brecht had been denounced in America as a communist who was therefore involved in 'un-American' activities. Back in Berlin in 1953 he declined to take any political stand on the Berlin workers' uprising, however, insisting rather that his company should remain in the theatre rehearsing his own political 'adaptation' of *Coriolanus* (an irony that later became the basis for a famed Günter Grass play – *The Plebeians Rehearse the Uprising*, 1966 – which portrays Brecht as a lonely, guilt-ridden and politically insecure figure).

Brecht's main contribution to world theatre, apart from his half-dozen classic plays, was his theory of detachment. By this he felt that an actor should not merely play a role but also within his or her performance become detached from it to comment on that role. It is a theory that cannot always be successfully applied by directors of Brecht's plays, and one that Brecht himself was willing to forget in the occasionally stronger interests of great theatre, something about which he knew more than most.

Benjamin Britten (1913–76) British Composer

Benjamin Britten, the leading English composer of his time, was born in Lowestoft, Suffolk, a county with which he was connected for most of his life. He displayed a talent for musical composition at a very early age, and by the time he left his preparatory school he had written ten piano sonatas, six string quartets, an oratorio and dozens of songs. At the age of eighteen Britten went to the Royal College of Music, and three years later joined the film unit of the Post Office to provide incidental music for documentary films. This brought him into contact with the poet W.H. Auden (*q.v.*) who became a close friend and a strong influence on his literary and artistic tastes.

The earliest of Britten's compositions to attract international attention was his *Variations on a Theme of Frank Bridge* which caused a sensation when it was played at the Salzburg Festival in 1937. In 1939 Britten and his friend the tenor Peter Pears left England to spend two and a half years in the United States. There

Benjamin Britten in 1943 by K. Green (detail)

Britten completed two important vocal works, dedicated to and first performed by Peter Pears: *Les Illuminations* and *Seven Sonnets of Michelangelo*. To a libretto by W.H. Auden, Britten also composed an operetta, *Paul Bunyan*, which was staged in 1941.

The majority of Britten's major works were written for the stage, and it was with *Peter Grimes*, his first opera, that the Sadler's Wells Opera Company returned to their own theatre in London at the end of the Second World War. In 1948 Britten and Pears established the Aldeburgh Festival in the Suffolk fishing village where they lived, and Britten wrote a number of operas, almost all of which were given their first performances at Aldeburgh. Among his most successful operas are *Billy Budd* (1951), *Gloriana* (1953), *The Turn of the Screw* (1954), *A Midsummer Night's Dream* (1960) and *Owen Wingrave* (1971), which was written for television. His last opera, *Death in Venice* (1974), was based on the Thomas Mann (*q.v.*) novel of the same name.

Britten was one of the greatest English composers since Purcell in the seventeenth century. His music has a rare spontaneity and freshness that makes it easily accessible to the ordinary listener: it was here that his genius lay.

Robert Broom (1866–1951) South African, ex-Scottish
Palaeontologist

No worker in palaeontology worked faster than Broom – 'moving along the corridors of the museum at a jog trot', they said of him – and a penetrating mind enabled him to çut through inessentials. Darwin's theory of evolution had burst upon him in his youth. Finding evidence to support it – and 'the missing link' – became the obsession of Broom's life, first in Australia, where he studied marsupials, then, from 1897 until his death, in South Africa.

His first papers concerned the many fossils of mammal-like reptiles he dug up there, spanning some sixty million years and pointing to the gap between the oldest form of reptile and the earliest mammals. When the Taungs skull, Australopithecus, was found in Southern Africa, Broom quickly recognized that it was close to the line leading to man. He was in his seventies when, notably at Sterkfontein, he chanced upon the fossil remains of hundreds of these Australopithecine creatures, now regarded with Australopithecus as being among the most primitive early beings known. Like fossils recovered in East Africa and the Orient, they showed that most of the Old World was populated by primitive human beings of their type from two or more million to 500,000 years ago.

Critics regarded some of Broom's claims as hasty or doubtful; he was always more rugged than the conventional scientist blinking behind his spectacles, a fighter who delighted in controversy. But his work, his influence and the impetus he gave to research in his chosen subject remain unchallenged. Fellowship of the Royal Society of London and numerous honorary doctorates from universities around the world bear testimony to this.

Luis Buñuel (b. 1900) Spanish
Film director

An attractive girl hurries along a station platform calling after a man on a train about to leave. Without a word he empties a bucket of water over her. He then offers an explanation to his startled fellow passengers. The opening scene of Buñuel's most recent film, *That Obscure Object of Desire* (1977), demonstrated that the master had lost none of his skill in combining imagination with a simple, straightforward narrative. Buñuel's imagery constantly surprises and intrigues, but he achieves his most powerful effects with a minimum of cinematic tricks. He is a great artist because he has consistently presented through the medium of the cinema his view of life: anti-cleric, anti-bourgeoisie, pro the unfettered liberal spirit.

Buñuel was educated by Jesuits. At the University of Madrid he met Salvador Dali (*q.v.*), and in 1926 entered the film industry while still a student at the Paris Académie du Cinéma. He made his first film in conjunction with Dali in 1928, the twenty-four-minute fantasy *Un Chien Andalou*, a series of astonishing and apparently unrelated images. It was followed in 1930 by *L'Age d'Or*, in which the foundations of Buñuel's

RIGHT *Palaeontologist Robert Broom by W.H. Coetzler*

ABOVE RIGHT *Luis Buñuel*

life-long obsessions were laid, with its vigorous attack on the Church, the Establishment and middle-class social ethics. The film was banned and Buñuel produced little original material in the 1930s, working mainly for American companies dubbing Hollywood films, and later going to Hollywood on unsatisfactory and lowly assignments. In 1947 he resumed his directorial career in Mexico with *Los Olivados*, which won the best direction award at Cannes in 1950. Its strong anti-clerical feeling was echoed in his later works, *The Criminal Life of Archibaldo de la Cruz* (1955), *Nazarin* (1959) and *Viridiana* (1961).

The apotheosis of Buñuel's mockery of bourgeois convention is reached in two of his later films, made in France, *Belle de Jour* (1967), in which a respectable upper middle-class wife realizes her fantasies by becoming an afternoon prostitute, and *The Discreet Charm of the Bourgeoisie* (1972), in which a party of dinner guests are unable to complete their meal in the face of an escalating series of bizarre interruptions. As a voice chiding human frailty, Buñuel is a unique force in the cinema, and while his later works have outraged less than previous ones the style is as sharp and to the point as ever.

C

Maria Callas (1923–77) Greek
Opera singer

The world-famous soprano Maria Callas was born Maria Kalogeropoulou of Greek parents in New York. She first went to Greece when she was thirteen, and studied music at the Athens

Conservatorium where her singing teacher was Elvira de Hidalgo, a celebrated soprano of the 1920s. Callas made her first appearances in opera with the Athens Opera, but her international career really began after her return to America. She was heard there by the well known tenor Zenatello who recommended her to the organizers of the open-air performances at the Arena in Verona, and it was there that Callas made her Italian debut in 1947 in the title-role of Ponchielli's *La Gioconda*. The performance was conducted by the veteran Tullio Serafin who saw her great potential and engaged her to sing Isolde in Wagner's *Tristan und Isolde* and the title-role in Puccini's *Turandot* in Venice.

The turning-point in Callas's career came when she took over the role of Elvira in Bellini's *I Puritani* at short notice when another soprano fell ill. A singer who could encompass both the great dramatic soprano roles of Wagner and Puccini and the lyrical and more colourful heroines of Rossini, Bellini and Donizetti was a great rarity, and Callas was soon very much in demand. Gradually, she gave up the heavier roles to concentrate on reviving the operas of Bellini and Donizetti in particular. She was highly regarded as an actress, and although her dramatic performances may have lacked the subtlety of such great operatic actresses of the past and present as Lotte Lehmann (*q.v.*), Elisabeth Schwarzkopf or Ileana Cotrubas, she was immensely impressive in such imperious parts as the title-roles in Bellini's *Norma* and Cherubini's *Medea*.

Callas's voice, with its slightly metallic tone, was not consistently beautiful and her technique was not without faults (while quite young she developed an uneven beat or wobble on her highest notes). But she was unique: her interpretive powers and magnetic personality made her an electrifying performer who is widely regarded as one of the greatest opera singers of all time. She made her last appearance, at the age of forty-one, as Puccini's passionate heroine Tosca in 1964.

Melvin Calvin (b. 1911) American
Chemist

Melvin Calvin was born in St Paul, Minnesota, and educated at the Michigan College of Mining and Technology. Since 1937 he has been Professor of Chemistry at the University of California.

Early in the history of the Earth, before there was any life, its atmosphere was largely carbon dioxide. Somehow, the earliest forms of green plants evolved. These took in carbon dioxide and converted it, using the energy of sunlight, into oxygen. The carbon from the carbon dioxide was combined with water to form sugars and starches, which are essential foods. This process, using the energy of sunlight to convert carbon

LEFT *Maria Callas, a charismatic personality as well as one of the world's greatest sopranos*

Dr Melvin Calvin, who discovered photosynthesis

Camus is one of the most important novelists and philosophers to have emerged from France in this century. He was born in Mondovi, Algeria, and after studying philosophy at the University of Algiers he organized, in 1935, an avant-garde theatre group with which he worked until 1938, when he became a journalist until the beginning of the war. It was during this time that he wrote his earliest successful works, the novel *L'Etranger* (*The Outsider*, 1942) and the play *Caligula* (1944). After the German occupation of France, Camus became one of the intellectual and practical leaders of the Resistance movement. He helped to found the underground newspaper *Combat* in 1943 and was for a time its chief editor and a regular contributor to it until after the Liberation of France.

In *The Outsider* (known in America as *The Stranger*), Camus took as his starting-point the proposition that the universe is absurd and without meaning, and pitted rational man against universal irrationality. The same theme underlies *Caligula*, but in his later work, beginning with the novel *La Peste* (*The Plague*, 1948), he moved towards a position in which the possibility of order being imposed upon the world was admitted and argued for. In his last years, Camus renewed his interest in the theatre, writing and directing stage adaptations of two novels which he greatly admired: William Faulkner's *Requiem for a Nun* and Dostoevsky's *The Possessed*. In 1957 he was awarded the Nobel Prize for Literature.

A humanist unable to accept the comfort of religion, Camus moved from the nihilistic

dioxide and water to oxygen and sugar, was essential to the evolution of animal life, and is essential to its continuance: if there were no green plants, the oxygen of the atmosphere would have disappeared by now. The chain of reactions is called photosynthesis, and it was Melvin Calvin who discovered how it works. For this he was awarded a Nobel Prize in 1961.

The difficulty about studying photosynthesis is that the reaction doesn't work in test-tubes, and living, green plant cells are needed. Another problem is that the reaction is very rapid. It takes place in a number of stages, but they follow each other so quickly that they cannot be separated. Calvin devised an original technique for a long, painstaking research project. He used carbon dioxide whose carbon atom was radioactive, so that it could easily be traced. He used simple, one-celled plants in his experiment, which he exposed to the radioactive carbon dioxide and sunlight for very short periods. He then checked the chemicals that contained this radioactive carbon, using a technique called chromatography. The plants were mashed with water and the solution run over a type of blotting-paper. The different chemicals spread to varying extents, and could be identified by the distance they had spread. The smears on the paper could also be checked for radioactivity to see if they had taken up the carbon from the carbon dioxide.

The results of these experiments showed the process of photosynthesis, by which plants absorb carbon dioxide and, with water, convert it to oxygen and the foodstuffs they need.

RIGHT *Albert Camus, winner of the Nobel Prize for Literature in 1957*

Absurdism of his youth to a more complex attitude in which, through his essays and novels, he strove continually to assert the dignity of man and to find ways of building bridges of understanding and affection between people, across chasms of indifference. Politically, he appeared to move from left to right in the conventional swing to conservatism that seems to accompany the ageing process. However, a close and sympathetic reading of such late works as the essay *L'Homme Revolté* (*The Rebel*, 1953) or the novel *La Chute* (*The Fall*, 1956) reveals Camus' apparently conservative stance to be basically non-political and founded rather on a concern with moral values and meaning.

Chester Carlson (1906–68) American
Inventor

The story of Carlson's invention of xerography as a copying process, and its commercial triumph many years later, follows closely the classical pattern of a brilliant invention struggling for recognition.

Chester Carlson was born in Seattle in 1906 to a family that was never rich – his father was a travelling barber, soon to be crippled with arthritis – and the boy worked to earn money while he studied. One of his employers was a local printer in San Bernadino, California, where the family had settled, and from him Carlson gained a small, worn-out printing-press; this taught him the difficulties of producing copies of a text. He started to keep a notebook of his ideas.

Carlson studied chemistry in junior college and physics at the California Institute of Technology, and then tried a number of jobs before joining an electronics company, P.R. Mallory. He earned a law degree in his spare time and became manager of Mallory's patent department. There he discovered the need for a copying process – patent lawyers need many copies of specifications, and there was then no quick, cheap way of making them. Carlson started to look for new processes and came across the experiments with electrostatic images of Paul Selenyi, a Hungarian physicist.

The principle behind electrostatic copying is simple. Some substances, such as sulphur, conduct electricity when a light shines on them. If a sheet of zinc covered with sulphur is given an electrostatic charge and is then illuminated by light shone through the document to be copied, the parts of the plate that the light strikes will become conductors and lose their charge. If a fine powder is dusted over the plate, the remaining electricity will hold it to the parts that were not exposed to light, which correspond to the original print. The printing will be reversed left to right, but a permanent copy can be made by laying a piece of charged, waxed paper over the plate – the paper will pick up the dust – and then heating it so that the dust sinks in. Carlson first got this process to work on 22 October 1938.

His invention was turned down by more than a score of companies, but eventually, in 1944, the Batelle Memorial Institution signed a royalty agreement, started to develop the process commercially, and signed an agreement with a small photopaper company called Haloid. This company, in 1959, twenty years after Carlson's first invention, demonstrated the first office copier. The rest is legend. Carlson became rich, the company, renamed Xerox, became outstandingly successful, and a new verb – 'to xerox' – entered the language.

Henri Cartier-Bresson (b. 1908) French
Photographer

On the street he is hardly noticed, an anonymous grey man in a raincoat, although closer observation might reveal a 35mm camera in his hand. Cartier-Bresson, the greatest living photographer, cultivates invisibility, rarely allowing himself to be photographed, retreating when his identity is revealed. His first exhibition, in New York in 1933, revealed the power of the image achieved by the new miniature photography. With a small Leica Cartier-Bresson depicted an extraordinary world of people going about their

The first xerox machine and its inventor, Chester Carlson

discovered that he possessed a voice of great natural beauty. He made his debut with a touring opera company at the age of twenty-one, but it was four years later that he achieved his first real success, singing the tenor role of Loris in Giordano's *Fedora* at La Scala, Milan. After this his rise to international fame was meteoric. He appeared at Covent Garden as the Duke in Verdi's *Rigoletto* in 1902, and subsequently often sang at Covent Garden. In 1903 he was heard for the first time at the Metropolitan Opera, New York, where he became a great favourite, appearing there virtually every season for the rest of his life.

Caruso's voice was a full-throated Italian tenor, more suited to the operas of Puccini, Leoncavallo and Mascagni than to those of Verdi or the earlier, more elegant composers of *bel canto* operas. Indeed, it was in the operas of Puccini that he had some of his greatest successes; he was chosen by Puccini for the role of Dick Johnson in *La Fanciulla del West* (*The Girl of the Golden West*) at its premiere at the

lives, yet forming astonishing rhythmical compositions in the most mundane settings.

Cartier-Bresson forswears all contrivance in his work. He never retouches his negatives or crops his prints. His compositions are formed in the camera at the moment he presses the shutter release, not later in the darkroom. He never sets up his photographs, but shoots spontaneously. He dislikes colour, choosing to work in black and white for greater truth. He has a fanatical puritanism towards his work, preferring to return from an assignment empty-handed rather than compromise his standards. Whether it be picnickers on a river bank, children among ruins, a prison camp informer denounced before newly liberated internees, there is an astonishing integrity that makes his photographs unique. Cartier-Bresson's range is broad, his subject mankind. His eye will note the humorous incident, a strange gesture, or a wry expression, and a moment later it is preserved forever by his lens. If sent by a magazine to cover an event of great pageantry he will turn his back on the spectacle and shoot faces in the crowd, discovering details of the day that would have gone unnoticed. His genius is that of perfect timing, of instinctively knowing the split second in which he has to make a picture. It is a skill to which all photographers aspire. Henri Cartier-Bresson is the master.

Enrico Caruso (1873–1921) Italian
Opera singer

Caruso was brought up in a Naples slum, so it was only with great difficulty that he was able to afford to study singing when, in his teens, it was

Metropolitan Opera in 1910.

Caruso's career also coincided with the invention and early popularity of the gramophone record. He made his first records of arias and Neapolitan songs in 1902, and continued to record until a few months before his death: the finest are those made between 1905 and 1908, when he was at his peak.

It was while he was singing in New York in the winter of 1920 that Caruso caught a bronchial infection which developed into pneumonia. He returned to Naples to recuperate, but died there. He was the best-known opera singer of his time, bringing his art to a wider public and becoming a household name through the medium of the gramophone. Even today his name is still synonymous with the art of the Italian tenor.

Pablo Casals (1876–1973) Spanish
Cellist, conductor and composer

Pablo Casals was the most famous cellist of the century. He was born in Vendrell, Tarragona, the son of an organist who supervised his early musical education. By the time he was twelve Casals was able to play most orchestral instruments, but decided to concentrate on the cello; by his late teens he had become an accomplished performer, and during his twenties he gave cello concerts throughout Europe and America. Slowly he became renowned as a specialist in the music of Bach and as a musician of unusual stature who brought a number of innovations to the technique of his instrument. He brought the solo cello suites of Bach, formerly regarded as of little interest musically, into the forefront of the cello repertory.

In 1919 Casals founded the Barcelona Orchestra, which he conducted for many years. He was not, perhaps, a great interpreter among conductors but he was generally recognized as an inspiration to his players and as a fine teacher of orchestral musicians. Another important aspect of his all-round musicianship was his collaboration with two other musicians; together they formed a chamber music trio that was to become famous. It consisted of Casals himself, the pianist Alfred Cortot and the violinist Jacques Thibaud and their playing and recording of the great classical trios became legendary.

Casals conducted his Barcelona Orchestra for the last time in 1936, when the Spanish Civil War caused him to leave his native land. Subsequently he lived in the south of France, and after the Second World War he helped to found a music festival in the small town of Prades, close to the Spanish border, in which he performed and taught. When he died in his late nineties, Casals had long been recognized not only by the musical public but also by his fellow musicians as an artist of unique quality, and a human being of rare moral conviction. As a performer he has left his mark upon succeeding generations of cellists, and indeed upon string players in general.

Fidel Castro (b. 1929) Cuban
Revolutionary

Castro is a phenomenon, a contradiction even. He is a Third World leader who is white, but the idol of non-white revolutionaries. He preaches independence and non-alignment, but his own country survives only on massive subsidies from the Soviet Union, and Cuba's actions abroad are mostly determined by Moscow. Yet there is something so powerful and extraordinary about the impact of his personality that it cannot be denied that Castro has 'star quality', an amazing magnetism that exudes naturally from this large, untidy man in a green uniform, a cigar constantly grasped in his hand.

Born on a large sugar estate owned by his father, who had come to Cuba from Spain about the turn of the century, Fidel's mother was a white Cuban cook in his father's household. He was educated at one of the finest Jesuit schools in Havana and at the university there. From the first he was a restless nationalist who disliked the American dominance of Cuba, and he was continually involved in revolutionary activity against Batistá, then the ruler of Cuba. With all his men dressed as sergeants in Batistá's army, Castro was captured leading an attack on the Moncado barracks in 1953 and sentenced to fifteen years' imprisonment. When Batistá granted an amnesty, Castro was released and went to Mexico, where he gathered together a group of guerillas – not all Cuban – and, on the yacht *Gran-ma*, landed on 24 November 1956 with eighty-two men who took to the Sierra Maestra mountains. The rebels succeeded and by January 1959 Castro had occupied Havana. He became Prime Minister in the same year.

From then on Castro gradually revealed himself as a Marxist-Leninist, but of a curiously chaotic and personal kind. He is an immensely undisciplined person, hating routine and desk-

LEFT *Spanish cellist Pablo Casals, whose technical and interpretive powers have influenced performers all over the world*

Fidel Castro, volatile, magnetic, undisciplined and the idol of revolutionaries everywhere

Pskov. His fame then began to spread abroad, and in 1901 he appeared at La Scala, Milan, in the title role of Boito's *Mefistofele.* A formidable actor as well as a rich and resonant bass, Chaliapin is said to have influenced the entire style of Italian operatic acting with his performance in Boito's opera. In Paris and London he created an outburst of enthusiasm and excitement when he appeared in the Russian operas under Diaghilev's (*q.v.*) management.

At the outbreak of the First World War Chaliapin returned to Russia but left again during the communist Revolution of 1917, never to return. In the 1920s he frequently appeared at the Metropolitan Opera, New York, and also embarked on a series of world tours as a concert singer. In 1933 he appeared in his only film, *Don Quichotte,* with music by Ibert. His numerous recordings of arias and Russian songs made him a household name, second only to Caruso (*q.v.*).

During the years of his greatest fame Chaliapin was acclaimed both as a singer and as an actor. Though by all accounts his acting was wildly undisciplined, he had immense power and authority as a stage personality. He was heard at his best in the Russian repertoire, especially as Mussorgsky's Boris, a role he made his own. Traces of Chaliapin's Boris are still to be found in the performances of eastern European interpreters of the role today.

work. He is unpunctual, volatile, and given to marathon speeches many hours long, their form often taking shape from the vibrations he picks up from his audience. For these peasant and worker audiences sense that, possessing as he does all their un-western and un-bourgeois qualities, Castro has much in common with them. He has a lively spontaneity and audacious bravery, which gives him an appeal to the illiterate and exploited masses of Latin America and other parts of the developing world, especially to those who do not know the darker side of his record in Cuba. This includes, in the early days, a contempt for human life, for human rights, the incitement of mob rule, and 'justice' shown in televised mass 'trials'. He does not like to delegate authority, and the economy of Cuba stagnates – even sugar, the agricultural staple, is rationed.

Feodor Chaliapin (1873–1938) Russian
Opera singer

Feodor Chaliapin was born into a humble peasant family in Kazan. He had little formal education and after working at various jobs he joined a travelling operetta company touring southern Russia. He studied briefly with the tenor Dmitri Usatov in Tiflis, where in 1893 he made his operatic debut as Mephistopheles in Gounod's *Faust.* The following year he appeared in St Petersburg, but his great success came only after 1896 when, in Moscow, he sang such roles as Boris in Mussorgsky's *Boris Godunov* and Ivan the Terrible in Rimsky-Korsakov's *Maid of*

RIGHT *Feodor Chaliapin, Russian bass, in his most famous role as Boris Godunov*

Coco Chanel (1886–1971) French
Fashion designer

Almost alone during the First World War, Chanel welcomed working clothes for women and provided her earliest customers with pullovers, sailor sweaters, pleated skirts and workmen's jackets in jersey: garments that were unlike anything worn before by fashionable women. She had a perfect sense of proportion and never changed her convictions about clothes and what they should do for women: primarily,

that they should be flattering, comfortable and practical, and make women look a little younger. She insisted that clothes should be effortless and quite plain – what she called 'chic on the edge of poverty'. Her pockets were meant to be used and, contrary to the old ideas, her buttons were meant to fasten. Saying 'I make fashions women can live in, breathe in, feel comfortable in and look younger in', she gave working clothes the style they had always lacked, and turned sports clothes into everyday clothes.

Among Chanel's many innovations are trousers for women, horn-rimmed spectacles as a fashion accessory, costume jewellery that was smarter than the genuine article ('It does not matter if they are real so long as they look like junk!') and real-life clothes for Hollywood filmstars – when invited there to design costumes for Ina Claire, Chanel dressed her in tweed suits and white silk pyjamas. Every part of the Chanel look became a much-copied hallmark, from the bow in the hair to the quilted bag on a chain, from the

beige and black sling-back shoes to the world-famous scent, Chanel No. 5, that made her a substantial fortune.

In 1954, at the age of sixty, Chanel made a comeback: she re-opened her salon and showed a collection that was rapturously received and which was a unique phenomenon during the 1950s – comfortable and fashionable clothes that did not date. Her classic cardigan suit came back with new details: edged with braid and gilt buttons, lined in quilted silk, gilt chains adding weight and swing to the jacket, tucked silk blouse with bow inside, and in the skirt, as before, deep pockets for cigarettes and money. If women could not afford the real thing they bought a copy and wore that until it wore out. New generations of women benefited from Chanel's contribution to ease and elegance, and reinforced her position among the most influential and longest-remembered designers in the history of fashion.

Charlie Chaplin (1889–1977) British
Actor, director, writer and composer

There was a time when the 'little fellow', Chaplin's tramp with the baggy striped trousers, black derby and cane, was the most evocative symbol of the screen in virtually every country of the world.

After an impoverished London childhood Chaplin learned his acrobatic skills in the music hall, reaching America with the famous Fred Karno troupe. Mack Sennett invited him to work for Keystone in Hollywood in 1913, and after a shaky initial start Chaplin evolved the tramp disguise in his second film, *Kid Auto Races at Venice*. In his first year he made thirty-five films, some of which he wrote and directed himself. By 1916 he had been signed by Mutual for an unprecedented $10,000 a week, and it was during this period that some of his greatest early films, such as *The Rink*, *Easy Street*, *The Cure* and *The Immigrant*, were made.

A period at First National followed, with *Shoulder Arms* and *The Kid* among the results. In 1919 he co-founded United Artists with Mary Pickford (*q.v.*), Douglas Fairbanks and D.W. Griffith (*q.v.*). His later silent features were suffused with sentiment and pathos, in contrast to the anarchic spirit of the early two-reelers. An exception to this was *A Woman of Paris* (1923), a serious drama in which Chaplin's only appearance was in an uncredited walk-on. The critical acclaim was high, but the public stayed away, and Chaplin withdrew the film from circulation. The tramp resurfaced triumphantly in the comic masterpiece *The Gold Rush* (1925). Chaplin faced the arrival of the talkies by ignoring them – his *City Lights* (1931), apart from the synchronized score, is a silent film. It is doubtful if any other performer could have

LEFT *Gabrielle 'Coco' Chanel in a braided cardigan suit typical of the style she made fashionable in the 1950s*

Charlie Chaplin with the baggy trousers, black derby and cane that were his trademark

his years in Switzerland with his last wife Oona, who bore him eight children. In 1972 he briefly returned to America to accept a special Academy Award, and in 1975 he was knighted.

Noam Chomsky (b. 1928) American
Linguistic theorist and political activist

Born in Philadelphia, Chomsky is one of the most influential thinkers in linguistic theory of the present century, and the only linguist whose works are widely read. His entire teaching career has been at the Massachusetts Institute of Technology, where he has trained many followers and built up a strong group.

At the centre of his thinking is the problem not of the function of language, but how it is that humans have the capacity to learn and use language. This problem partly has to do with a child's readiness to absorb linguistic information, but partly also with the ability to generate from that information new, as yet untaught but correct uses of language. Children have the ability to utter new sentences correctly, i.e. strings of words they have never before heard or spoken. Grammar, therefore, is no mere matter of simple rules to be learned and obeyed, but must also be a matter of understanding deep rules that allow the words of some sentences to be used differently in others.

In his *Syntactic Structures* of 1957 Chomsky suggested that rules for phrase-structure must reveal deep grammatical structures that control correctness and ambiguity and determine the surface structure of what we hear and write. Since that time Chomsky has expanded and to a considerable extent revised his views several times. In particular he has argued that there must

succeeded by so blatantly ignoring the new medium.

Five years passed before the next Chaplin film, *Modern Times*, in which apart from a nonsense song he again remained mute. But by the *Great Dictator* (1940), a parody of fascism, he at last accepted the talking picture, and buried the character of the tramp. *Monsieur Verdoux* (1947) was a brilliant black comedy and *Limelight* (1952) a paean for the lost world of the London music hall. His last two films, *A King in New York* (1957) and *A Countess from Hong Kong* (1966) were disappointments to a world conditioned to wait long periods for a Chaplin film.

Chaplin's private life was controversial, his political simplicity looked on as ultra left wing. His resistance to American citizenhood and his much-publicized sexual involvements created unpopularity in the United States, and in 1952, while en route with his wife and family to Europe to promote *Limelight* (1952), his right of re-entry was withdrawn. Chaplin spent the remainder of

RIGHT *Noam Chomsky*

be something like an inherent mental capacity or linguistic ability built into every human that enables him or her to learn language. This belief arose because of the phenomenon that, from a finite set of rules and examples, once we are linguistically competent we can generate an infinite number of sentences. Two of Chomsky's best-known books on the subject are *Cartesian Linguistics* and *Language and Mind.*

As the Vietnam War escalated in the 1960s Chomsky gained another sort of fame by criticizing the war and those intellectuals and academics who supported it. A youthful radical and Zionist, he came in middle age increasingly to ally himself with those who mistrusted the governing elites of the United States and of Israel. He made some attempt to establish a connection between his radical politics and his linguistic theories, but these are not widely held to be successful; it is Chomsky's linguistic theories alone that are generally considered to be of major importance.

Winston Churchill (1874–1965) British
Political leader

Churchill was one of the greatest politicians that Britain has ever had. Most of his life was spent in public service, and he came to be regarded as the greatest living Englishman. He led the country to victory in the Second World War, and his powerful and emotive speeches of that time united the country in a passionate determination to win.

Churchill regarded himself as a man with a destiny, which his early adventurous life on the world's battlefields at the turn of the century, and his brushes with death, underlined. Like his great ancestor, Marlborough, he was to make his impact on history.

To Britain's trade unionists, Churchill was seen as a reactionary. It was often claimed that before the First World War he had 'told the troops to fire on the miners striking at Tonypandy'. In fact, he never did and the troops never fired. He was also supposed to have crushed the 1926 General Strike. The truth of the matter was that he was far less harsh in Cabinet against the TUC than others, but Churchill had an aggressive public image that went against him.

To Britain's rich ruling class, tightly knit as it was until 1945, Churchill was a man not to be trusted. He had switched parties twice. He was an orator: they thought him an agitator, and never forgot his attacks on the rich when he was a Liberal Cabinet Minister before the First World War. To them he was unprincipled, an opportunist. Even his imagination and his skill with words, his very cleverness, counted against him. Their judgement was: an unsound man, a 'brilliant wayward child'.

Churchill's inner secret was his immense energy and his sensitive creativity. He was the last British statesman ever to be able to shape events like an artist, to bring imaginative rather than administrative powers to politics. This quality enabled him, in that 'darkest hour' of 1940, to speak for the British people, to provide, as he himself said, the 'lion's roar'. He saw things against the long view of history; he had a good grasp of strategy, and undoubtedly, in spite of subsequent debate and controversy, his direction of the war could have been bettered by no other man in Britain, let alone any politician.

He had been prepared for that, his very own finest hour, by almost continuous involvement in government in a great variety of offices of state from 1906 to 1929. Even the period in the wilderness, from 1929 to 1939, had the value of enabling him to think deeply about, and to fight, the Nazi menace.

Towards the close of the war he saw the dangers that would come from Stalin (*q.v.*), and,

Winston Churchill: a Second World War poster

defeated at the 1945 election, he was to play a great part in persuading the west to stand firmly together to resist the potential aggressor. His period as peace-time Prime Minister, 1951–5, was a benign twilight, during which he was made a Knight of the Garter, and after that he remained in old age a backbench Member of Parliament for some years. When he died in 1965 he was given the grandest state funeral of any subject since the Duke of Wellington.

Colette (1873–1954) French
Novelist

Sidonie Gabrielle Colette, known simply as Colette, wrote at least a dozen books which have become landmarks in literature, including *Chéri* (1920), *Sido* (1930), *La Vagabonde* (1931–2) and *Le Pur et l'Impur* (*These Pleasures*, 1934). The most famous woman writer in her lifetime, she

A poster advertising Colette's Claudine à Paris

was a member of the Belgian Royal Academy and the first woman member of the French Académie Goncourt. Born in the beautiful Burgundy countryside of St Sauveur-en-Puisaye, she went to Paris at twenty, already married to a bohemian hack-writer, Henri Gauthier-Villars (pen-name Willy). In collaboration with him she wrote a series of provocative stories between 1900 and 1903. After an early divorce she became a music hall performer, recording her stage experiences in three books, of which *La Vagabonde* is one. She lived for several years with a woman and then in 1912 married Henri de Jouvenel, a newspaper proprietor and politician.

Colette expressed in words exactly what her senses conveyed, and she remains the most sensual of all writers. In *Les Vrilles de la Vigne* (1923) she gave a lyrical series of descriptions of animals and flowers, and her later autobiographical work, including *Sido* and *La Maison de Claudine* (*The Mother of Claudine*, 1922), has perhaps her finest character portraits of her mother, and a description of her happy childhood. Not interested in ideology or twentieth-century preoccupations, Colette always wrote about instinctive human behaviour, the pleasures of the senses and what that great novelist Tolstoy called 'the tragedy of the bedroom'. She divorced Jouvenel in 1924 and married her third husband, Maurice Goudeket, in 1935. From 1949 she suffered from bad arthritis but continued to write, usually from her divan-bed among her collection of paperweights and framed butterflies, her fur blanket and flowers. A legendary figure, in 1953 she was made grand officer of the Légion d'Honneur. She died in Paris in August 1954 and received official honours at her funeral.

Joseph Conrad (1857–1924) British, ex-Polish
Novelist

Although all Conrad's novels are written in English, until he was about twenty he spoke no English at all. His real name was Teodor Józef Konrad Nalęcz Korzeniowski, and he was born in the Ukraine of Polish parents. His father was a revolutionary and writer who was exiled to Russia, and it was there that Conrad was orphaned at the age of eleven. Spending most of his early years at sea, he eventually joined the

British merchant navy and gained his certificate as master in 1884, at which time he took up British nationality. In 1890 he commanded a river steamer on the Belgian Congo, but after his first novel, *Almayer's Folly*, was published in 1895 he gave up his profession to concentrate on writing. He married in 1896, and wrote and published a number of novels before achieving immense popularity with *Chance* in 1913, a novel which is not now generally regarded as one of his most successful.

Many of Conrad's novels are set in exotic, far-away places, and concerned with the sea and sea-faring men. Developing an apparently impersonal method of story-telling as opposed to straight narrative, Conrad used the device of a narrator, Marlow, in novels such as *Chance* and *Lord Jim* (1900) and in short stories, analysing and commenting on the significance of the events that he narrated. However, the sea was not Conrad's only theme and one of his finest novels, *Under Western Eyes* (1911), is an account of political oppression in Tsarist Russia. The obsessive theme in all his work was the testing of character under conditions of extreme stress and danger, and the stresses and dangers were as frequently moral as physical. He wrote two novels in collaboration with the English writer Ford Madox Ford, *The Inheritors* (1901) and *Romance* (1903), but these are inferior to his own creations, which gained Conrad his reputation as a major novelist who explores human motives and aspirations with immense skill and penetration. *The Secret Agent* (1907), under the guise of a spy story, examines the nature of anarchy through techniques which typify Conrad's methods as a novelist.

Le Corbusier (1887–1965) Swiss
Architect

An erratic and complex man, Le Corbusier (born Charles-Edouard Jeanneret) was also the greatest architectural innovator the twentieth century has seen. He designed several brilliant buildings, notably the Villa Savoye at Poissy (1929–31), the Unité d'Habitation at Marseilles (1947–52) and the Ronchamp Chapel (1950–4). Unfortunately, he spread his genius in many different directions, with different degrees of success, and his reputation has suffered as a result.

Like Frank Lloyd Wright (*q.v.*) and Mies van der Rohe (*q.v.*), he had no formal training. But he gave *himself* an architectural education by walking across Europe on a four-year study tour, having built his first house at the age of seventeen. In 1917 he returned to Paris and immersed himself in the world of art, architecture and criticism.

Le Corbusier's early work – the Citrohan house plans (1920–22) and the Pessac housing estate near Bordeaux (1922–6) – represented a determinedly 'modern' approach to the post-war housing problem. He preached rationalism, insisting that 'a house is a machine for living'. Modern people, he proposed in his unfortunately very influential project for a 'contemporary city of three million inhabitants' (1922), would live in blocks of flats set in parkland, work in huge skyscrapers, and travel between zones on expressways.

Most of his realized projects of this period were individual villas, like the Maison Stein on the outskirts of Paris (1927) and the Villa Savoye. They were revolutionary but also remarkably elegant, rectangular and formal but lightened by the delicate use of glass, metal and space. When the private commissions from rich patrons dried up during the austere 1930s, Le Corbusier turned his attention to larger-scale projects, town plans (none of which were implemented) and public buildings, including the Salvation Army Hostel and Maison Suisse in Paris (1931–2).

But it was in the 1940s and 1950s that Le Corbusier's architectural genius was fully manifested, in buildings suggesting huge, expressive sculptures rather than machines for living. The chapel at Ronchamp was revolutionary in form, extraordinary even by Le Corbusier's standards: an apparently casual design executed in massive materials, it has a curved, almost billowing concrete roof, and three thick walls pierced irregularly with small windows. The Unité d'Habitation offered a revolutionary concept, that of a town in one block (a scheme which was taken up by countless unsuccessful imitators); again the building was immensely big and strong, like a concrete whale beached in the suburbs of Marseilles.

Yet after fifteen years pursuing this rich stylistic vein, Le Corbusier's work seemed

The sculpturally beautiful Ronchamp Chapel – Notre Dame du Haut at Haute Saône – designed by Le Corbusier

suddenly – with the Corbusier Centre at Zurich (completed in 1968) – to be about to embark on a new style, using steel, glass and colour. This phase, however, ended before it began, with Le Corbusier's death in 1965.

Jacques-Yves Cousteau on board Calypso

Jacques-Yves Cousteau (b. 1910) French
Aquanaut and environmentalist

A lawyer's son, Cousteau's passion for the sea developed when he joined the French navy in 1931. After breaking both arms in an accident he took up swimming in the Mediterranean as therapy; on donning goggles, he caught his first glimpse of the undersea world that was to dominate the rest of his life.

In 1943 Cousteau and the engineer Emile Gagnon invented the aqualung, used by millions of divers since. After the war he helped organize the French navy's first undersea unit, and then developed underwater filming to new levels of expertise. In 1950 he purchased a former naval minesweeper, the *Calypso*, and embarked on annual oceanographic expeditions, winning accolades and an Oscar with his first full-length film, *The Silent World*. He has won two Oscars since, made approaching a hundred films for cinema and television, and written over thirty books.

Although Cousteau's approach is non-academic he has increasingly stressed environ-mental concerns, his popularity deriving from his ability to combine persuasive instruction with elements of personal daring by himself and his devoted team of diving cameramen. His most striking success has come in the United States, where more than 150,000 people have joined the Cousteau Society, a registered non-profit-making organization that lends powerful support to the ecological lobby. Cousteau has no specific political aims of his own, preferring to quote the Spanish proverb: 'The road to paradise *is* paradise'.

Noël Coward (1899–1973) British
Dramatist, actor and songwriter

Noël Coward was the jack of all theatrical trades and the master of most of them – actor, playwright, songwriter, author, director, cabaret entertainer and wit – who across half a century brilliantly sustained a talent to amuse. Born into a lower-middle-class suburban London background in Teddington he became at the age of ten a professional child actor, much to the delight of his ambitious mother, and went on from there to film for D.W. Griffith (*q.v.*) in *Hearts of the World* (1917) and to star at the age of twenty-one in his own first West End comedy, *I'll Leave It To You* (1920).

It was in 1924, with *The Vortex*, a play about drug addiction and perhaps indirectly also about homosexuality, that Coward first made his name as actor, author and director. The play hit London with all the 'scandalous' impact that John Osborne (*q.v.*) achieved with *Look Back in Anger* exactly thirty years later, and overnight the boy actor and aspiring songwriter had become the playboy of the West End world.

Within a year he had another play, *Hay Fever*, and a revue running simultaneously in the West End. Broadway was conquered in the same year, and from then on the Coward career reads almost like a mid-century history of the British theatre: after *The Vortex* and *Hay Fever* came *This Year of Grace*, *Bitter Sweet*, and then in 1930 the play with which, more than any other, Coward was to be forever associated, *Private Lives*. Written for his beloved close friend, the actress Gertrude Lawrence (they had acted together as children), and also starring a young Laurence Olivier (*q.v.*), Coward's *Private Lives* was the perfect summary of the way in which that generation hid its post-First World War disenchantment under a tight-lipped and some-times cynical smile.

The 1930s also brought *Cavalcade*, a patriotic epic, comedies like *Design For Living* and *Present Laughter*, the one-act play cycle *Tonight at 8.30* (also written for Gertrude Lawrence) and such musicals as *Conversation Piece* and *Operette*. In the 1940s, between wartime troop concert tours, he wrote *Blithe Spirit* and made the Oscar-winning navy film *In Which We Serve*, in which he played a lightly fictionalized Lord Mountbatten.

The post-war years brought a change in theatrical fashions and a period in which Coward was exiled both geographically and theatrically from England. These were the years of his American cabaret seasons and such Broadway musicals as *Sail Away* and *The Girl Who Came To Supper*. They were followed by a return to London favour when in 1964 the National Theatre made *Hay Fever* their first revival by a living playwright. In 1970 Coward received a knighthood.

He will be remembered not only for his plays and films but also for more than three hundred songs, among them 'Mrs Worthington', 'The Stately Homes of England' and 'Mad Dogs and Englishmen'. He has left a memory of the most theatrically and musically blithe of all show-business spirits.

Francis Crick (b. 1916) British & James Watson (b. 1928) American Biologists

Francis Crick and James Watson, as Watson reports, went into their usual bar one evening in 1953 and announced that they had just found the Secret of Life. It was a dramatic statement, but in a way true. They had solved one problem that is fundamental to understanding reproduction, and which is unique to living creatures. They had worked out how a living cell can divide to produce two identical cells. It turned out to depend on the size and shape of simple chemical molecules. The discovery won them the 1953 Nobel Prize.

Francis Crick, born in Northampton on 8 June 1916, and James Watson, born in Chicago on 6 April 1928, joined forces at Cambridge in 1951. Crick had been educated at University College, London, and Cambridge University, Watson at the University of Chicago and then at the Universities of Indiana and Copenhagen. The problem they turned to was that of inheritance: how does a cell in the liver, for example, divide to give two identical liver cells? The characteristics of a cell are carried by units called genes, and these are 'assembled' to form chromosomes, which can easily be seen under a microscope as black woolly strings. When a cell divides, each chromosome duplicates itself. The process is called replication, and it is the key to heredity.

Chromosomes were known to be composed of a chemical, called DNA (the full name is deoxyribonucleic acid). Crick and Watson analysed DNA and made a model of the complex structure of the sugars, phosphates and chemical bases in it. By doing so they realized how DNA

replicated. The reason that cells produce similar cells, that donkeys give birth to donkeys and that humans give birth only to humans, ultimately depends on the chemistry and shape of the chemical bases.

LEFT *The immaculate Noël Coward*

BELOW LEFT *Dr Francis Crick and Professor James Watson with a model of the DNA molecule whose structure they analyzed in 1953*

BELOW *Bing Crosby*

Bing Crosby (1904–77) American
Singer and actor

After studying law, Crosby – born in Tacoma, near Seattle – became a member of the vocal trio The Rhythm Boys, which, after touring in vaudeville, joined the Paul Whiteman band in 1927. He appeared with Whiteman in the film *The King of Jazz*, and he then left to begin a solo

career of extraordinary commercial success, becoming the most famous and popular singer in the world, unchallenged till the rise of Frank Sinatra (*q.v.*) in the 1940s.

Crosby's fame was built on a carefully staged informality which enabled him to move into acting fairly easily. With his pipe-smoking, casually dressed image, he created an illusion of an ordinary man whose style of singing – as relaxed as if he were singing in the bath – made him the crooner *par excellence*. Throughout the 1930s he steadily increased his range as a light comedian in Hollywood, where his career reached its climax with an Academy Award for his portrayal of a whimsical singing priest in 'Going My Way'.

Crosby's phenomenal success with Irving Berlin's (*q.v.*) 'White Christmas' – said to have sold thirty million copies – topped a long line of recording hits, such as 'When the Blue of the Night', which he part-wrote, 'Just One More Chance' and 'Can't We Talk it Over'. His professional double-act with comedian Bob Hope in the long series of 'Road' films retained wide popularity for many years. He was also well known for his exploits as a golfing charity fundraiser.

Marie (1867–1934) & Pierre Curie
(1859–1906) French
Physicists

Marie Curie was born in Warsaw on 7 November 1867 as Marya Sklodowska and eventually left her native Poland to study science in France, having struggled to save enough money for the fare and a bare subsistence. She qualified in physics and mathematics and in 1895 married Pierre Curie. They were awarded jointly a Nobel Prize in 1903. (Their first daughter Irène, by then Irène Joliot-Curie, was to share a Nobel Prize with *her* husband in 1935.)

Marie's earliest research was connected with Pierre's work on the magnetization of iron, but as soon as she heard of the discovery of the penetrating rays given off by minerals containing uranium, she adopted this subject as her own. It was she who coined the name 'radioactivity' to describe this occurrence. She quickly found a way of measuring radioactivity, and showed that its intensity depended on the amount of uranium present in the uranium mineral. This was predictable. But then she found that some samples of minerals containing uranium had much more radioactivity than they would have had even if they had been pure uranium.

She realized that these samples of mineral must contain a second radioactive element, and set out to separate it. It was clearly such important research that Pierre abandoned his work to become her assistant. After some

months they extracted from a large mass of uranium a tiny amount of a highly radioactive element that they called polonium (after Marie's native country). But the polonium in the uranium did not account for all the radioactivity, and eventually they detected yet another element; this they called radium. It was available only in minute quantities, however, and in order to produce more of it they embarked on an almost interminable series of chemical experiments. In December 1898 they were given a ton of scrap uranium mineral from the state mines; it took until 1902 to produce a tenth of a gramme of radium.

Pierre was killed in a road accident in 1906 and Marie continued his lectures at the Sorbonne, as well as her own studies of radioactivity and radium, after his death. For her work in isolating polonium and radium and her research in radioactivity Marie was awarded a Nobel Prize in 1911. She died in 1934 of leukaemia, a form of radiation sickness contracted from her work with radioactive materials.

D

Salvador Dali (b. 1904) Spanish
Painter

The life and personality of Dali have attracted as much public interest as his art. Born near Barcelona, Dali, like Picasso (*q.v.*), was a child prodigy. His stormy artistic career began in 1921 at the San Fernando Academy in Madrid, from which he was later expelled.

Among his most impressive early works are the paintings and collages of 1927. By the following year his art had begun to reflect the Surrealism for which he is best known: this was an attempt to reveal subconscious states by using dream-like images and hallucinatory forms with an eerie use of light and space. (In his autobiography he explained that since childhood he has been subject to hallucinations and acts of violence.)

Dali's first mature works, a series of small

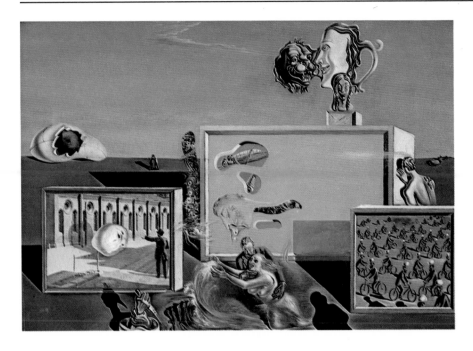

Illumined Pleasures *by Salvador Dali, 1929*

pictures of 1929, are, in their compactness and in the intensity of his vision, among his finest creations. It is the precision and clarity of his irrational dream images and settings which seem to have an almost hypnotic effect on Dali's admirers. He was obsessed with abnormal mental states, with putrefaction, castration, voyeurism and masturbation – and it is not always easy to interpret his private obsessions and dreams. For example, the idea for the soft watches in his famous painting *The Persistence of Memory* (1931) came, Dali said, from eating ripe camembert cheese.

Undoubtedly, Dali's major contributions to twentieth-century art were his early Surrealist paintings and his early films, such as *Le Chien Andalou* (1929). Although his later paintings, which include a number of Christian subjects, are greatly admired by the general public for their technical skill and compositional and optical tricks, they appear self-conscious and contrived. Nonetheless Dali's eccentric personality and outrageous showmanship have made him one of the best-known artists of the century.

Simone de Beauvoir (b. 1908) French
Philosopher and novelist

Distinguished author and existentialist philosopher, Simone de Beauvoir became world famous with the success of her intellectual and passionate book *The Second Sex* (1949), which exploded the myth of the *éternel féminin*. Educated in Catholic schools and at the Sorbonne, she passed her aggregation in philosophy in 1929, the year she met Jean-Paul Sartre (*q.v.*), who was to be her lifelong companion. Together they established a provocative monthly mag-

azine, *Les Temps Modernes*, in 1945.

De Beauvoir became a leading existentialist with the success of her first novel, *L'Invité* (*She Came to Stay*) in 1943, and followed it with a stream of critical writings and novels. She always placed the individual at the centre of the world, in control of his or her actions and responsible for them. Her non-fiction work included *Pour une Morale de l'Ambiguité* (*The Ethics of Ambiguity*, 1947) and *Faut-il brûler Sade* (*Must we Burn de Sade*, 1951). She was a vivid travel writer, publishing *L'Amérique au Jour le Jour* (*America Day by Day*) in 1948 and *La Longue Marche* in 1957. Her novels were intended to instruct as well as to explore the conflict between a personal commitment and a public duty. *Tous les Hommes sont Mortels* presented a picture of the psychological pressures attendant upon a hypothetical immortality. De Beauvoir's important three-volume autobiography began in 1958 with *Mémoires d'une Jeune Fille Rangée* (*Memoirs of a Dutiful Daughter*) and was followed by an

RIGHT *Simone de Beauvoir*

ing year that he began to reach a comparatively wide public. His opera *Pelléas et Mélisande* (1902) brought him international recognition; he was by this time much in demand abroad as a conductor of his own music.

His private life, however, was complicated and unhappy: in 1899, threatening suicide if she refused him, Debussy had married Lilly Texier. Five years later the situation was reversed and Lilly actually attempted suicide when Debussy left her for Emma Bardac, whom he eventually married after his divorce from Lilly in 1908. In 1915 he underwent an operation for cancer, and was thereafter a semi-invalid.

Debussy wrote for the orchestra as well as for the piano, and is generally considered to be the first of the French 'impressionist' composers. He himself maintained that in music impressionist theories could be put into practice more fully than was possible in painting. He was perhaps not the most original of melodists, but certainly one of the most poetic of composers, and one whose rich orchestral harmonies have been much copied by later generations. His songs, delicate and sensitive settings of the French poets, are valuable additions to the concert singer's repertoire.

Charles De Gaulle (1890–1971) French
Political leader

'All my life I have had a certain idea of France.' That certain idea, a deep patriotism, the conviction that France stood for something valuable and unique in human civilization, burnt like a star in the able mind of Charles De Gaulle.

It was a faith he needed. A professional soldier, he survived the First World War and foresaw that the next would not consist of static trench warfare; it would be mechanized. He wrote about his theory and urged in vain that tanks should be used properly as the new cavalry. (Early in the Second World War, the Germans, with their Panzer tanks, were to demonstrate precisely how.) In 1940 De Gaulle was made general and also became Under-Secretary of War. The Government collapsed shortly afterwards and an armistice was to be signed with the Nazis. De Gaulle opposed it to the end. His arrest was imminent, but by a clever ruse he got away in a small aeroplane, carrying with him, said Churchill (*q.v.*), 'the honour of France'. Once in London he appealed to 'Free France' to continue the struggle against the German occupation, but at first it was a small force of only seven thousand men who joined him in uniform and fought alongside the Allies.

Gradually, De Gaulle's faith, persistence and courage made headway. His symbol, the Cross of Lorraine, eventually flew over most of the French overseas empire, and the Resistance grew

account of her own mother's death of cancer, written with chilly detachment, in 1964. Her belief that the individual is at the heart of all action distanced her from some causes and movements, including women's liberation, although she remains one of the most independent women of her generation.

Claude Debussy (1862–1918) French
Composer

Debussy showed a precocious musical talent, which his aunt encouraged, and at the age of ten he left St-Germaine-en-Laye, the town of his birth, to enter the Paris Conservatoire. He was soon acknowledged to be a superb pianist, and at the age of eighteen he secured a post as pianist in the house of Tchaikovsky's wealthy patroness, Nadezhda von Meck, travelling with her to Switzerland, Italy and Russia. He had already begun to compose, mainly songs and piano pieces, and the influence of the Russian composers he encountered through his employer was soon evident in his own music. In 1884 Debussy won the prestigious Prix de Rome with a cantata, *L'Enfant Prodigue*, but it was not until his string quartet of 1893 and his orchestral tone-poem *Prélude à l'Après-Midi d'un Faune* in the follow-

President De Gaulle on a visit to Romania

Diaghilev was the father of twentieth-century classical ballet, freeing it from the hidebound traditions of the Imperial Ballet of St Petersburg (now Leningrad). Soon after his arrival in Moscow from his birthplace, Perm, he realized that he was unlikely to achieve great success as a musician and settled for being an organizer. He had the vision to see how choreographers, dancers, painters, designers and composers could be brought together to create ballets which would unify all the elements involved. The greatest result of his aim was to be *Petrouchka*, created by the choreographer and dancer Mikhail Fokine in 1911.

Meeting a group of painters and designers in St Petersburg, Diaghilev was instrumental in producing an influential magazine, *The World of Art*, in 1898, which gave him access to the Imperial Theatres, where he tried to introduce some of his ideas. Unsuccessful, he turned his energies to organizing exhibitions of Russian art, and it was the success of the one he mounted in Paris in 1905 which led him to present, with even more success, recitals and opera in 1907 and 1908. In the following year he introduced to Paris the choreography of Fokine, a breakaway from the formula used in the Imperial Theatres, as well as dancers such as Pavlova and Nijinsky (*q.v.*). These performances, including the exotic ballets

to heroic proportions. After D-day in 1944, the allied armies advanced to Paris, and De Gaulle and his supporters entered a city full of snipers. Bullets were fired, scattering many as they entered Notre Dame, but De Gaulle kept on walking. He then presided over the interim French Government fighting for the interests of France, as he did throughout the war when he felt they were threatened by Britain or America. He resigned in 1946, still with a political following, holding himself ready for the 'next call from the nation'. Some laughed, but De Gaulle sensed that disaster would come, and that France would need new institutions.

The call eventually came in 1958 when the French colony of Algeria refused to recognize the French Government. De Gaulle was elected president in that year and subsequently Algeria was granted independence.

De Gaulle re-wrote the Constitution so that it became a kind of synthesis of French history, combining both the tradition of liberty and that of order and strong central government. Under it, France advanced phenomenally, her economic strength grew, and she followed a very independent foreign policy. De Gaulle left office in 1969, but his Constitution survived him. He had given France a new unity and restored much of her greatness.

RIGHT *Founder of the Ballets Russes, Sergei Diaghilev*

The Firebird and *Scheherazade* as well as vigorous male dancing, mark the re-birth of ballet in the west.

It was Nijinsky's sister, Bronislava Nijinska, who choreographed the first two great ballets of what would become known as Diaghilev's 'cocktail period', *Les Noces* (1923), with music by Stravinsky (*q.v.*), and *Les Biches* (1924), the epitome of 1920s chic. During this time Diaghilev was obliged to produce a number of fashionable rather than lasting ballets to please the type of audience on which he relied for money. Mixed-media events, avant-garde decor and outrageous ideas became more important than choreography, though many of these ideas were way ahead of their time.

Diaghilev had discovered in turn Fokine, Nijinsky, Leonid Massine (who produced a stream of works for the company, by then called Ballets Russes) and, lastly, George Balanchine (*q.v.*). The strain of coping with the many talented and often temperamental people about him, of producing something new and spectacular each season, and the continual financial problems finally proved too much. Diaghilev died in Venice in 1929, but many members of his Ballets Russes went on to found their own companies around the world; it is largely from them, from the tradition which Diaghilev began, that ballet in the west today has grown.

Marlene Dietrich (b. 1901) American, ex-German
Actress

The early life of Marlene Dietrich is a mystery, her origins obscured by Hollywood press agents in the early 1930s. It is known that she was born in Berlin in 1901, had an upper middle class upbringing, and appeared in films as an extra possibly as early as 1918. She was in a chorus line of a musical revue in the early 1920s and later studied at the Max Reinhardt Drama School. By the late 1920s she had played leading roles in German films, and was spotted by the director Josef von Sternberg, who cast her in *The Blue Angel* (1930). He brilliantly projected Dietrich's sensuality as a male-destroying cabaret vamp, Lola-Lola, revealing to the world in all their glory the celebrated Dietrich legs. She was an immediate hit, and was whisked off to Hollywood with Sternberg, who was to make six more films with her, turning her into a screen goddess – a romantic star possessed with an unassailable and mysterious beauty, which was evident whether she was swathed in furs and diamonds or a simple peasant costume, or attired in male evening dress, complete with top hat.

The Dietrich legend was already obvious by *Blonde Venus* (1932), where she makes her entrance in a night club act as a gorilla, delicately removing a furry paw to reveal her elegant

Marlene Dietrich

feminine hand beneath, then slowly and sensuously performing a striptease. The Sternberg association ended with *The Devil is a Woman* (1935), in which the Lola-Lola role of the male-dominating female reached its peak. From then on she varied her parts: comedy with *Desire* (1936) and *Angel* (1937) and even farce with *Destry Rides Again* (1939), a spoof Western.

Meanwhile, having spurned an invitation to return to Nazi Germany, she was placed high on the Gestapo extermination list. She became an American citizen and worked earnestly and valiantly entertaining troops, while denouncing the regime in her former country. When her film career sagged after the war she turned to the stage and recording studio, with fresh triumphs from a cabaret performance of stunning glamour and sophistication. And always the song that had to be included in her act was the one that Lola-Lola first sang in 1930, 'Falling in Love Again'.

Christian Dior (1905–57) French
Fashion designer

No fashion innovation today could equal the excitement generated by Dior's New Look on 12 February 1947 because it had been preceded by thirteen uninterrupted years of a square-shouldered, clumpy silhouette reinforced in Britain as the wartime Utility Suit. Dior's gloriously nostalgic suits and dresses, with their tiny waists, rounded hips, enormous hats and

Christian Dior's 'New Look' coat of 1947

full, rustling skirts, seemed to the audience like forbidden fruit after the depressing war years. The models swept along with fifteen, twenty-five, even eighty yards of fabric in their skirts: ashtray stands went crashing as they pirouetted.

The new salon was hardly equipped for such success. The staff were working eighteen hours a day and buyers were still in the salon at two o'clock in the morning; one of them bought an unprecedented forty garments. Dior's two first private customers were the Duchess of Windsor and Eva Perón.

Dior said, 'I designed clothes for flower-like women, with rounded shoulders, full, feminine busts, and hand-span waists above enormous, spreading skirts'. The dressmaking techniques were immensely complicated, with hips swelling over shells of cambric or taffeta worked into the lining, or fine pleats stitched down and released over stiff petticoats. Back in Britain, the Board of Trade was outraged to see that 'man-tailored' suits in the yardages they recommended were ignored while the non-Utility New Look copies were selling out as soon as the manufacturers could get them into the shops. Unknown to the Government and the press, a private showing of Dior's collection was given to the Queen, Princess Margaret, and the Duchess of Kent. To all critics Dior simply replied, 'I brought back the neglected art of pleasing'.

This was a late and overwhelming reception for a shy designer who had only recently emerged from the ranks at couturier Lucien Lelong's. Dior was forty when, with the cotton tycoon Marcel Boussac as backer, he opened his own premises at 30 Avenue Montaigne in Paris at the end of the war. The New Look re-established Paris as the undisputed centre of international fashion, and for the rest of his life Dior was to dictate to women what they should wear. With his tulip line, his H, A and Y lines, he maintained a climate in which women rushed to see what he decreed, terrified that their clothes might be outdated overnight, as they had been in 1947. When he died in 1957, he left the field open to the fashion revolution of the 1960s.

Walt Disney (1901–66) American
Animator and film producer

Disney's contribution to the entertainment of millions is probably unequalled by any other person, and continues long after his death. He was not the inventor of animated films, but he made that medium almost synonymous with his name, bequeathing to the world of cinema a cartoon superstar who was to be as universal a symbol of films as Chaplin (*q.v.*) or Garbo (*q.v.*) – Mickey Mouse.

Disney was born in Chicago, and at nineteen worked in a Kansas City commercial art studio. In conjunction with a friend, he began making animated commercials and shorts called Laugh-o-Grams, which were shown at local theatres. After a bankruptcy he went to California and began producing cartoons mingled with live action, the series called *Alice in Cartoonland*.

Mickey Mouse was born in 1928, at first in a silent cartoon, but after two shorts Disney introduced sound to animation with *Steamboat Willie*, himself dubbing Mickey's voice in a high-pitched falsetto. The *Silly Symphonies* followed, in which cartoons illustrated well-known music pieces, and a gallery of characters emerged, characters such as Donald Duck, Pluto the Dog, Goofy, and Minnie Mouse.

Disney pioneered three-colour Technicolor and by the mid-1930s all his output was shot in that process. He also invented the multiplane camera, which brought depth and moving perspective to animation. In 1934 he embarked on the first full-length cartoon, *Snow White and the Seven Dwarfs*, which was premiered three years later. It still attracts large audiences whenever it is revived, and the Disney Organization has wisely kept it off television. It was followed by *Pinocchio* (1939), and the ingenious but controversial *Fantasia* (1941), in which music was allied to cartoon imagery.

During the Second World War the Disney studio turned out propaganda films. In post-war years there was a move into live action features, the first of which was *Treasure Island* (1950), and nature documentaries under the generic title

True-Life Adventures. As always, the emphasis was on family entertainment. A weekly television series was launched in 1954 and lasted more than a quarter of a century. But the most significant development of the 1950s was the opening of Disneyland, an amusement park at Anaheim, California, which rapidly became the most important tourist attraction in western America. Disneyworld at Orlando, Florida, followed in 1971, and a third park is under construction in Tokyo.

Marcel Duchamp (1887–1968) American, ex-French
Painter

Duchamp was born at Blainville, France. In 1911 he came under the Cubist influence of Braque (*q.v.*) and Picasso (*q.v.*), and the first work of his maturity was the famous study of movement, *Nude Descending a Staircase No. 2* (1911–12), which caused a sensation when first exhibited in New York in 1913. It reflects both the Cubist use of faceted form and limited colour, and an interest in 'simultaneity', which is concerned with the depiction of time, movement and change. Duchamp has admitted the influence of chronophotography, in which figures are shown in continuous motion in a sequence of photographs, like consecutive stills from a film.

In one of the most revolutionary decisions in the history of modern art, Duchamp decided to abandon traditional easel painting and to concentrate on ideas: in his own words, 'I wanted to put painting once again at the service of the mind'. His 'ready-mades' were the logical step in this direction, using man-made objects themselves rather than pictorial representations of them; his first works of this type were a bicycle wheel placed upside down on a stool (1913) and a bottle rack (1914), everyday objects shown in isolation in a new context. This anti-art – Dadaism, as the movement became known – had Duchamp as its pioneering figure; it contradicted all the accepted ideas of beauty in painting and sculpture.

In 1915 Duchamp arrived in New York with plans for what was to become his most important work and one of the most enigmatic creations of the twentieth century – *The Bride Stripped Bare by Her Bachelors Even*, known also as the *Large Glass* (1915–23). In this, the Bride is represented in the upper section, the Bachelors in the lower, in a combination of oil paint, wire and foil, dust and varnish on a sheet of clear glass. When the glass was accidentally broken in transit, Duchamp was philosophical, and later spent many months piecing the work together. This baffling masterpiece has lost none of its powerful, erotic presence, and will continue to suggest many layers of meaning.

It was thought that after completing this work Duchamp gave up all activity as an artist, but following his death it was found that he had in fact continued to work on a number of projects. His ideas and his small body of work have had an inestimable influence on the course of post-Cubist twentieth-century art, first shattering and then revising our definition of 'a work of art'.

Isadora Duncan (1878–1927) American
Dancer

Isadora Duncan led a life of such high drama that she overshadowed many of the other pioneers of modern dance, and to some extent these dramas became more important than her actual achievements in helping to found a new way of dancing. Her message was freedom, freedom from the rigid methods of the classical ballet, from the restricting costumes that went with them, and from the artificial stories on which they were often based. By the turn of the century, after dancing-lessons as a child in San Francisco (and an early foray into teaching other children in order to help the family finances), she obtained work in revues in Chicago and New York, but was soon striving to do something more serious. She and her family moved to Britain in 1899, where Isadora was fortunate enough to find patrons for her free-dance

ran into the Seine). After a life which inspired others to develop the young art of modern dance, Isadora Duncan herself died tragically: her long scarf caught in a wheel of her lover's open car and strangled her.

LEFT *Isadora Duncan* c. *1920*

E

George Eastman (1854–1932) American
Inventor

Eastman had advanced from an office boy to a twenty-four-year-old bank clerk in Rochester, New York, when he bought a tripod camera to take on holiday. It was so bulky, unwieldy and complicated that Eastman paid a photographer five dollars for lessons before deciding to stay at home to see if he could simplify it. Working away in the family kitchen during the evenings, Eastman perfected the first, simple, dry photographic plates before his great breakthrough in 1884 that made every man a photographer: roll film. Four years later, Eastman began packaging the film in 100-exposure strips in simple box cameras he had designed himself. He called the cameras Kodaks, which was meaningless but, he hoped, catchy, and sold them under the slogan

George Eastman and his original box camera, the Kodak

recitals, and then on to Paris, which became her home for the rest of her life; from there she set out on recital tours which took her to Vienna and Berlin. She also visited Greece, which had been a source of influence since both the ideals and the costumes she had seen on vase paintings and sculptures in the British Museum had first inspired her. Following the success of these tours Duncan decided to found a school in Berlin in 1904, and soon afterwards visited Russia. Her appearances there had a profound effect on the younger generation of classical dancers and choreographers as well as people in the dramatic theatre.

In contrast to the formality of classical ballet, her solos were very much free expressions of her own inner feelings; what technique there was did not become a 'school' of dance and is now largely lost. Her subject-matter suited the drama of the times, often combining revolutionary ideals with heroic music. Indeed, after the Russian Revolution of 1917 the new Soviet Government invited her to found a school in Moscow. Like so many of her enterprises, this came to nothing, as her burning desire to create was not matched by a complementary skill at organization.

Duncan married the Russian poet Serge Essenine in 1922, but he later committed suicide, one of the many tragedies that dogged her life (of her three children by her two lovers, one died young and the other two drowned when their car

'You press the button, we do the rest'.

Eastman-Kodak's American and English laboratories were soon processing rolls of film by the thousand as amateur photography boomed. Within a year, the first American motion picture was shot on Eastman film, launching the movie boom; in 1900 came the $1.00 box Brownie camera; and by the mid-1920s Eastman-Kodak dominated the entire American film industry.

Eastman gave away over a hundred million dollars – to universities, dental clinics, for the welfare of British troops in the First World War – and in 1930, when he celebrated the fiftieth anniversary of his first photographic patent, he gave half a million Brownies to children whose twelfth birthday was in the same year.

After a long illness Eastman shot himself, and in his Rochester mansion he left pinned to his pillow his epitaph: 'To my friends – my work is done. Why wait? GE.'

Paul Ehrlich (1854–1915) German
Bacteriologist

Before the beginning of this century, the drugs used to cure illnesses were frequently ineffective and most of the successful drugs were folk remedies, like quinine for malaria, that were used without understanding. Scientific medicine, the preparation of particular drugs to cure specific illnesses, was virtually invented by one man, Paul Ehrlich, who coined the word 'chemotherapy' to describe the process.

Paul Ehrlich was born in Strehlen, Silesia (now Poland), on 14 March 1854, and soon after graduating in medicine he turned to studying dyes that would colour particular kinds of bacteria. This research was to lead to his greatest discoveries.

For a while, however, Ehrlich concentrated his attention on producing injections that would cure diphtheria. In 1896 the German Government set up a research institute for him (he was by then a professor at the University of Berlin), and although the institute was originally intended for research into the properties of blood and into methods of inoculation, Ehrlich soon returned to his interest in dyes that stain bacteria.

His argument was that if a particular dye stained the bacteria, then the chemicals of the dye attached themselves to the cells of the bacteria, which meant that the dye must have a strong chemical attraction to the bacteria, stronger than to the cells of an animal or human. If the dye were poisonous, it could kill the bacteria that caused a disease without damaging the cells of the patient. He would have what he called a 'magic bullet' to fight a disease.

Quite quickly, Ehrlich found that there was a dye, trypan red, that attacked the tiny organisms that caused sleeping sickness. He made hundreds of compounds and tested each one to see if it attacked the organisms but was harmless to the patient. By 1907 he had produced a drug called simply 606 (its number in the series) which was more efficient than any others but not good enough. Determinedly he carried on, and by 1909 had tried more than 900 compounds, still with no great success.

By then, however, it had been discovered that the dreaded disease syphilis was caused by tiny organisms called spirochetes. One of Ehrlich's assistants tried 606 on spirochetes and found that it was marvellously effective, and in 1910 the compound, to be called Salvarsan, was available as a cure. It was followed by neo-Salvarsan, which was even more effective. Ehrlich had shown that by painstakingly making and testing drugs on a logical basis, it was possible to find compounds that would cure.

Albert Einstein (1879–1955) American, ex-Swiss, ex-German
Physicist

The Theory of Relativity is Einstein's greatest achievement – scientists and mathematicians are still working out its consequences – and yet Einstein would have been a world-famous scientist had he never discovered it. Indeed, he was awarded a Nobel Prize for research in a completely different branch of science.

Albert Einstein was born in Ulm, Germany, on 14 March 1879, the son of an unsuccessful businessman. Albert himself was not very successful at school, but eventually scraped into the Technical High School in Zurich and graduated from there in 1901. His choice of career was limited because he was a Jew and eventually he took a junior post in the Patent Office in Berne. While there he worked at theoretical physics in his spare time, and by 1905,

Paul Ehrlich

when he was still only twenty-six, had achieved enough for even the most distinguished scientist's lifetime. He made three major, completely different discoveries.

His first explained Brownian motion. A Scottish botanist, Robert Brown, had noticed that pollen particles suspended in water could be seen to jiggle about when looked at under a microscope. Einstein realized that this was because the pollen particles were continuously being struck by molecules of water, and they are so small that they are not struck evenly on all sides. The uneven battering juggled the pollen. Einstein showed how to work out the weight of a molecule of water by measuring the distance the pollen particles were jiggled.

Another discovery, which earned him the Nobel Prize in 1921, was an explanation of what is called the 'photoelectric effect'. Some chemical elements send off a stream of electrons – tiny particles with a negative electrical charge – if a beam of light is shone on them. A brighter beam of light would be expected to make the electrons fly off at a higher speed, but this is not so. Instead, a brighter beam produces more electrons at the same speed. Einstein showed that this 'photoelectric effect' could be explained by Planck's (q.v.) theory, that the energy of light existed in packets, which Planck called quanta. Violet light, which has more energy, would have a larger quantum – or packet – than red light, which has less. Red light shone on a photoelectric element would release those electrons that needed quanta of just that size, and they would come off with a speed that corresponded to that energy. If the red light were twice as bright, it would affect twice as many electrons, but they would come off at the same speed. The more energetic violet light would liberate electrons that needed the larger quanta, and they would therefore come off faster. It was a brilliant, basically simple theory.

Nowadays, Einstein is most famous for his Theory of Relativity. Again, the basic ideas are brilliant and simple and the consequences are rich, complex and fascinating. To make sense of some very odd results in experimental optics, Einstein said that, firstly, the speed of light in a vacuum is constant at about 186,000 miles per second even if the source of the light is travelling at, say, 500 miles a second. His second idea was that there are no fixed points in the universe. Any movements or speeds measured are relative to some chosen point somewhere on Earth, or on the surface of the Moon, or at a point in a moving railway carriage, for example. Einstein said that the laws of motion in particular, and in fact all the laws of physics, must hold whatever place is chosen as the fixed point. All motion, in other words, is relative; hence the phrase 'the Theory of Relativity'.

The consequences of the theory are startling. It

turns out that anything that is moving very quickly gets heavier (strictly it gets more massive); that any moving object gets smaller; and that a clock aboard a moving object ticks more slowly.

The theory also says that matter can be turned into energy, and this, it was later discovered, is what happens in the atom bomb (the famous equation is $E = MC^2$). Einstein was eventually to write to President Roosevelt during the Second World War advising him to set up research into the atom bomb.

By then Einstein, as a refugee from the Nazis, had become an American citizen and was working at the Institute for Advanced Studies at Princeton. He continued to work there until his death, researching theoretical physics and studying means by which the terrifying energy of the atom could be controlled.

ABOVE *Albert Einstein as the eccentric genius in a portrait by Hans Erin*

OPPOSITE, ABOVE *The great Russian film director Eisenstein*

OPPOSITE *Sir Edward Elgar, Master of the King's Musick, 1934*

Sergei Eisenstein (1898–1948) Russian
Film director

Eisenstein's stature as the leading theorist of cinema has undergone many upheavals, and today he is regarded more as a provoker of ideas than as the fountainhead of all wisdom. The son of a Jewish architect in Riga, Eisenstein first

trained in that profession, but after the 1917 Revolution and service in the Red Army he became a theatrical designer. A man of culture and an accomplished linguist, Eisenstein quickly became a leading figure in the debate on the arts in revolutionary Russia, and began to evolve some of his most famous cinematic theories, such as the use of individual shots linked by 'montage'. He made his first film in 1923, and won international recognition with *The Battleship Potemkin* (1925). His passionate belief in the Bolsheviks was enshrined in all his early films, particularly *October* (1928) and *The General Line* (1929).

Abroad Einstein was regarded in left-wing circles as the outstanding creative force in the cinema, able to flourish in a socialist environment untrammelled by the pressures of commerce. However, in 1930 he went to America, amid great controversy, and attempted to work in Hollywood. His project for a film came to nothing and he went south to Mexico, shooting many thousands of feet of film for an uncompleted documentary epic on the oppressions of the peasants, *Que Viva Mexico*. Ill and tired, he returned home.

The influence of Hollywood was visible in his spectacular *Alexander Nevsky*, in which thirteenth-century Russian history was invoked as anti-Nazi propaganda, with a powerful score by Prokofiev (*q.v.*). Eisenstein's last work was the gloomy, melodramatic *Ivan the Terrible*. The first part was shown in 1945, but the second, which Stalin (*q.v.*) allegedly disliked and ordered to be banned, was not finally released until a decade after Eisenstein's death. Forced to recant by the authorities, his third part of *Ivan* was abandoned (Eisenstein, even without external pressures, retracted many of his views). There is a characteristic heartlessness in Eisenstein's work that puts audiences at bay, but his sense of imagery and design is unsurpassed.

Edward Elgar (1857–1934) British
Composer

It was Edward Elgar's father, organist at Worcester Catholic church for nearly forty years, who encouraged Edward's early musical interests. The boy learned the organ, so that he could deputize for his father, and taught himself the violin. He was also to a large extent self-taught in composition. Leaving school at fifteen he worked for a year in a lawyer's office before taking up a career in music. For the next fifteen years or so his career centred entirely on Worcester: teaching, playing in concerts and conducting a staff orchestra at a nearby lunatic asylum for whose inmates he also wrote dance music, and producing choral music for the Catholic church. At the age of thirty-two Elgar married a woman nine years his senior, and it was her encouragement that led him to seek success beyond his immediate surroundings.

For many years Elgar concentrated on composing oratorios for provincial music festivals. This led to a knighthood in 1904, but perhaps more importantly it led to the composition of his masterpiece, *The Dream of Gerontius*, a musical setting of Cardinal Newman's poem, first performed at the Birmingham Festival in 1900. In 1901 his *Pomp and Circumstance* March No. 1 appeared, its central section later to be adapted by Elgar as *Land of Hope and Glory*, which became a second national anthem. His First Symphony (1908) was so successful that it was played nearly a hundred times during the year of its appearance. His Second Symphony (1911) was less well received, but his Violin Concerto has endured, despite its length and difficulty.

Elgar's musical style seems to today's audiences to belong essentially to the Edwardian years, an era of expansive serenity and confidence. The music he composed during and after the First World War is less impressive, though the Cello Concerto (1919) is an exception; the last of his major works, it has an affecting, autumnal beauty.

T.S. Eliot (1888–1965) British, ex-American
Poet, playwright and critic

Thomas Stearns Eliot is probably the most famous and most important poet of the twentieth century. He was born into a business family in St Louis, Missouri, and was subsequently sent east to be educated at Harvard. Already determined to make his reputation as a poet, and considerably more interested in European culture than his native American, Eliot made his way to England in 1915 and lived there for the rest of his life, becoming a British citizen in 1927. His extraordinary gifts were quickly recognized by the American poet Ezra Pound (*q.v.*), who was largely responsible for the publication of Eliot's early work. By the time his innovatory, major poem *The Waste Land* appeared in 1922, Eliot had become generally recognized as the leader of his generation of poets. He had been supporting himself by working in a bank and by reviewing copiously for *The Times Literary Supplement*, but by the end of the 1920s he had become a director of the publishing firm of Faber and Gwyer, later Faber and Faber, with whom he remained for the rest of his life.

Of conservative and religious temperament, Eliot became a member of the Anglican church. His Christianity continued throughout his life to influence both his critical essays and his poetry, though he always encouraged and helped other talented poets even when their political or religious beliefs differed widely from his own.

One of the earliest and most successful of Eliot's religious poems is *Ash Wednesday* (1930), which celebrates the peace and content to be found in orthodox Christianity. His masterpiece is generally reckoned to be *Four Quartets* (written between 1936 and 1942), four long poems which constitute Eliot's statement of his philosophical and religious position, and which meditate on time, the soul and the meaning of life.

Eliot also wrote a number of plays. Those with modern settings are only partially successful in their mixture of verse and prose, with the exception of *The Family Reunion* (1939) which has something of the power of classical Greek tragedy. The earliest play, *Murder in the Cathedral* (1935), dealing with the assassination of St Thomas à Becket, is a remarkably fine example of modern religious drama.

Eliot was awarded the Nobel Prize for Literature in 1948 and the Order of Merit in the same year. He is not only universally regarded as the leading poet of his time in the English language but is still, without doubt, the most influential.

T.S. Eliot, the most important poet of his time; TOP *some of his plays and collected poetry*

Duke Ellington (1899–1974) American
Pianist, composer and bandleader

One of the century's most prolific musicians, Duke (christened Edward Kennedy) Ellington graduated from leadership of a quintet in the early 1920s to the triumphant inspiration of the greatest large orchestra in jazz history.

His methods and style can be compared to those of no other musician, classical or jazz, in the world, and may be defined as the evolution of a system of utilizing the orchestra as an instrument on which the composer-leader might improvise. Each of his musicians was hand-picked for the degree to which his personal style could be integrated into the orchestral texture Ellington desired; most of his famous soloists, once recruited, stayed with him for twenty or thirty years. He composed over 2,000 pieces, ranging from sketched trifles to major concert works, and his mastery extended from three-minute arrangements of astonishing density and richness, to the composition of popular songs like 'Solitude' and 'Sophisticated Lady', which gave him a second profession alongside George Gershwin (*q.v.*) and Cole Porter (*q.v.*). As a pianist he derived from the old 'Stride' school exemplified by his teacher, James P. Johnson and by his friend and contemporary Thomas 'Fats' Waller. Ellington, however, brought to the style an impressionistic, romantic flair of his own which transformed the style and made it something so personal that he remains one of the most easily recognizable soloists in jazz.

His major works include 'Black, Brown and Beige', a history of the Negro in America, 'The Tattooed Bride', and some witty paraphrases of Greig and Tchaikovsky. Time will reveal him to have been one of the century's major musician-composers, not just in the jazz field but in music generally.

Duke Ellington and his orchestra

Charles Elton (b. 1900) British
Ecologist

We all know that some species of animals and plants are at risk nowadays. We plough up hedgerows and thus destroy the homes of a rich variety of birds and small animals; we dam a lake and totally alter the conditions for the creatures that live in the area. We now understand that there is a close interaction between different kinds of living creatures and also between the creatures and their environment. The whole subject of ecology – the complex relationships between forms of life and the environment – is founded on the research of Charles Elton, although others, of course, have played important parts in its development.

Elton was born on 29 March 1900 in Liverpool and educated at Liverpool University and Oxford. He studied zoology, and his particular interest was in the relationship of animals to nature. By studying the links between their lives and their environment, he discovered the factors that regulate the size of animal populations and the significance of food chains. For example, the number of owls in an area depends in part on the number of mice available as food; this in turn depends on the amount of grain that the mice

feed on, and if there is a lot of grain one season, causing the mouse population to rise, this would have a similar effect on the number of owls.

He developed, too, the idea of an ecological 'niche'. We are used to the thought of the 'survival of the fittest', but, as Elton saw, this means the fittest for a particular environment – or niche. A woodpecker, for example, can thrive because it has virtually no rivals for the food it digs out of trees. Animals and plants can exploit all sorts of unlikely niches, from deserts to the polar icecaps. As he realized, the creature selects the environment and migrates when it changes.

Charles Elton turned his discoveries to great practical use. Having applied his work on the variations in the populations of fur-bearing mammals in the Arctic to the variations in the populations of mice and voles in Britain, he used his research during the Second World War to find ways of reducing the populations of rodents that were a threat to the nation's crops. The Bureau of Animal Populations that he founded at Oxford in 1932 is still a major international centre for studies in ecology.

F

Juan Manuel Fangio (b. 1911)
Argentinian
Racing driver

Until the watershed of the Second World War, motor racing was largely a dangerous and dilettante recreation; since the mid-1960s it has become a furious battle of high technology, sponsorship and expensive manufacturing expertise. In the years between, the sport was shaped by a band of highly skilled and highly courageous professionals, the Grand Prix drivers of the 1950s and 1960s who lived, and often died, moulding the gentlemanly sport of the vintage years to the terrifying speeds with which the new car designers had endowed their machines. The greatest of this breed, both in his performances and in the judgement of all his rivals, was Fangio.

An Italian born in Argentina, he made his name in his twenties with a string of spectacular triumphs in South American competitions, but the much more fragmented nature of top-class motor racing in those days meant that he did not make the big leap to the European-dominated Grand Prix circuit until he was nearly forty years old. Yet there, in ten seasons, until his retirement (still at the top) in 1958 – including the barren 1952 when he broke his neck at Monza – he led four different and successful racing teams (Alfa Romeo, Maserati, Mercedes-Benz and Ferrari) and won the world drivers' championship an unequalled five times.

His most-quoted triumph was his 'impossible' victory at the Nurburgring in 1957, when a forced pit stop had put him nearly fifty seconds behind the two leaders, Hawthorn and Collins. He tamed that most demanding of circuits, broke the lap record time and again, and overtook both leaders within 200 yards of each other to grab the lead and the race.

It was victories like this that gave Fangio an air of invincibility, but his brilliance at the wheel was only part of the story. His concentration was superb, his knowledge of what was going on

Fangio in a Mercedes at Le Mans, 1955

William Faulkner

ty, in which many of his subsequent novels were set.

Faulkner did not achieve instant success as a writer. After service in the Royal Canadian Air Force towards the end of the First World War, he briefly attended the University of Mississippi and then turned to a variety of jobs. At this period in his life he wrote verse, and a volume of his poems, *The Marble Faun*, appeared in 1924. His first novel, *Soldier's Pay*, was published in 1925. Neither this nor a second novel, *Mosquitoes* (1927), excited much interest in the literary world, and it was only with *Sartoris* and *The Sound and the Fury*, both published in 1929 and both dealing with the breaking-up of old southern families, that Faulkner began to acquire his reputation as a novelist. *Sanctuary* (1931) gave him his first popular success. Among the finest of Faulkner's later works are *Absalom! Absalom!* (1936) and the collection of stories *Go Down, Moses* (1942), all but one of which are concerned with members of a Yoknapatawpha family throughout several generations.

The strength of Faulkner's novels lies in their concern for the tragic history of the American South, their complex portrayal of human behaviour as influenced by personal and public history, and their use of almost melodramatic over-emphasis to present a picture of a unique but, even during the novelist's life-time, rapidly disappearing segment of American life. Faulkner was no mere propagandist for the South: his subject was mankind. It was through the particular – the Mississippi that he knew so intimately – that he reached out to embrace the universal. He was awarded the Nobel Prize for Literature in 1949.

beneath the shuddering bonnet of his cars was uncanny, and his ability to nurse disintegrating machines to victory against all the odds was legendary. In Argentina the word '*fangio!*' entered the language as a friendly, admiring accusation of breathtaking lunacy.

William Faulkner (1897–1962) American
Novelist

William Faulkner's imaginative recreations of life in the southern regions of the United States earned him recognition as a great American novelist. He was born in New Albany, Mississippi, into an old Mississippi family, and he drew on much of his own family's past in his novels. His third novel *Sartoris* (1929), for example, tells the story of the descendents of Colonel John Sartoris, a character based on the novelist's great-grandfather, Colonel William C. Faulkner (himself the author of a popular romantic novel, *The White Rose of Memphis*). It was in *Sartoris* that Faulkner invented Yoknapatawpha Coun-

Federico Fellini (b. 1920) Italian
Film director

Fellini approaches the cinema with the enthusiasm of a small boy playing with a new toy. He is a romantic, a poet of the medium, frequently using it as an autobiographical vehicle to assail, delight and confound his audiences. He is the most successful of Italian film directors, with a world-wide reputation, a quadruple Oscar winner who has spurned all invitations to work outside his homeland.

He was born in Rimini, his father a travelling confectionery salesman. When he was seven he ran away for a few days with a circus, an event that left an indelible mark on his outlook. At twenty he reached Rome, already one of the young street-smart set who were to form the subject of one of his great early films, *Il Vitellone*. Fellini worked briefly as a journalist and cartoonist, and for a time as general helper to an itinerant actor, experiences which formed the basis of his first film as director, *Lights of Variety* (1951). He entered the film industry as a screenwriter and worked on *Open City* (1945) and *Paisa* (1946), as well as acting in *L'Amore* (1948). In 1943 he had married the actress Giuletta Masina, who was to be essential to many of his films, most notably *La Strada* (1954), in which a circus strongman attempts to enslave her, *Cabiria* (1957), a heart-rending story of a prostitute which formed the basis for the Broadway musical *Sweet Charity*, and *Juliet of the Spirits* (1965), his first colour film.

Fellini's arrival as an international celebrity director was occasioned by *La Dolce Vita* (1960), a send-up of Roman high-life. Then in $8\frac{1}{2}$ (1963) he offered his most self-indulgent exercise to date, presenting a film director/ringmaster played by the actor Marcello Mastroianni, in the guise of Fellini himself, undergoing a mid-life crisis and encountering various mistresses, freaks and assorted grotesques in a picaresque nightmare. Self-indulgence became a weakness in subsequent films such as *Fellini Satyricon* (1969), *Fellini Roma* (1972) and *Fellini Casanova* (1976), all of which were marred by a deliberate pursuit of outrageous effects for their own sake. But there was a fleeting return to a dramatic narrative with *Amarcord* (1973), set in Fellini's hometown of Rimini in wartime. Fellini infuriates critics by his excessiveness and lack of serious purpose, but he has never been guilty of dullness.

Ronald Fisher (1890–1962) British
Geneticist and statistician

The son of an auctioneer, R.A. Fisher excelled at school and university, and became a professor at University College, London, in 1933. From 1943 until he retired in 1957 he was Professor of Genetics at the University of Cambridge.

Fisher contributed to two separate subjects, statistics and biology. He was jointly responsible, with Karl Pearson, for the modern form of the subject of statistics. He was especially interested in applying small-scale sampling techniques to the analysis of natural selection, the process by which adaptations that evolve within species either survive or not. His classic work on the subject is *The Genetical Theory of Natural Selection* of 1930.

Fisher's work on the dominance of traits through gene selection has provided the basis for much modern research concerning population. It has also led to a clearer understanding of the rhesus blood group. Biologists still use his methods and techniques in their work. Fisher was little known outside the academic community as he had no gift for writing or lecturing, and many of his important and influential ideas entered the mainstream only after others had succeeded in making them more readily intelligible.

Kirsten Flagstad (1895–1962) Norwegian
Opera singer

Federico Fellini directing Fellini Satyricon

Kirsten Flagstad was to be acclaimed for her magnificent soprano voice in most of the major opera houses around the world. She came of a musical family in Hamar and studied singing with her mother and another teacher, making her debut in Oslo at the early age of eighteen in the opera *Tiefland*. For the next twenty years she sang only in Scandinavia, where she appeared in a huge variety of roles, in comic operas and operettas as well as more serious works. Her international success did not come until she was in her late thirties, when she was invited in 1933 to sing small roles in the annual Wagner Festival at Bayreuth in south-eastern Germany. The following year in Bayreuth she sang the leading role of Sieglinde in Wagner's *Die Walküre*. As a result of her immediate success as Sieglinde, Flagstad was engaged by the Metropolitan Opera, New York, where she made a sensational debut in 1935, again as Sieglinde, and was acclaimed as one of the leading Wagner sopranos of the day. From this time on she specialized in the operas of Wagner.

At the Metropolitan Flagstad went from triumph to triumph in most of the great Wagner roles: Kundry in *Parsifal*, Brünnhilde in *The Ring*, Isolde in *Tristan und Isolde*. In 1936 and 1937 she was heard at Covent Garden to great acclaim as Brünnhilde and Isolde and as Senta in *The Flying Dutchman*. During the war, Flagstad returned to Norway to be with her husband, but his association with the Quisling Party (Quisling, the Norwegian wartime premier, collaborated with the Nazis) caused a decline in her popularity when she sang in America again after the war. She herself was charged in Norway with political offences but was acquitted by a tribunal. She

Sir Ronald Fisher

Kirsten Flagstad as Brünnhilde in Wagner's The Ring

specks of mould had fallen into the dish. This ruined the experiment, but Fleming spotted that the bacteria had been killed in a ring around each speck of mould. Obviously, the mould was producing a chemical that killed bacteria, and as the mould was called *penicillium notatum* Fleming called the unknown chemical penicillin. He found that the mould did not harm the white cells in human blood, so that penicillin might be valuable as a medicine. But he knew no way of continuing the research, and he set it aside and published his results. It was these results that led Howard Florey, with Ernest Chain, to produce penicillin. In 1945 Florey, Chain and Fleming shared the Nobel Prize for Medicine for their work on this highly efficient drug.

Howard Florey was born in Adelaide, Australia, and attended university there before coming to England to study at Oxford and Cambridge; in 1935 he accepted a post at Cambridge. By this time the idea of 'wonder drugs' was in the air and Florey turned to Fleming's abandoned research, spurred by the outbreak of the Second World War.

He and Ernest Chain first set out to identify the active chemical in the mould. Then he had the problem of extracting the penicillin on a small scale in the laboratory and testing it. Later, an enormous research project in both Great Britain and the United States was devoted to making the drug on a large enough scale to be useful. Though production techniques were difficult and cumbersome, they served to produce the drug in time to be used in the war.

Penicillin is still the most useful of the antibiotics, and nowadays improved versions of it will attack infections that resist the original form. Florey, Chain and Fleming were knighted for their research, and Florey was made a life peer in 1965.

BELOW *Lord Florey by H. Carr (detail);* RIGHT penicillium notatum, *the mould from which Florey extracted penicillin*

sang again in opera and concerts in London, her noble and radiant voice hardly impaired at all by the intervening years.

Flagstad made her last stage appearances in 1955, and then took over the directorship of the opera in Oslo, emerging occasionally from retirement to sing in concerts. She was never anything other than the stateliest of actresses on the operatic stage, but she expressed everything through the splendour of her voice and the solid dependability of her technique.

Howard Florey (1898–1968) British Pathologist

In 1928 the Scottish bacteriologist Alexander Fleming, working at St Mary's Hospital in London, made a curious accidental discovery. He had been growing some bacteria – staphylococci – in an open dish, and he noticed that

Margot Fonteyn (b. 1919) British
Ballet dancer

For most audiences today Fonteyn is the contemporary image of a prima ballerina.

Her early training was largely in Shanghai, where she was taught by Russian emigrés escaping the Revolution, and in 1934 she joined the Vic-Wells Ballet School, founded three years earlier by Ninette de Valois. Soon she began dancing small roles with the company and working with the choreographer Frederick Ashton; it was as his 'muse' that she first became famous. Though she danced *Swan Lake* and *Giselle*, it was her performance as Aurora in *The Sleeping Beauty* in 1939 which marked her emergence as a classical ballerina. In this role she and the Sadler's Wells Ballet (as it was known at the time) opened the Royal Opera House in 1946 and, three years later, their first New York season. The 1940s saw her taking part in more great ballets, in particular Ashton's *Symphonic Variations*, one of his masterpieces.

By the late 1950s it seemed that Fonteyn had reached a peak of technical and interpretive powers, unrivalled as the leading ballerina of the time. According to her autobiography, she believed herself to be already past that peak when Nureyev (*q.v.*) left Russia and chose to dance with her. 'Mutton dancing with lamb' was her own description of a partnership that carried sensitivity and understanding to a point of perfection that is very rarely seen. Apart from great performances of the classical ballets like *Giselle*, they also danced many new works, such as *Paradise Lost* (choreographed by Roland Petit), *Lucifer* (choreographed by Martha Graham [*q.v.*]) and *Marguerite and Armand* (choreographed by Frederick Ashton), very much 'their' ballets and never danced by anyone else.

Fonteyn has not perhaps been an active innovator in twentieth-century ballet, but as the first British-trained prima ballerina and the most celebrated performer of her time, she has made a unique contribution both to the world of ballet in this country and to the tradition of classical dance throughout the world.

Henry Ford (1863–1947) American
Car manufacturer

Brought up on a Michigan farm, Ford was captivated by machinery from the moment he first saw a steam engine, and by sixteen was making his way in the machine-shops of Detroit. An early car venture flopped with only twenty-five sold, but in 1904 he set up the Ford Motor Company with $100,000, mostly raised from friends, and set about planning the Model T. For the T, Ford invented mass-production techniques, using the first assembly lines and

transforming the economics of car-making. Until the T, cars were hand-built exclusively for the rich, but Ford's methods cut prices (customers could have any colour as long as it was black), from $950 in 1909 to only $600 four years later, and sold fifteen million Model Ts up to 1928. The Model T's record sales were not surpassed until Volkswagen's Beetle. By enabling the average family to buy a car, Ford laid the foundations of today's auto-dominated American society.

Always stubborn, Ford made the mistake of clinging to his one-colour, one-model policy for too long. In the mid-1920s the Ford Motor Company was valued at a billion dollars and dominated nearly half the American car market, but General Motors were making cars in a range of colours, with modern hydraulic brakes and six cylinders. Belatedly Ford developed the A series and struck back in 1932 with the V-8, but he never recovered market leadership from GM. However, in 1935 the £100 Ford Popular became Britain's bestseller as Henry Ford, with rubber plantations, coal mines, railways, timber and iron ore interests, began to develop his business into today's multinational corporation.

He was often guilty of flagrant anti-semitism and was a brutal opponent of trade unions, fighting them off throughout the 1930s with a 3,000-strong gang of thugs. But Henry Ford, diet faddist and practical joker, was also a philanthropist who paid an unheard-of $5 a day minimum wage in 1914, and, in sharp contrast to the criticisms levelled at capitalists such as Rockefeller (*q.v.*), he won popularity with the American public as well as respect for his achievements and financial success.

John Ford (1895–1973) American
Film director

Born in Maine of Irish parents, John Ford, still known by his Irish name of Sean O'Fearney, migrated to Hollywood as soon as he was out of high school, in pursuit of his older brother Francis who had become a writer-director. He acquired work in the free-and-easy atmosphere as a stuntman and extra (he was a hooded Ku Klux Klan rider in D.W.Griffith's [*q.v.*] *The Birth of a Nation*), eventually embarking on a directorial career that was to last more than half a century. His most notable silent film was *The Iron Horse* (1925), which embodied much of Ford's romantic view of the West, with men taming the frontier through the railroad. But it was the coming of the sound film that gave Ford the opportunity to secure his reputation as a great populist of the cinema, and while at the time of their release *The Informer* (1935), *How Green Was My Valley* (1941) and *The Grapes of Wrath* (1950) were the films hailed as his

masterpieces, in retrospect it is seen that his best work was in the most commercial of his Westerns, such as *My Darling Clementine* (1946), *Fort Apache* (1948), *Wagonmaster* (1951), *Rio Grande* (1951) and *The Searchers* (1957), where a simplistic American faith in the community is proudly presented. Ford's view of the West, with its dashing, powerful cavalrymen and resourceful, pretty women set against a spectacular backdrop of empty plains, was greatly over-romanticized, and he denigrated the Indians until his last homage to the frontier, *Cheyenne Autumn* (1965), belatedly makes recompense to them. Ford's long association with John Wayne, who first worked for him as the young cowboy in *Stagecoach* (1939), resulted in the projection of a popular but chauvinistic masculine stereotype, not confined to Westerns but also evident in such brawling extravaganzas as *The Quiet Man* (1952) and *Donovan's Reef* (1964). The macho philosophy of Ford may become increasingly dated, but the power of his images, the skilful construction of his narratives, and the breathtaking craftsmanship of his films will always excite. Nine of his works were shot in Monument Valley in northern Arizona, a strange and mysterious landscape that somehow has become a memorial to him in its own right.

Sigmund Freud (1856–1939) Austrian
Founder of psychoanalysis

Freud was one of the most influential figures of the twentieth century and his theories have profoundly affected modern views of human nature. It is due to him that the idea of the

Film director John Ford

Sigmund Freud, whose theories introduced into everyday life an awareness of the unconscious mind: a portrait by Victor Kraus

American poet Robert Frost

repression of sexual desires is the major cause of neurosis and that human beings have powerful sexual drives from birth. Each person goes through the 'Oedipus complex', sexual hunger for the parent of the opposite sex and fierce jealousy of the other parent. The sex-drive, Freud thought, can be 'sublimated' into providing the energy for finer ambitions and achievements.

Freud's contemporaries in the 1890s and 1900s were outraged and denounced him, but he was a persuasive lecturer and writer, and the time was ripe for his ideas. Though he himself was a puritan, Freudianism has contributed to modern permissiveness and the collapse of nineteenth-century standards. Both C.G. Jung (*q.v.*) and the psychiatrist Alfred Adler (1870–1937) were Freud's disciples for a time but, like Breuer before them, were unable to accept his emphasis on sexuality. In 1938, when the Nazis took power in Vienna, Freud fled to England, where he died. His books include *The Interpretation of Dreams* (1900), *The Psychopathology of Everyday Life* (1904), *Totem and Tabu* (1913), *The Ego and the Id* (1923) and *Moses and Monotheism* (1939).

Robert Frost (1874–1963) American Poet

Although born in San Francisco, Frost moved east to New England while still a child and became renowned for his poetry dealing with life in that region of America; he came to be known as the voice of New England. His education was generally sporadic and later he studied between odd jobs, although he did for a time attend Harvard. In his twenties he was for five years a farmer in New Hampshire, but poetry had by then become his chief interest in life. He failed to achieve publication in the United States and consequently went to England where his first two volumes, *A Boy's Will* (1913) and *North of Boston* (1914), were published.

Continuing to remain aloof from literary fashion, on his return to America in 1915 Frost began to find acceptance as a poet with his simple verses of country life and concerns. *Mountain Interval* (1916) contains two of the best known and most anthologized of his poems, 'The Road Not Taken' and 'Birches'. For *New Hampshire*, a volume of poems published in 1923, Frost was awarded the first of his four Pulitzer Prizes, others following in 1931, 1937 and 1943. By this time his poetry had acquired a deeper complexity beneath its apparent simplicity, and a tendency to abstract philosophizing became more prevalent, especially in his post-war verse dramas *A Masque of Reason* (1945) and *A Masque of Mercy* (1947). Frost's *Complete Poems* (1949) was followed by a final volume, *In the Clearing* (1962).

unconscious mind has become commonplace. Freudianism is not a scientific system, however, and whether it is a path to truth or a blind alley is still a matter of dispute.

Freud based his theories partly on his memories of himself as a child. Born at Freiberg in Moravia (now Pribor, Czechoslovakia), the son of a Jewish wool merchant, he took his medical degree at Vienna University and lived most of his life in Vienna. Psychoanalysis was born of his interest in the use of hypnosis in the treatment of hysteria, which convinced him that neurosis has unconscious roots and is caused by emotional disturbances early in life. Under hypnosis patients recalled and relived traumatic forgotten experiences, and so freed themselves of them. For a time Freud collaborated with the physician Josef Breuer (1842–1925) and with him wrote *Studies in Hysteria* (1893).

Freud dropped hypnosis and devised the technique of 'free association', in which the patient relaxes on a couch and says whatever comes into his mind as a way of releasing material from the unconscious. He found clues to the unconscious in dreams. He believed that

In his lifetime Frost was often thought to be opposed to the mainstream of contemporary poetry, a writer concentrating on clear moral issues and simple country joys, a lover of nature and a homely philosopher. He was, however, a poet of sufficient stature to impose his own vision of the world upon the contemporary landscape, and he was also by no means a mere chronicler of country life. Though he wrote in traditional verse forms, Frost was a sophisticated poet, dealing in irony and ambiguity within the context of his verses about New England life. The best of his work is full of wit and imagination, and is the product of a temperament that fully comprehends the melancholic and pessimistic as well as the placid and rustic.

Wilhelm Furtwängler (1886–1954)
German
Conductor

Born in Berlin, the son of a professor of archaeology, Furtwängler began his musical studies in Munich at the age of eight and gained early experience as a conductor in Zurich, Strasbourg and Lübeck. Furtwängler's first big opportunity came when he was engaged to conduct both opera and concerts at Mannheim, an engagement that led to his conducting important orchestras in Vienna and Berlin. In 1922 he became the conductor of both the Berlin Philharmonic and the Leipzig Gewandhaus orchestras. The success of his concerts in both cities led to his being offered engagements to conduct abroad. He began to visit England in 1924, and soon became a regular guest conductor of the leading British orchestras. He also brought his Berlin Philharmonic Orchestra to England on several tours.

Furtwängler elected to remain in Germany, where his position remained a privileged one, after the Nazis rose to power in 1933 and throughout the Second World War. He appears not to have been an enthusiast for the Nazi regime and is said to have tried to ease the plight of Jewish musicians of his acquaintance. But he also allowed his name to be used by the Nazis for propaganda purposes and accepted whatever official posts he was offered. This led to difficulties for him after the war, and there was much reluctance both in England and America to offer him engagements. However, in due course Furtwängler re-established himself in England on purely artistic grounds. He was, after all, one of the three leading conductors of his generation of the great Austro-German classical repertoire, especially of Beethoven and Wagner. (The other two, Bruno Walter [q.v.] and Otto Klemperer [q.v.], were Jewish and had left Germany in 1933.)

As a conductor, Furtwängler's technique was visually somewhat eccentric and nervous in gesture, but it resulted in interpretations of the classics which, though personal and romantic rather than classical, had the stamp of authority. He was especially effective in the operas of Wagner, and his interpretations of *The Ring* and *Tristan und Isolde* are fortunately preserved on gramophone records.

G

Indira Gandhi (b. 1917) Indian
Political leader

Indira Gandhi was the only child of Jawaharlal Nehru (*q.v.*), the first Prime Minister of independent India. After her mother died she acted as political hostess for her father. Educated in India and Switzerland and at Oxford, she married Feroze Gandhi in 1942; they had two sons, Rajiv and Sanjay. Indira served on the Congress Party working committee from 1955 to 1959, when she was elected Party president. When Shastri

Wilhelm Furtwängler, renowned especially for his interpretations of Wagner

Indira Gandhi, political leader of India in her fourth term of office

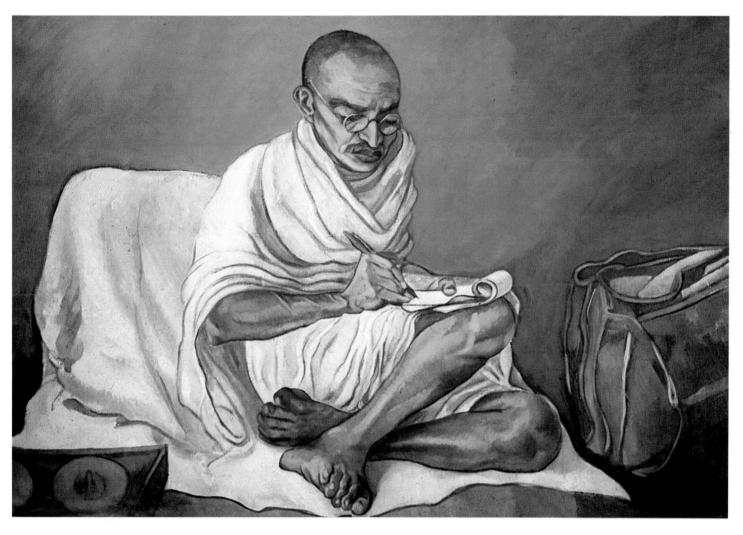

Mohandas Karamchand Gandhi, known as 'Mahatma' – 'the great soul'

succeeded Nehru as Prime Minister in 1964 he brought her into his Cabinet as Minister of Information and Broadcasting. After Shastri's sudden death in 1966 Mrs Gandhi became the third Prime Minister of independent India.

Although the Congress Party suffered setbacks and her leadership was questioned, she again won the leadership in 1967 and 1971. During the 1977 elections, however, she was defeated in the north partly because of the increasing power of another party, the Janata, and partly because of the unpopular sterilization programmes instigated in northern India by her son Sanjay. Commissions were formed to inquire into the excesses and alleged crimes committed by Mrs Gandhi's family during her leadership and she was arrested as a result, but although Sanjay served a term in prison Mrs Gandhi retained the sympathy of the public. She soon demonstrated once more that she could win seats in the north, and as the power of the Janata Party waned she was swept back to power in a landslide victory. On 14 January 1980 Mrs Gandhi became Prime Minister of India for a fourth term. A ruthless and aggressive politician, she has established her name almost as a symbol of modern India.

Mahatma Gandhi (1869–1948) Indian
Politico-religious leader

'Mahatma' ('the great soul') Gandhi was born in the small state of Porbandar, of which his father was the chief minister. It was a poor place, not directly ruled by the British like the rest of India. Gandhi's mother was a deeply religious Hindu, and following custom, Gandhi was married at thirteen. Money was scraped together for him to train as a lawyer, which necessitated his attending the Inns of Court in London. He entered the Inner Temple in 1888.

In London Gandhi became a leading member of the vegetarian movement, which included George Bernard Shaw (*q.v.*). The philosophy of many vegetarians included the simple life, pacifism and socialism, ideas which, with his intense religious feelings, Gandhi was to bring to the Indian independence movement during the 1920s and 1930s.

He first practised law successfully in South Africa from 1893. But even as a lawyer he was thrown out of a first-class railway compartment because he was Indian. He decided that racial indignities should not be accepted, a view that evolved into *Satyagraha* ('firmness in truth') or passive resistance.

He returned to India in 1914, and from 1919 became the leader of nationalism there, his non-violent methods and philosophy of peace incomprehensible to the officials of the viceroy's glittering court. From the ancient Hindu scriptures came further ascetic ideas – non-possession, indifference to material things, indifference to pain or pleasure, triumph or tragedy. Clad only in a pair of steel spectacles and a *dhoti* (a loin-cloth, spun by himself), his only other possession a cheap pocket-watch, this 'naked fakir' challenged the might of the British Empire. His method was non-cooperation, non-violent civil disobedience. The Government had a tax, and a monopoly, on salt. Very well, Indians would march 200 miles to the sea and make salt. All, especially the poor and the Untouchables (the lowest caste of peasants), were drawn into the independence movement, which until then had been almost exclusively middle class.

Gandhi fasted, went on hunger-strike, and generally mortified himself for India's cause. His routine included a daily enema, and he considered it a sign of his esteem to his associates if he offered to perform this service upon them. His moral authority on the masses of India was enormous; but he could not prevent partition. In 1946 the British gave in, granting India independence in 1947. Some months later Gandhi was assassinated by a fanatical Hindu extremist.

Greta Garbo (b. 1905) American, ex-Swedish
Actress

Although Garbo's last screen appearance was in 1941, she remains a great star, her mystique as powerful now as it was at the height of her career. In her teens she was an assistant in a Stockholm department store, and was selected for publicity work. Attracted by acting, she enrolled in the Swedish dramatic academy, where she caught the eye of the director Mauritz Stiller, who signed her for *The Atonement of Gösta Berling*, and became her Svengali-like sponsor. She appeared in Pabst's *Joyless Street* in 1925, then went with Stiller to Hollywood as part of his contract with MGM. Her first American film, *The Torrent*, revealed her astonishing effect on the camera, and from then on the temperamental Stiller was pushed into the background while the MGM machine was activated to exploit their new star. Recent researches have revealed that she handled her progress with shrewd assurance, and that Louis B. Mayer on more than one occasion was forced to yield to her wishes. Her series of films with the actor John Gilbert resulted in some of the most compulsive yet restrained erotic counterplaying in the silent cinema, and audiences, aware that the romantic interest went beyond the film set, responded, to ensure their box-office success.

By the time Garbo made her talkie debut in 1930 in *Anna Christie* ('Garbo Talks!') the affair with Gilbert was over, although it was at her insistence that the flamboyant actor, whose sound career had been a failure, was co-starred with her in *Queen Christina* (1933). She later reappeared as *Anna Karenina* in a 1935 sound version (the silent one with John Gilbert had been called *Love*) and played *Camille* and Maria Walewska in *Conquest*. Her penultimate film was a satirical comedy, *Ninotchka* ('Garbo Laughs'). With the advent of the Second World War a large section of Garbo's overseas audience was removed, and MGM fatally cast her in a contemporary American comedy, *Two-Faced Woman*, with undistinguished results.

Garbo never made another film, although over the years several projects were mooted. Her reticence at personal publicity had always been a characteristic, but from then on she became an international hermit, a mysterious cloaked figure in dark glasses, often travelling under an assumed name, fervent in keeping journalists, photographers and the public at a distance, and thus helping to ensure that the Garbo magic was kept intact.

The legendary Greta Garbo

George Gershwin

George Gershwin (1898–1937) American Composer

Gershwin was born in New York City on 26 September 1898, the son of Russian Jews. He was raised in poverty but proved so precocious that before he was twenty he was famous as the composer of 'Swanee'. One of the few Americans who established an indigenous American school of songwriting for the theatre in defiance of European domination, Gershwin struck a perfect balance between pure jazz and popular music. Throughout the 1920s he became established as a virtually infallible composer of musical comedy, beginning with *Lady Be Good* (1924) and developing with *Oh, Kay!* (1926) and *Funny Face* (1928). A self-taught man with disarming vanity, Gershwin chafed against the constrictions of shallow lyrics, and throughout his career sought to find ways of making his songs meaningful. Concurrent with his musical career he made several more formal compositions, and his *Rhapsody in Blue* (1924) remains the most widely popular and most-quoted concert work of the century. In 1934 he composed America's first folk opera in *Porgy and Bess*, after which he went to Hollywood and wrote several brilliant scores for the performer he so admired, Fred Astaire (*q.v.*).

Most of Gershwin's songwriting was done with his elder brother, the gifted lyricist Ira Gershwin. George was also a painter of considerable talent, a mordant wit, and the embodiment of such musical potential that contemporaries like Arnold Schoenberg (*q.v.*) felt that by the time of his death (after surgery for a brain tumour) he had hardly begun to express his full range. Dozens of his best songs remain in circulation, and the opinion of posterity is at one with the description of him as 'an extraordinary being too great to be real'.

John Gielgud (b. 1904) British Actor

The child of a theatrical family (his great-aunt was Irving's leading lady Ellen Terry), John Gielgud was to become Olivier's (*q.v.*) only true rival as Britain's leading classical actor from the 1930s through into the 1960s. Where Olivier's theatrical talent is primarily physical, however, Gielgud's is vocal; he is, wrote Kenneth Tynan, 'the best actor in the world – from the neck up', and Gielgud himself has frequently acknowledged his awkwardness of movement on stage, though it cannot be said to have impeded his career.

From Lady Benson's drama school in the Cromwell Road in 1922, Gielgud got his first job as an understudy and assistant stage manager for his cousin Phyllis Neilson-Terry at £4 a week. He first came to Londoners' attention when he understudied and later replaced Noël Coward (*q.v.*) in two long-running West End hits, Coward's own *The Vortex* (1924) and Margaret Kennedy's *The Constant Nymph* (1926). But it was as a classical actor that Gielgud was soon to establish himself, notably in the Old Vic seasons of 1929–31 when he played Romeo, Richard II, Macbeth, and the role that was to be most closely associated with his Shakespearian career, that of Hamlet. In 1934 he took *Hamlet* back into the West End, and a year later was alternating Romeo and Mercutio with Olivier at the New Theatre before a triumphant *Hamlet* on Broadway.

In 1937–8 at the Queen's Theatre and in 1944–5 at the Haymarket he formed his own companies working in classical repertoire, and in this period also added *Richard of Bordeaux* and *The Importance of Being Earnest* to his most characteristic and important stage successes. Soon after the war he was at Stratford with the young Peter Brook for a 1950 *Measure For Measure* and, also at Stratford, he premiered the *Much Ado About Nothing* which he later took around the world. In the 1950–1 season at Stratford he also played Cassius in *Julius Caesar*, a role he was to repeat a year later on film opposite Marlon Brando (*q.v.*) as Mark Antony.

From the early 1950s Gielgud worked with increasing frequency in films, finding that highly paid though often small 'guest star' roles would allow him the financial freedom to do uncommercial work in the live theatre. His film career had in fact started in 1932 with *The Good Companions*, and its highlights include *Disraeli*, Olivier's *Richard III* (in which he was the unfortunate Clarence), Orson Welles' (*q.v.*) *Chimes at Midnight* (he was Henry IV) and Otto Preminger's *St Joan* (he was Warwick).

In 1955 Gielgud played King Lear at Stratford and at the Theatre Royal Drury Lane in Japanese settings by Noguchi, and three years later he pioneered a solo Shakespearian evening called *The Ages of Man* which also took him around the world. In the 1960s he began to work for the first time in his career with several young contemporary dramatists, among them Harold Pinter, Alan Bennett, David Storey and Peter Shaffer.

A veteran of more than fifty films, almost a hundred theatrical productions as director and more than two hundred as an actor, Gielgud is also the author of three autobiographies; in one of them he wrote of himself, 'I have three besetting sins both on and off the stage – impetuosity, self-consciousness and a lack of interest in anything not immediately concerned with the theatre or with myself.' But few actors of this century can rival his experience, and none can bridge as he does theatrical history from Ellen Terry to Harold Pinter. Gielgud was knighted in 1953 and in 1977 he was made a Companion of Honour.

Carlo Maria Giulini (b. 1914) Italian
Conductor

Giulini studied both composition and the viola at the Accademia di Santa Cecilia in Rome, where he also took his conducting course. As a student he played in the Augusteo Orchestra, and learnt much about conducting technique by studying the methods and results of the many distinguished conductors of the Orchestra. At the end of the Second World War, in 1944, he was appointed assistant conductor of the Rome Radio Orchestra, and the following year became Musical Director of Radio Italiana. In 1951 he was invited to become assistant to Victor de Sabata at La Scala, Milan, and this was the real beginning of Giulini's strong interest in opera. He is, however, unusual among Italian conductors in being renowned as much for his handling of the Austro-German orchestral repertory as for his interpretations of Italian opera.

Giulini collaborated with the film and stage director Luchino Visconti in many of the operas

he conducted at La Scala, and has always insisted that the operas he conducts should be properly staged in accordance with the wishes of the composer; more than once he has withdrawn from a project because he disapproved of the staging, and in recent years he has moved away from opera altogether, except for the occasional recording or special project.

In the 1950s and 1960s he was especially admired for his performances of the operas of Rossini and above all of Verdi. He first visited Britain in 1955 to conduct Verdi's *Falstaff*, but his greatest success in Britain was the Royal Opera's centenary production of Verdi's *Don Carlos* in 1958, which he conducted and which Visconti produced. The production is still in the 1981 repertory of the Royal Opera House, Covent Garden.

Sir John Gielgud, one of the greatest stage actors of our time

Carlo Maria Giulini

For many years the chief conductor of the Vienna Symphony Orchestra and, more recently, of the Los Angeles Philharmonic Orchestra, Giulini does not conduct a great deal of contemporary music, preferring to present the music he loves and which he is so superbly equipped to interpret: the classical symphonic repertory from Mozart to Mahler.

Martha Graham (b. 1894) American
Choreographer

Of all the pioneers of modern dance, Graham has been influential in founding a school of dance in both senses of the word: she created a style which is followed by many companies around the world and is taught according to her basic principles, and she founded and still directs her own school of dance in New York. Her company too has survived, a testimony to the remarkable deter-

Martha Graham, a pioneer of modern dance, in a painting by Paul Meltsner, 1940

mination and strength of character which she has consistently shown since the days of her own recitals in 1924. Born in Allegheny, Pennsylvania, into an old American family, she was prevented from dancing until she was almost nineteen because of parental opposition, but she then joined the Denishawn School, the first school of modern dance, which also taught ethnic dance and ballet. Much that she learned there was in a decorative, exotic style, and it was not long before Graham rejected it as she had done the even more exotic and artificial classical ballet. She felt that dance had to say something deeper, make more psychological statements than would ever be found in classical ballets that were rooted firmly in the nineteenth century. To express her ideas she had to evolve her own system of movement, replacing the striving for grace and airiness of the classical ballet by an affinity with the ground and an acceptance of the force of gravity. At its simplest this idea was expressed by dancing in bare feet and using many 'falls' in place of leaps and jumps. The power of the movement came from the solar plexus, and the sudden intake and release of breath and the resultant contractions of the spine made the back expressive through movement. Subject-matter, too, was carefully considered. In the early years of her group and throughout the 1930s she created important works that explored different psychological aspects of womanhood. By the end of the Second World War she had already discovered the power of Greek mythology and drama to express universal psychological situations, and embarked on a series of works ranging from her key work *Night Journey* (1947) to the ambitious full-length dance-drama *Clytemnestra* (1958). This brought to a peak of perfection her method of showing the heroine, or of telling the story, from different points of view, so that in a dance such as *Seraphic Dialogue* (1955) Joan of Arc is shown watching herself in her various roles – Maid, Warrior and Visionary – before being received into heaven. As her company became more established, Graham broadened her technique to include complementary ideas from the classical ballet, even creating a work for Rudolf Nureyev (*q.v.*) and Margot Fonteyn (*q.v.*).

Graham Greene (b. 1904) British
Novelist and playwright

Born in Berkhamsted, Hertfordshire, Graham Greene was educated at Berkhamsted School, where his father was headmaster, and at Oxford, after which he became a journalist on the editorial staff of *The Times*. He was converted to Catholicism in 1927, and his religion plays an important and integral part in almost all his novels and plays. His first novel, *The Man Within* (1929), was an historical romance about

D.W. Griffith (1875–1948) American
Film director

David Wark Griffith was the single most influential figure in the American silent cinema, the innovative pioneer who explored and enlarged the infant medium and laid down many of the conventions that are current to this day. Raised as a Kentucky farm boy, the son of an impoverished ex-officer in the Confederate Army, Griffith became an actor in touring companies in his early twenties. After repeated attempts to write for the stage he eventually had a play produced, and in 1908, after working as an actor, became a writer for the Biograph Studio in New York.

There he quickly became a director, and in five years turned out some 450 films, albeit most of them one-reelers. Nevertheless, it was a prodigious and unparalleled achievement, particularly as he freed the camera from many of the stylistic limitations of viewpoint. Griffith used close-ups, inserts, long-shots, medium-shots and cutaways to progress the action at a time when such devices were virtually unknown. But it would be wrong to regard Griffith merely as a cinematic technician. He cherished good acting and evolved through his players, who included Mary Pickford (q.v.), the Gish sisters, Henry Walthall and Mae Marsh, a style that was far removed from the standard stage-derived acting of the day. He created in Hollywood the first American

nineteenth-century smugglers, but it is hardly typical of his work. Greene soon found the genre that suited his talent and produced a series of novels which he called 'entertainments', using the world of intrigue, international espionage and murder to make statements about faith, betrayal and personal morality. Among them are *Stamboul Train* (1932), *A Gun for Sale* (1936) and *Brighton Rock* (1938); but the religious views they reflect are discussed more explicitly in what Greene considers his more serious novels. Of these the two finest are probably *The Power and the Glory* (1940) and *The Heart of the Matter* (1948), both concerned with an individual's struggle to believe in the Catholic faith, a struggle between faith and rational intelligence.

It is this moral struggle that has dominated most of Greene's work in the post-war years, a struggle set against life in a variety of countries – Mexico, Haiti, Cuba, West Africa, Indo-China – in such novels as *The End of the Affair* (1951), *Our Man in Havana* (1958) and *A Burnt-out Case* (1960). His more recent novels, such as *The Honorary Consul* (1973) and *The Human Factor* (1978), have tended to blend the earnestness of the novels with the espionage world of the 'entertainments'.

A number of Greene's novels have been made into films, among them *England Made Me* (1935) and *Our Man in Havana*. He has also written plays – *The Living Room* (1953), which is concerned with religious issues, and *The Complaisant Lover* (1959), a comedy – but his art is essentially that of the novelist, using his well-rounded and convincingly drawn characters to make his comment on the modern world and to explore his obsessive concern with the relationship of morality to religion.

ABOVE LEFT *Graham Greene*

BELOW *Director D.W. Griffith (left) in Hollywood with producer Carl Laemmle Jnr (centre) and theatre magnate Sid Grauman (right)*

Che Guevara, hero of young revolutionaries throughout the 1960s

Che Guevara (1928–67) Cuban, ex-Argentinian
Revolutionary

Born an aristocrat, Ernesto (Che) Guevara was encouraged by his parents to read widely. He was a sickly, asthmatic boy, but his resolve to strengthen his body by sport revealed a single-minded determination at an early age.

While still a student he hitch-hiked all over Latin America and saw the grinding poverty. He qualified as a doctor in 1953, and a year later went to Guatemala, at that time a left-wing outpost in Central America. Exiles from Cuba were among the revolutionaries there, and it was they who gave Guevara his nickname, adopting his own habit of calling everybody 'che', which in Argentina means pal.

In 1955 Che met Fidel Castro (*q.v.*). They were drawn to each other at once and talked of nothing but revolution. Che left Guatemala with Castro and eighty-two others in December 1956 with the intention of landing in Cuba and deposing the Government. Che was one of the twelve who survived and retreated to the mountains. He proved to be one of the most successful commanders in the Cuban revolution, a favourite of Castro's, who was to say: 'If, as a guerrilla, he had his Achilles' heel, it was his excessively aggressive quality, his resolute contempt for danger.'

By January 1959 the revolutionaries had triumphed. Che was made commander of Havana's La Cubana fortress, and a Cuban citizen. He worked on land and farming reform and became head of the National Bank. He kept no regular hours, but sometimes worked for thirty-six hours at a stretch. He always wore the gear of the guerrillas – battle fatigues and boots – even when attending the meetings of pin-striped bankers. This behaviour endeared him to the world's youth, and he became to many of them a symbol of challenge to all accepted and conventional values.

Che wanted to see a 'new' socialist man created. This must, he considered, be implemented throughout the developing world. Love, he said, cannot exist between master and slave; that relationship must be utterly destroyed before love can be built. Che left Cuba once he felt that the creation of this new society was under way, and went to Vietnam, the Congo, his native Argentina, and finally Bolivia. There, he led guerrilla raids, but was increasingly disappointed by the slow progress of the Bolivian revolution. He became careless, and finally, racked by asthma and swollen by countless mosquito bites (to which he reacted strongly), he was captured and shot in Bolivia.

Che's appearance is firmly imprinted on the minds of all who saw his image staring out from hundreds of thousands of posters throughout the

epic feature, *The Birth of a Nation* (1915), a film about the Civil War of astonishing breadth, followed two years later by the grandiose *Intolerance*, with its monumental sets. Its four stories from varying periods were intercut to reach almost simultaneously a final message. *Intolerance* was something of a financial disaster, forcing Griffith into less ambitious but artistically more satisfying works, such as *Hearts of The World* (1918), *True Heart Susie* and *Broken Blossoms* (1919), *Way Down East* (1920), his second biggest box-office success, and *Orphans of the Storm* (1922).

Although a co-founder with Chaplin (*q.v.*), Pickford and Douglas Fairbanks of United Artists, his career tailed off in the 1920s and died out in the early days of sound. Griffith's last years were sad, and he died a forgotten alcoholic in a Hollywood hotel at the age of seventy-three.

1960s. His reasoning and his speeches, always rambling and even incoherent, struck a sympathetic chord in America's 'love generation' of which he will always be a symbol, as he was of the world-wide student protests of his time.

H

William Randolph Hearst (1863–1951)
American
Newspaper proprietor

The arch-exponent of the strident tabloid press, Hearst immortalized himself with his response to a reporter who cabled from Havana to say there would be no war: 'You furnish the pictures and I'll furnish the war', replied Hearst, who proceeded virtually single-handed to foment the Spanish-American war. He had no compunctions – he is even suspected of murder – and his journalism reflected his lack of scruple. 'What we're after', said one of his staff, 'is the gee-whiz emotion.' If there was a quotation to be distorted or a story to be invented, Hearst's highly-paid editors were willing. He played on patriotism and stuck out for the underdog against the bosses. There was little that he did not appreciate about the mechanics of the popular press. No expense was to be spared in getting the story or capturing readers' attention with screaming headlines, stunts and lively stories. 'Putting out a newspaper without promotion is like winking at a girl in the dark – well-intentioned but ineffective', he once said. And in most newspapers, never mind the popular press, something of his influence can still be seen today.

Hearst started at the top. His father had become a multi-millionaire as one of the founders of the Anaconda Copper giant, and gave his twenty-three year old only child the loss-making *San Francisco Examiner* to play with. The young Hearst lost even more with it, but after his father's death his mother continued to finance him, selling out her interest in Anaconda. He moved into New York with the *Morning Journal*, and won a long, bitter and costly circulation war with Joseph Pulitzer's *World*. Duplicating his formula from city to city, he became America's biggest newspaper proprietor. But weakened by his own extravagance and the Wall Street crash, his empire went into decline.

His attempts to move into politics were unsuccessful. He flirted with the Republicans and the Democrats, but his dreams of the White House took him no further than Congress. He spent lavishly in an effort to promote the career of his mistress, the actress Marion Davies, and was a profligate collector of antiques, raiding many stately homes to furnish his Welsh castle,

William Randolph Hearst, ruthless and single-minded, and the most powerful of American newspaper proprietors. He took over the San Francisco Examiner, *a present from his father, at the age of twenty-three*

St Donat's. His remarkable life inspired a masterpiece in Orson Welles' (*q.v.*) *Citizen Kane*, which is set against the backdrop of Hearst's extraordinary Renaissance palace in California, St Simeon.

Ernest Hemingway (1899–1961)
American
Novelist

Born in Oak Park, Illinois, where his father was a doctor, Hemingway started his career as a journalist, beginning to write fiction only after he had left America and was living in Paris. He was one of the generation of expatriate writers who made Paris their base in the 1920s, among them the Americans Ezra Pound (*q.v.*) and Gertrude Stein, both of whom encouraged Hemingway. His first published volume was *Three Stories and Ten Poems* (1923), which was followed in the next year by *In Our Time*, a collection of fifteen stories, many of them dealing with the development of young Nick Adams, a semi-autobiographical character. Hemingway's first

Ernest Hemingway

novel, *The Torrents of Spring* (1926), was quickly followed in the same year by *The Sun Also Rises*, which established his reputation and which is still considered by many to be one of his finest works.

Big-game hunter, deep-sea fisherman, traveller, war correspondent, and bull-fighting enthusiast, Hemingway lived a life of restless intensity, seeking adventure – even violence. He interpreted the world more easily through action than through character, and was always at his best when describing physical incident. In *Death in the Afternoon* (1932), a non-fiction work in which he romanticized bullfighting, the feeling may be sentimental but the prose in which it is expressed is always strong and taut. His style became somewhat more poetic in *A Farewell to Arms* (1929), one of his most popular novels, and reached its full maturity, combining both strength and poetic expression, in the novel that is probably his masterpiece, *For Whom the Bell Tolls* (1940), which tells the story of an idealistic American academic who goes to fight with the Republican army in the Spanish Civil War. It was ten years before his next novel, *Across the River and Into the Trees*, which was generally thought disappointing, but in 1952 Hemingway found his best form again in a short novel, *The Old Man and the Sea*. In 1954 he was awarded the Nobel Prize for Literature. Unable to submit to incarceration when he became mentally ill in the last few years of his life, he shot himself in 1961.

Thor Heyerdahl (b. 1914) Norwegian
Writer, anthropologist and adventurer

Heyerdahl's taste for anthropological exploits was acquired when he spent a year in the Marquesas Islands in the south Pacific after graduating in zoology from Oslo University. During the war he saw active service as a parachutist with the Free Norwegian Forces, and then, in 1947, embarked on the expedition that brought him international fame. On a balsa-wood raft named *Kon-Tiki*, he and five Norwegian companions floated from Peru to Polynesia. His aim was to prove that archaeological similarities between South America and Polynesia could be explained by trans-Pacific exploration by the peoples of ancient times. His success, engendered by post-war Europe's eagerness for peacetime heroes, far transcended such modest academic intentions. His account of the epic journey sold over twenty million copies and his crude film of the voyage won an Oscar.

The acclaim gave Heyerdahl the financial strength to embark on further similar ventures: an expedition to the Easter Islands in 1955–6 was followed more strikingly a decade later by the *Ra* voyages, when Heyerdahl and a cosmopolitan six-man crew sought to demonstrate that Egyptians, in a papyrus boat, could have crossed the Atlantic centuries before Christopher Columbus. They made it on their second attempt, narrowly escaping disaster on their first bid when their craft foundered 500 miles from their goal. Heyerdahl's written output has been prolific, and he has won a measure of academic respect for his theories. Like Cousteau (*q.v.*) he has recently used his popularity to campaign against pollution and other ecological crimes.

Edmund Hillary (b. 1919)
New Zealander
Mountaineer

It was ironic that as a New Zealander, Hillary should crown three decades of strictly British mountaineering endeavour by becoming the first man to stand on the summit of the world's highest mountain. A beekeeper and wartime navigator on flying-boats in the Pacific, Hillary was chosen for the 1953 Everest expedition after a New Zealand party had virtually gate-crashed the 1951 British Everest reconnaissance. But he amply proved his worth, and leader John Hunt nominated him and Sherpa Tenzing, an Everest veteran, for the second summit bid. Hillary mounted the final snow-cone first at 11.30 a.m. on 29 May 1953, followed a few steps behind by

ABOVE *Thor Heyerdahl afloat on his balsa-wood raft* Kon-Tiki *during his epic voyage from Peru to Polynesia*

Edmund Hillary (right) with Sherpa Tenzing on the slopes of Everest

Tenzing; they shook hands and then embraced each other. On returning to the climbers anxiously waiting at Camp VII, Hillary's now famous first words, in the modern unheroic style, were: 'We knocked the bastard off.'

Hillary was appointed leader of the New Zealand Antarctic expedition which reached the South Pole in 1958. But afterwards he was increasingly drawn back to the Himalayas, feeling a particular debt to the Sherpas of Nepal for the valiant support they had given to the world's mountaineers, and becoming the major inspiration behind the building of schools, hospitals, bridges and airstrips in the region. Hillary also capitalized on his achievements by becoming an author and lecturer and consultant on camping and outdoor equipment supplies.

Alfred Hitchcock (1899–1980)
American, ex-British
Film director

Son of a north-east London shopkeeper, Alfred Hitchcock was educated by Jesuits and entered the film industry in 1920 as a title writer. His ascent was rapid: by 1925 he had directed his first film, and in the following year enjoyed success with his third, *The Lodger*, in the genre that was to be his special preserve, the suspense thriller.

His career falls into distinct sections: first, the British period, ending in 1939, which includes the first British talkie, *Blackmail*, and a series of Gaumont-British thrillers such as *The Man Who Knew Too Much*, *The Thirty-Nine Steps*, *Sabotage* and *The Lady Vanishes*; then his

Master of the suspense thriller, film director Alfred Hitchcock

Hollywood years, spanning nearly four decades, with memorable films such as *Rebecca*, *Shadow of a Doubt*, *Notorious*, *Strangers on a Train*, *Rear Window*, *Vertigo*, *Psycho*, *The Birds*, and his last, *Family Plot*, in 1976. Noted for his careful pre-planning ('My films are made on paper'), he was nevertheless one of the most innovative forces in the history of the cinema, ever ready to experiment with overlapping sound, shock cuts, ten-minute takes, low-key colour lighting, techniques in which he was usually way ahead of the field. He was a master at invoking terror from the most normal of settings, subjecting innocents to satanic ordeals.

Audiences saw him as a consistent and reliable entertainer, but critics recognized a deeper, more complex moral purpose, as well as an astonishing control of the medium.

Adolf Hitler (1889–1945) German, ex-Austro-Hungarian
Dictator

A number of myths have grown up around the life of the twentieth century's greatest mass murderer: he was really called Hitler, not Schicklgrüber, though his illegitimate father was known by that name until he established his right to the family name of Hitler; in early adulthood Adolf was a painter of insipid scenes, not a house painter; and he chewed not carpets but nuts and raw vegetables.

Hitler was totally undisciplined: he could never follow routine, only whim, even when,

between 1940 and 1944, he was master of most of Europe. He had no friends, established no close personal relationships, except with his mistress, Eva Braun, whom he married a few hours before their suicide on 30 April 1945, just before the Russians stormed his bunker in Berlin. And it was Eva's blind loyalty and domesticity rather than any mental affinity – she was totally empty-headed – that attracted Hitler.

Hatred was Hitler's driving force. His early days had been miserable, as he scraped in Vienna for a few coins and went from one shabby lodging to another. He blamed not his own faults and fecklessness but the rich middle classes, the Jews – Vienna was a centre of Jewish culture, which had spawned an anti-Semitic party – and the trade unions, controlled, he thought, by the Jews. When war broke out in 1914, Hitler went to Munich. He enlisted in the German army, and won two Iron Crosses. After the war he was a spy for the German army in the fermenting right-wing political scene. While an informer his power of magnetic oratory became apparent, and, by 1921, he was head of the tiny Nationalsozialist-ische Deutsche Arbeiterparti: National Socialist German Workers' Party, NAZI for short.

Germany had lost the First World War, for which Hitler blamed the Jews. Then came economic depression: Hitler blamed the Jews. Germany and the west were threatened by the Bolsheviks: Hitler said they were all Jews. A pure race (*Volk*) was the destiny of the world. The Germans were the purest Aryans, the master race. Their blood must be kept pure and free

Adolf Hitler

RIGHT *Ho Chi Minh, communist leader of North Vietnam*

from Jewish or Slavic pollution. Hitler said the Aryans would overcome and dominate the others so that their 'will' and race would emerge and triumph. There would be a new world order, as history required, of masters and slaves. It would be the third German Empire, the Third Reich, which would last a thousand years.

The world depression of 1929, pathetically weak politicians, plus Hitler's appeal to the voters and the violence of his political private army, the Brownshirts, resulted in the German Parliament, the Reichstag, giving full powers to Hitler as Chancellor in 1933. A year later the old president, Hindenburg, died, and his powers were combined with the Chancellor's to make Hitler the supreme Führer, the Leader.

Then, with consummate skill, he exploited the weaknesses of the western leaders. He re-armed Germany and embarked on expanding the German Empire by occupying neighbouring countries. His demands on Poland led in 1939 to the Second World War. Hitler thought the war was going well until he made the mistake of attacking Russia, where he encountered severe opposition, and was faced with fighting on two fronts. The United States eventually joined in the conflict, and the Germans were beaten ultimately by their own weapon of overwhelming mechanical superiority. The war ended in 1945. Hitler had brought about the deaths of tens of millions of people, exterminating the Jews and others in forced labour camps and the gas ovens of concentration camps: he was the greatest criminal ever in the annals of genocide. Hitler shattered the world as it was before he appeared on the political scene, and today we live still with the consequences.

Ho Chi Minh (1890–1969) Vietnamese, ex-French Indo-Chinese
Political leader

The cry of 'Ho, Ho, Ho Chi Minh' was made in the streets of many western cities by protestors demonstrating against American involvement in the Vietnam War during the 1960s. Ho Chi Minh, leader of North Vietnam, with his frail figure and straggling old man's beard, seemed the embodiment of peaceful intent and of the suffering of the peasantry of his unfortunate country. Few of the protestors realized that he was a professional revolutionary, a man dedicated to the Communist Party and to nationalist ideology.

Unlike Lenin (*q.v.*) or Mao (*q.v.*), who were genuine intellectuals, or Stalin (*q.v.*), who pretended to be one, Ho made no contribution to communist theory. He was born in Vietnam, then a French colony, of poor peasant parents and spent his early years as a labourer, as an elementary schoolteacher and then as a seaman.

The First World War victory of the Allies in 1918 was supposed to be also a victory for the principle of national self-determination, and though this was applied only to Europe the colonial Third World also took up the new desire for freedom. Ho Chi Minh petitioned the statesmen settling the world's future at the Versailles Peace Conference to recognize Indo-China's rights also. In 1920 he joined the French Communist Party and took part in the international anti-colonialist movement, backed by Moscow, where he went for training.

In 1930 Ho Chi Minh founded the Indo-Chinese Communist Party, and for most of that decade he remained in Moscow. Fortunately for him, he left for China in 1938, thus escaping probable execution under Stalin. In 1945, his guerillas having fought the Japanese during the Second World War, he declared Vietnam independent. The French returned, however, and tried to re-establish their authority by a draining war (1946–54). The French withdrew from the country after the 1954 Geneva Agreement which partitioned Vietnam between the North, which Ho Chi Minh ruled, and the 'independent' pro-western South. The United States protected the South, and was steadily drawn to its military support as pressure from the North grew from 1959 onwards. The ensuing Vietnam War was to ruin the reputation of President Lyndon Johnson. It also shredded America's moral authority, and for some years gave her a distaste for involvement overseas, enabling the Russians to appreciably increase their influence. Ho Chi Minh died before President Nixon ended the war and the victorious North Vietnam forces occupied the South, whose capital, Saigon, is now named Ho Chi Minh City in his honour.

Frederick Gowland Hopkins
(1861–1947) British
Biochemist

Frederick, later Sir Frederick, Gowland Hopkins shared the 1929 Nobel Prize for Medicine with the Dutch physician Christiaan Eijkman for their contribution to the discovery of vitamins.

Born in Eastbourne, Sussex, Hopkins began his career in science with studies in analytical chemistry, and qualified as a doctor at Guy's Hospital, London. He became a lecturer in chemical physiology and then Professor of Biochemistry (the chemistry of life) at the University of Cambridge, where he remained for the rest of his life.

Hopkins was interested in the relation between diet and growth, and recognized that a nutritious diet needed 'additional food factors' as well as the basic carbohydrate, protein and fat. In order to identify these factors Hopkins carried out experiments on laboratory rats, feeding them on synthetic diets that were, as far as chemistry could tell, fully nutritious; but the rats did not grow normally. When he added milk to the diet, however, the rats prospered. Gowland Hopkins considered that vitamins in the milk were responsible. He was never able to isolate the vital elements, but the conclusions he drew from his experiments did much to establish an awareness of the essential role played by vitamins in diet. He also helped to demonstrate the astonishing fact that there were recognized diseases – scurvy and

Frederick Gowland Hopkins, biochemist, who discovered vitamins and recognized that diseases could result from dietary deficiencies

beri-beri for example – that were caused not by an infection but by a deficiency in diet.

In later researches Gowland Hopkins showed that muscles in action accumulate a chemical called lactic acid, which we now know to be a half-way stage in using the energy from sugar in the bloodstream. (If the lactic acid accumulates in the muscles, it causes muscle fatigue.) He also discovered a chemical, glutathione, that is essential to the basic function of body cells, playing a key part in their use of oxygen. His work thus helped towards our present understanding of how a living cell works.

Edwin Hubble (1889–1953) American
Astronomer

The two most important ideas in modern astronomy are that of the expanding universe and that of the Big Bang, the cosmic explosion that started the universe. The second idea comes from the first and both depend on the observations of the astronomer Edwin Hubble.

Hubble was born in Marshfield, Missouri, on 20 November 1889 and after gaining a degree from the University of Chicago he studied law at the University of Oxford. He intended to become a lawyer, but was invited to join the Yerkes Observatory to research in astronomy, which until then had been only a hobby. After the end of the First World War he joined the staff of the Mount Wilson Observatory and started to work with the 100-inch telescope, then the largest in the world.

Hubble was particularly interested in the nebulae, which look like shining clouds of gas, rather than in the bright, clear points that are the typical stars. Eventually, with the giant tele-

The beautiful Horsehead Nebula, made up of a mass of distant stars (see Edwin Hubble)

scope, he found individual, faint stars in a nebula. The nebula's cloudy appearance came from a mass of these faint stars, like those we see in the cloud-like streak we call the Milky Way. Hubble calculated that the stars in the nebula were 800,000 light years away – eight times the distance of the furthest star in our own galaxy. He showed, for the first time, that there were star systems outside our own, and these starry nebulae were renamed galaxies to emphasize this.

Hubble went on to study other galaxies and found that many of them were much further away still. When he measured both their distances and the speed at which they were travelling away from the Earth he uncovered an astounding fact: the further away a galaxy was, the faster it was travelling. It was remotely possible that every galaxy really was travelling away from the Earth, but Hubble decided that a better explanation was that the universe was expanding. If it is expanding at a constant rate, it is at some remote point expanding at the speed of light, and we can know nothing of what happens beyond that. From measurements, the knowable universe is twenty-six thousand million light years in diameter.

By working backwards astronomers can calculate when the universe started to expand – when the Big Bang occurred, in other words. Hubble's original calculation was that the universe is two thousand million years old, although it is now known to be much older even than this.

Aldous Huxley (1894–1963) British
Novelist and essayist

Aldous Huxley, one of the distinguished Huxley family of writers and scientists, was the grandson of T. H. Huxley and the brother of Julian, both of whom were eminent biologists. Born in Godalming, Surrey, Aldous was educated at Eton and Oxford. A serious eye disease prevented him from pursuing his medical studies and led to his being almost blind for the rest of his life. He became a journalist and, in 1920–1, drama critic of the *Westminster Gazette*, after which he went to live in Italy and began to write novels. It was in Italy that he met D. H. Lawrence (*q.v.*), on whom he based a character in his novel *Point Counter Point* (1928) and whose letters he edited after Lawrence's death. Huxley's earliest novels, *Crome Yellow* (1921), *Antic Hay* (1923) and *Those Barren Leaves* (1925), are brittle, witty and cynical satires on English post-war society. It was D. H. Lawrence who led Huxley to an interest in deeper values and encouraged him along paths of self-exploration.

Point Counter Point was followed by Huxley's best-known novel, *Brave New World* (1932), in which he voiced his concern at the dangers resulting from scientific progress. The more wholeheartedly Huxley embraced the novel of ideas, the less certain his grip upon characterization became, to the extent that his later novels are almost fictionalized essays. In 1934 he travelled in Central America and in 1937 settled permanently in California. Here he became converted to a form of mysticism and began to interest himself in the occult. His later work includes a number of lively and intelligent essays, brought together in *Collected Essays* (1960), and *The Devils of Loudun*, a famous study of mass-hysteria in the Middle Ages.

One of the later novels, *Time Must Have a Stop* (1944), with its popularization of his mystical beliefs, aroused interest, as did *The Doors of Perception* (1954) and *Heaven and Hell* (1956), describing his experiments with hallucinogenic drugs, but it is upon the earlier work, up to and including *Brave New World*, that Huxley's posthumous reputation most securely rests.

ABOVE *Aldous Huxley;* LEFT *some of his novels and essays*

BELOW *James Joyce, author of* Ulysses *and* Finnegans Wake; *a portrait by Jacques Emile Blanche, 1935*

J

James Joyce (1882–1941) Irish
Novelist and poet

James Joyce is regarded as one of the most imaginative and most innovatory literary talents of the twentieth century, whose use of language remains unequalled. The son of a civil servant and the eldest of ten children, he was born in Dublin and educated there at University College. His mother was a pious Catholic and it was to a large extent as a result of her influence that Joyce at first considered, under Jesuit pressure, becoming a priest. His eventual rebellion against not only Catholicism but also his family background and Irish nationalism is described in the largely autobiographical novel *A Portrait of the Artist as a Young Man*, first published as a series in a magazine in 1914–15. By then Joyce had lived for several years as a teacher of languages in Paris and Trieste with a young woman from Galway, Nora Barnacle. The couple did not marry until 1931, and then only to protect the legal rights of their two children. Between the two world wars they lived mainly in Paris, where Joyce wrote his masterpiece, *Ulysses*, published in 1922. In 1923 he began work on *Finnegans Wake*, a huge work in a difficult, punning style, which was to occupy him for the next seventeen years, achieving publication in 1939.

Ulysses, which for many years was banned in the United States, is now recognized as perhaps the greatest novel written in English in the twentieth century. It records the events of an average day in the lives of its three leading characters in Dublin. In *Finnegans Wake* Joyce

employed a 'stream of consciousness' technique, in which the thoughts and actions of the characters are conveyed by the reflections within their own minds, using a language of Joyce's own invention so elaborate that, to the uninitiated, the novel is barely understandable. Among those who have made a study of Joyce's highly individual use of language, however, it has enthusiastic admirers. His other major works include two volumes of verse, *Chamber Music* (1907) and *Pomes Penyeach* (1927), and a play, *Exiles* (1918).

Joyce left Paris in 1940 and returned to Zürich, where he had spent the years of the First World War. Throughout his life he had suffered from eye trouble, his vision deteriorating until he was almost blind. His daughter's mental illness, which caused her to be confined in an institution, was a source of great distress to him and contributed to his comparatively early death in Zürich the following year.

Carl Gustav Jung (1875–1961) Swiss
Psychiatrist

For the general public Jung is second only to Freud (*q.v.*) in his influence as a psychiatrist, though the value of his work is still disputed. He was born at Kesswil, the son of a Protestant minister, and took his medical degree at Basle University. He then worked at the Zürich University psychiatric clinic and the Burghölzli Mental Hospital in Zürich, where he was in charge of the hypnotism clinic. He coined the now familiar term 'complex' for a cluster of associated ideas and emotions, largely, if not entirely, unconscious.

From 1907 to 1912 Jung was Freud's favourite disciple, but he felt that Freud placed far too much emphasis on sex and experiences of early childhood as factors in human behaviour. His book *The Psychology of the Unconscious* (1912) criticized Freud and the two men quarrelled. Unlike Freud, Jung was more impressed by the differences between people than by the similarities. He went on to classify personality-types and drew what is now the well-known distinction between the 'extrovert' or outgoing personality and the 'introvert' or inward-turning one.

Jung is best known for his theory that besides the personal unconscious there is the 'collective unconscious', common to all human beings, which contains the 'archetypes' or common patterns of ideas that come to the surface in religion, art, philosophy, science, dreams and all forms of expression. He grew increasingly interested in religion, mythology, mysticism, alchemy and the occult, and believed that loss of religious faith was the prevailing disease of modern man. His psychiatric method became a spiritual journey towards the goal of 'individuation' or the achievement of wholeness, the development of a complete, fully integrated personality.

Jung lived most of his life in Switzerland. He was Professor of Psychology at Zürich University from 1933 to 1941, and from 1933 onwards his followers gathered at the Eranos Conferences, held at Ascona on Lake Maggiore. He was a prolific writer, but clarity was not one of his gifts and his books are not easy to grapple with. They include *Psychological Types* (1916), *Modern Man in Search of a Soul* (1933), *Psychology and Religion* (1938), *The Integration of the Personality* (1939), *Psychology and Alchemy* (1944) and *Memories, Dreams and Reflections* (1962).

Dr Carl Gustav Jung on his eighty-third birthday, July 1958

K

Franz Kafka (1883–1924) Austrian
Novelist

The writings of Kafka, a highly influential German-language novelist, owe much to the Danish philosopher Kierkegaard, as they deal mainly with modern man's search for a meaning to life in a world that Kafka saw as one of futility, paradox and absurdity.

Kafka was born in Prague, then part of the Austro-Hungarian empire, into a family of Czechoslovakian Jews. He was educated at the German grammar school there, and it was only when he became an adult that he began to think of himself as either Czech or Jewish. At Prague University he met Max Brod, his friend for life and future biographer (who was responsible for the publication of Kafka's novels). After leaving university with a doctorate in law, Kafka took a job as a clerk with the Government insurance organization for the kingdom of Bohemia and began to write in his spare time. He published little in his lifetime, but when he died prematurely, of tuberculosis, the manuscripts he left with his friend Brod, with instructions that they should be burned, included three novels, *Der Prozess* (*The Trial*), *Das Schloss* (*The Castle*) and *Amerika*. Brod disregarded Kafka's instructions and the novels were published in 1925, 1926 and 1927.

The form of these major works appears to be that of a dream. Because of this they are full of symbols, many of which need explanation. In the years after Kafka's death, and even more so following the Second World War, a vast Kafka industry sprang into being, with critics and scholars offering conflicting interpretations of his novels. It is difficult to separate the subject of the novels from the structure Kafka uses to describe it, but the subject could be thought of as a lonely and confused individual's search for identity, a voyage of self-discovery, combined with a great bitterness at the transience and futility of life as Kafka saw it. Some of these themes emerge more clearly from his diaries and letters. By giving artistic shape to his pessimistic fears in his novels, Kafka helped to dispel those fears and created in the process some of the most obsessively fascinating works of this century.

Wassily Kandinsky (1866–1944) Russian Painter

Kandinsky, like Mondrian (*q.v.*), was one of the pioneers of abstract painting. He was born in Moscow and studied law and political economy before devoting himself to painting at the age of thirty, when he left for Munich. By 1909–10 Kandinsky was starting to use colour with an expressive power as he moved towards abstraction, a course that has certain parallels in the career of Mondrian. 'One thing became clear to me', he wrote, 'that objectiveness, the depiction of objects, needed no place in my paintings and was indeed harmful to them.' By 1911, his work had at first glance an abstract appearance, although recognizable forms are discernible. Two years later Kandinsky's work had reached the brink of abstraction. *Improvisation No. 30 (Cannon)* of 1913 (a musical title, in common with many 1910–14 pictures) is one of the most dynamic semi-abstract compositions of the period.

Like Mondrian, Kandinsky was involved in a number of group activities – he organized the

LEFT *Franz Kafka;* BELOW LEFT *Kafka's entry in a friend's album: 'There is a coming and a going – a parting, often for ever'*

BELOW Improvisation No. 30 (Warlike Theme) *by Wassily Kandinsky, 1913*

Blaue Reiter group in Munich in 1911 – and also wrote theoretical essays on art. In his essay of 1910–11 'Concerning the Spiritual in Art' he justifies the development of non-objective painting and discusses art's spiritual value.

He returned to Russia after the Revolution and in 1918 was appointed professor at the Moscow Academy of Fine Arts. He lived and taught in Germany from 1922 to 1933, and spent his last eleven years in Paris. The geometric compositions of his German (Bauhaus) period gave way to a greater abstraction and fantasy at the end of his life. As one of the founders of abstract art, Kandinsky's painting and writings have enormous historical importance in the development of non-objective art in this century.

Buster Keaton (1895–1966) American
Actor, director and writer

Where Chaplin (*q.v.*) expressed emotion in the face of adversity Keaton stayed impassive. Where Chaplin evoked pathos, Keaton remained stoic and aloof. Where Chaplin erupted into joyous laughter, Keaton retained an unsmiling gravity. Yet the two rivals had notable similarities. Both were skilled acrobats who had learned their tumbling on the vaudeville stage. Both achieved overall responsibility for their films, controlling every stage from screenplay to edited print. Both gave the silent cinema the benefit of their unique comic genius.

Keaton initially made a number of two-reelers with Fatty Arbuckle, many of which are now lost, before becoming a star in his own right with *The Saphead* (1920). His highly original visual sense and extraordinary comic timing was developed and refined in the features he made during the 1920s, most notably *Our Hospitality*

(1923), *Sherlock Jr* and *The Navigator* (both 1924), *The General* (1927) and *Steamboat Bill Jr* (1928). The arrival of sound virtually extinguished his career, which had in any case suffered a setback when he relinquished artistic and production control of his films to MGM. His personal life was also wracked with problems, to which he reacted with recurring bouts of alcoholism.

Although Keaton frequently appeared in cameo parts – most importantly in Wilder's *Sunset Boulevard* (1949) and Chaplin's *Limelight* (1952) – his full return to popularity did not occur until the Venice Film Festival of 1965, when he received a tumultuous reception following a major retrospective of his films. A few months later he was dead.

With hindsight it is possible to see that the 'Great Stone Face' was perhaps the greatest of all film comedians as well as the purest, projecting his skills with a delicate, dignified subtlety without any recourse to sentiment. The incident in which he bounces one railroad cross tie off another to enable his locomotive to get through in *The General* is one of the best sight gags in the history of the movies, invariably raising cheers from the audience whenever it is shown.

John Fitzgerald Kennedy (1917–63)
American
Political leader

When John Fitzgerald Kennedy was elected President in 1961 it seemed to much of America and the world that a new era of hope had dawned. JFK, or Jack as his intimates called him, had a magnetic quality that drew the best men to his side. There had been no one like him since Franklin Roosevelt (*q.v.*).

The impassive face of Buster Keaton: a still from Go West, *1925*

This was a man with style, the style of leadership. Handsome, carelessly elegant (few people were aware that, for most of the time, he was painfully strapped into a surgical corset) his distinctive Bostonian voice brought out the memorable phrases which stirred the Western Alliance. Let the word go forth, he said in his inaugural address, that the United States is ready to accept any challenge, at any time, at any place.

He showed, when Russia prepared to install missile sites in Cuba in 1962, that he meant what he said. JFK, at the risk of nuclear war, firmly induced Russia to cancel its plans, and from that crucial turning point came a vital improvement in east-west relations and the partial nuclear test-ban treaty between the two super-powers.

Kennedy came from a rich and secure background, though his family's wealth and social standing were of recent origin. His parents were tough Boston-Irish Catholics, with deep roots in that ethnic Democratic Party stronghold, and their money came from successful business ventures. JFK's father, Joseph Kennedy, former ambassador to Britain, and his remarkable mother, Rose, put all their children through a rigorous physical and mental training – preparation for a life of achievement. JFK, in London with his ambassador father, saw the results of Chamberlain's appeasement policy in 1939. His book *Why England Slept*, published while he was still a student, is an account of Britain's lack of preparation for the approaching Second World War. He became a voracious reader, and indeed his personal tastes, like those of the beautiful Jacqueline Bouvier, whom he married while he was a senator, were cultivated and solidly intellectual. It was said that as President his White House was like a royal court: 'Camelot', they called it.

He was the first Catholic to become President, beating Richard Nixon by a whisker and defeating a long tradition of religious prejudice, yet the ease with which he assumed office and his treatment of the Cuban missile crisis brought him acceptance even in the bigoted South; the blacks trusted and approved of him. But his planned programme of social reform at home and his stepping-up of America's involvement in Vietnam had to be left to his successor, Lyndon Johnson, to implement. At the age of only forty-six Kennedy was cut down by an assassin's bullet in Dallas, Texas, a tragedy which was felt across the world.

André Kertész (b. 1893) American, ex-Hungarian
Photographer

The photographic career of André Kertész spans nearly seventy years. It began in his native Budapest two years before the outbreak of the

First World War, but it was not until he was in military service that his hobby became a lifetime vocation. He went to the Front with a camera and glass plates in his pack, but it was not scenes of battle that interested him. He observed the quiet details of war – a soldier saying farewell to a girl, tired soldiers trying to relax in a field, men having their wounds dressed, troops moving up to the line watched by anxious peasants. He himself was wounded, barely escaping with his life from a bullet that just missed his heart but partially paralyzed him.

In 1926 Kertész migrated, like many fellow Hungarians with ambitions in the arts, to Paris, where he began photographing the painters there. In 1927 he had his first one-man show. Favouring small cameras, Kertész was by 1928 working with an early Leica, enabling him to capture his moments with the minimum of fuss. Kertész experimented and demonstrated the capabilities of 35 mm photography so effectively that even Henri Cartier-Bresson (*q.v.*) was influenced by him. Illustrated magazines were springing up in Europe using the work of

ABOVE *John F. Kennedy in the Oval Office at the White House*

OPPOSITE ABOVE Satiric Dancer *by André Kertész, 1926*

OPPOSITE BELOW *John Maynard Keynes: a watercolour by Gwen Raverat*

miniature cameras, and Kertész was an early star.

In 1936 he went to the United States, where the Museum of Modern Art in New York exhibited some of his pictures in its first major photographic show. He remained there during the Second World War, working in photojournalism. Then for many years he was under contract to Condé Nast, the publishers of *Vogue*. Kertész did not receive full critical recognition until the mid-1960s, in spite of the volume and range of his work. It was only after his one-man exhibition at the Museum of Modern Art in 1964 that his greatness was formally acknowledged, and since then his reputation has consolidated with each year. Even more remarkably, the octogenarian photographer is still at work, and his most recent photographs demonstrate that he is still using the camera as a means of revealing his special vision of the world.

John Maynard Keynes (1883–1946)
British
Economist, philosopher and civil servant

Keynes was born in Cambridge, the son of J.N. Keynes, a logician and economist. After a brilliant career at Eton and Cambridge (in mathematics and economics), he combined university teaching with a public career. He was a member of the Bloomsbury Group of artists and intellectuals, and took a strong interest in philosophy, the arts and music throughout his life.

Keynes's principal interest and contribution was in the field of economics. At the height of the Depression in 1936 he published his *General Theory of Employment, Interest and Money*, which challenged the conventional economic beliefs of the time. In particular he believed that deflationary policy and resulting unemployment were not self-correcting phenomena. In retrospect the ideas are simple enough: that reducing payrolls by dismissal or wage reductions may drive prices down, but not enough to rekindle demand and start the upward cycle again. He argued that the Government should change its policy, that it should invest, spend on public works, and manipulate interest rates and money supply to make buying and borrowing more possible and attractive. Such injections of money are multiplied as they circulate through the economy and so enhance the demand for goods and services, which in turn creates employment. His theory is one for a liberal capitalism, but a liberal capitalism that recognizes the commanding position of the central Government in managing economic affairs and, moreover, urges the commitment of the central Government to that management and to the maintenance of full employment.

The most striking initial impact of Keynes's thinking was on Roosevelt's (*q.v.*) New Deal and the policy of National Reconstruction. Only subsequently did the orthodox economics of the time give way to Keynesianism.

During the Second World War Keynes played a highly influential role in the Treasury and it was he who negotiated the post-war loans and credits with the United States, and designed the International Monetary Fund.

Keynes was married to the Russian ballerina Lydia Lopokova and with her founded the Vic-Wells Ballet. Elevated to the peerage, he died in 1946 just before he was to receive the Order of Merit.

Martin Luther King (1929–68) American
Religious and civil rights leader

The son of a black Baptist minister, Martin Luther King was born in Atlanta, Georgia. After obtaining a doctorate in philosophy, he became attracted by the ideas of Mahatma Gandhi (*q.v.*), seeing a great similarity between the great Indian's ideal of non-violence and the Christian ideals of love, goodness and forgiveness.

He had gone to Boston to study for his doctorate, but while completing it he returned to the South in 1954 to become the pastor of Dexter Avenue Church, Montgomery, Alabama. Blacks in the South were still subject to segregation, with separate and usually far inferior facilities for them, if any. But with the rise of independent states in Africa and the beginnings of a general current of change in attitudes to race, the black people of the South were stirring against the burden of centuries of subjection.

Blacks were relegated to the backs of the buses and had to give up their seats to whites whenever 'necessary'. In 1956 Montgomery blacks decided to boycott the system, and Dr King led the boycott. The overwhelming majority of the bus customers were black, and for the first time blacks were able to exert economic power. After this show of solidarity, buses were desegregated in nearly every Southern city.

King's success with the Montgomery boycott had made him a public figure, and he was elected President of the Southern Christian Leadership Conference. He returned to Atlanta to further his work. He was an inspiring preacher and speaker, and recordings of his 'I have a dream' speech are still played with great effect. He moved through the South, fearlessly confronting brutal local police chiefs and leading his followers with prayer and songs like the famous 'We shall overcome' when confronted by guns, tear gas and fierce police dogs.

His devotion to non-violence and to passive resistance found an ideal expression in sit-ins, in which blacks, sometimes with white sympath-

izers, sat in seats in public places which were reserved for whites.

In 1961 he began his freedom rides, which ended segregation on inter-state travel. In 1963 there was the famous Freedom March on Washington, which indicated the size of the support for the Federal Civil Rights legislation that Kennedy (*q.v.*) was beginning to send to Congress.

But by now there was a tougher sound to black demands for a greater share in American life, and this in turn provoked a white backlash. King, though blameless, became a focus for the attention of white extremists. He frequently received death threats, and his home was bombed. On 4 April 1968 he was shot dead in Memphis, Tennessee. A national day of mourning was declared in the United States, services were held world-wide, a monument was erected in New York and an avenue named after him in Harlem. His example still continues to inspire blacks the world over.

Otto Klemperer (1885–1973) German
Conductor

Otto Klemperer was one of the last of the great generation of Austro-German orchestral conductors which flourished in the years between the two world wars. He was born in Breslau into a Jewish family, and studied music in Frankfurt and Berlin, where he made his debut at the age of twenty-one conducting the Offenbach operetta

Martin Luther King: the Freedom Speech, Washington DC, 1963

Otto Klemperer in rehearsal

Orpheus in the Underworld. The following year, on the recommendation of Gustav Mahler, he was engaged by the German Opera House in Prague as Assistant Conductor, where he remained for three years before accepting a similar position in Hamburg for a further three years (1910–12). After engagements in other provincial opera houses, Klemperer became Musical Director of the Cologne Opera from 1917 to 1924, and the Wiesbaden Opera from 1924 to 1927, when he was given the directorship of the Kroll Opera in Berlin. Klemperer's period at the Kroll saw the production of a number of important new operas, but this activity was ended abruptly when the Kroll was closed down in 1931. With the rise to power of the Nazi regime in 1933, Klemperer was forced to leave Germany.

Making his way to America, he became Principal Conductor of the Los Angeles Philharmonic Orchestra. From then until the end of his life he conducted very little opera, but made an immense reputation with his performances of the symphonies of Beethoven and Mahler, especially in the post-war years when he came to be seen as the guardian of a great tradition of classical performance. In the 1950s and 1960s his concerts in London with the Philharmonia Orchestra, whose Principal Conductor he became, were among the most exciting and valuable of London's musical events. In the symphonies of Beethoven, the strength, majesty and objectivity of Klemperer's performances have no rivals.

Triumphing over a series of illnesses which would have felled lesser men, Klemperer survived to become the remaining link with the life and times of Mahler, whose music he had helped to keep alive.

Fritz Kreisler in a watercolour portrait by Boris Chaliapin

Fritz Kreisler (1875–1962) American, ex-Austrian
Violinist and composer

Fritz Kreisler was the son of an eminent physician who was himself an enthusiastic amateur musician. Kreisler's musical gifts were recognized in his infancy, and he made his first appearance playing the violin at a concert when he was seven. The youngest child ever to have been admitted to the Conservatorium in Vienna, the city of his birth, he carried off the gold medal for violin playing at the age of ten. He was only twelve when, after further study in Paris, he won the Premier Grand Prix de Rome against forty competitors, all of them adults. In 1889 the fourteen-year-old Kreisler undertook a highly successful tour of the United States. However, on his return to Vienna he laid the violin aside for some years in order to study medicine, with a view to taking up his father's profession (an idea he was soon to abandon), and he joined the Austrian army.

At the age of twenty-four, Kreisler made a second brilliant musical debut, this time in Berlin, and left for another tour of the United States. He was now recognized as a master of his instrument, and for the next half-century was spoken of as one of the greatest musicians of his time.

Kreisler was typical of Viennese musicians in producing a tone of rare beauty, but he allied this to matchless phrasing and an instinctive sense of rhythm, a combination which brought him a much wider popularity than that enjoyed by any of his rivals. He was the Caruso (*q.v.*) of the violin. Understandably, his greatest successes were with the Viennese classics, especially the violin concertos of Beethoven and Mozart, but he also enjoyed playing lighter music both as encores at his recitals and on gramophone records. He composed a number of pieces for the violin which he at first announced were arrangements of older, classical music, admitting only some years later that they were his own work. He also composed a successful operetta, *Apple Blossoms* (1919), which was a Broadway hit.

Other violinists have equalled Kreisler in technique, but none in musicianship or sheer beauty of tone. His performances of the Beethoven Violin Concerto and of a number of his own compositions, pieces of great charm, are preserved on gramophone records.

Akira Kurosawa (b. 1910) Japanese
Film director

That the western world is aware of the Japanese cinema at all is to a large extent part of the achievement of Kurosawa, whose *Rashomon*, shown at the Venice Film Festival in 1951, was the first film from Japan to be shown widely to European and American audiences. It has since been recognized that he has absorbed the influences of Hollywood to a much greater degree than his contemporaries, adapting them into the traditional modes of Japanese expression. Kurosawa's receptiveness to western culture has led him to base several of his films on major European literary works: Dostoevsky's *The Idiot* (1951), Gorky's *The Lower Depths* (1957) and Shakespeare's *Macbeth* (filmed as *Throne of Blood* in 1957), in which the Scottish tragedy is transplanted to medieval Japan. The traffic has been two-way. One of Kurosawa's most famous films, *The Seven Samurai* (1954), was remade by Hollywood into a classic Western, *The Magnificent Seven*, and *Yojimbo* (1961) was the basis for *A Fistful of Dollars*.

Kurosawa began his career as a commercial artist, abandoning it for films in 1936 when he became an assistant director. He directed his first film in his own right in 1943 (*Judo Saga*). As a screenwriter he has also written more than a score of films for other directors. He exercises a powerful control over his own work, usually being responsible for his own editing and writing. *Dersu Uzala* (1975), a Japanese-Russian co-production, won an Academy Award for the best foreign-language film of the year. In 1980 his *Kagemusha*, the most expensive film ever made in Japan, was joint winner of the Golden Palm at the Cannes Film Festival, and was acclaimed as the master work of a great director who had by now reached the age of seventy. The film was widely shown in the west, having been part-financed by American film-makers. Kurosawa is one of the masters of the Japanese cinema, and it is to him that the credit must go for ensuring that not only his own but also the films of other Japanese directors, such as Mizoguchi, Ozu and Oshima, are now widely known and accessible throughout the world.

L

Freddie Laker (b. 1922) British
Aviation tycoon

Like so many successful ideas, Sir Freddie's was brilliantly simple: why should a traveller who wants to fly cheaply have to be one of a group booking or else book weeks in advance? Why, he reasoned, could passengers not just turn up at the airport and catch a plane as easily as a train? Laker's first low-price 'turn-up, take off' Skytrain left for New York in September 1977 after a six-year battle against airline and Government opposition. Within three years he had nearly 100 Skytrains a week shuttling between British airports and Miami, New York and Los Angeles, and was bidding for around-the-world routes;

ABOVE *Freddie Laker: 'Fly me, I'm Freddie'*

LEFT *Akira Kurosawa, director of* The Seven Samurai *and* Kagemusha

BELOW *Allen Lane, Managing Director of Penguin Books, 1940, with his secretary at Penguin head office;* INSET *the Penguin logo – elegant but flippant*

his service had made the other airlines closely examine their pricing and booking policies.

Success has brought Laker money, a knighthood and the satisfaction of confounding the cosy, uncompetitive airline cartel that said cheap, non-bookable seats were not viable. Once a tea-boy for a flying-boat maker, then an aircraft engineer in the wartime Air Transport Auxiliary, delivering anything that flew, he became an airline managing director and is now owner of one of the world's best-known airlines, Laker Airways. Like many post-war aviation hopefuls, his big break came in 1948, when the Russians blockaded Berlin, making flying the only means of delivering supplies and transporting people to and from the city; Laker had bought some planes for scrap only weeks before the Russian clamp-down gave them a highly profitable new lease of life. The post-blockade slump in the aviation industry saw a shrewd and unsentimental Laker surviving by melting aircraft down for aluminium pans.

Back in aviation, Laker built up a cargo airline, ran trooping flights, pioneered car ferry

aircraft and even had his own transport aircraft – the *Accountant* – built. Right at the top of the tree as managing director of British United Airways, the country's biggest independent airline, he gave up his job to start from scratch with Laker, or Fredair as he liked to call it.

Tough, impatient of any delay and particularly of trade unions, Laker attracts intense loyalty from employees, even though, as one quipped, it's 'work for Fred and sell your bed'. Aircraft salesmen say he has a mind like a computer and drives a very hard bargain. He venerated his mother until she died in 1979; 'Mum' to almost everyone in the airline, she had coached her son for success from the start, schooling his behaviour and table manners even though the cloth was sometimes a newspaper. He is still very much the earthy man of Kent, but he is also a superb publicist and showman whose energy and straightforward determination have struck an encouraging blow for private enterprise in Britain.

Allen Lane (1902–70) British
Publisher

Allen Lane's brilliant idea of publishing quality literature on a large scale in cheap, paperback form revolutionized twentieth-century publishing and left millions of readers in his debt. Of West Country yeoman stock, of which he remained intensely proud, Lane left Bristol Grammar School at the age of seventeen to work for his uncle's publishing firm, the Bodley Head, in London. By the time he was twenty-two, Lane was a Bodley Head director and had inherited his uncle's passion for adventurous publishing, high living and stylish presentation. An early Lane winner was the first British publication of James Joyce's *Ulysses* in 1936.

With his two brothers, Lane had formed an ambitious triumvirate which, after the death of his uncle in 1925, began increasingly to unsettle the staid Bodley Head board. When he showed them the first dummy of a Penguin paperback, to be priced at sixpence – the cost of a packet of cigarettes – like most other people Lane approached, they were hostile. Bodley Head distributed the first ten titles with the brothers' financial backing, but modest sales seemed to justify the pessimism.

Taking his co-directors' advice to 'go and work on something else', Lane left Bodley Head and went his own way. With his brothers and £100 capital, he rented the disused crypt of Holy Trinity Church in London's Great Portland Street and set up Penguin Books. Publishing books in paperback form was not a new idea, but Lane's notion of doing it in well printed and well produced editions was. Until then paperbacks had been of the penny dreadful variety, with lurid covers; the design of Lane's Penguins was to have what he described as an 'elegant flippancy', a characteristic implicit in their name. Lane had offered a £5 prize to his staff for the invention of a suitable imprint, and it was his secretary who came up with Penguin.

At first the new venture had a struggle to survive, but eventually Woolworths and then Selfridges placed small orders. The idea took off instantly. In a matter of days, public demand translated Woolworth's order for twelve gross into one of 80,000 copies. Success followed success, enhanced by the appearance of the political 'specials' on the eve of the Second World War – in 1939 ten million Penguins were sold.

Lane not only anticipated the rising public appetite for cheap, quality reading, which was encouraged by the spread of education, but also convinced his fellow publishers that they had nothing to lose by permitting paperback versions of their hard cover best-sellers. His battle to publish *Lady Chatterley's Lover* showed he had lost none of his taste for adventure, and the publicity surrounding the obscenity trial did nothing to harm the subsequent sale of Penguin shares to the public. When he died at the age of sixty-seven, Allen Lane, knighted in 1952, was probably the only man to have become a millionaire from book publishing.

Fritz Lang (1890–1976) American, ex-Austrian
Film director

The son of a Viennese architect and destined for the same profession, the young Fritz Lang ran away from home to study art in Paris before being conscripted into the Austrian army during the First World War. Wounded four times, he was discharged. He entered the film industry in Berlin after writing screenplays, and directed his first film in 1919. His dark vision was characterized by an almost paranoid distrust of power and organized authority. Of the films he made in Germany two stand out as classics: the astonishing, if simplistic, view of the future in *Metropolis*, in which Lang foresaw an urban world where mankind was subordinate to the machine; and *M*, the case history of a child murderer at large in a fear-stricken city with mob law taking over from the official order.

Lang's next film, *The Testament of Dr Mabuse* (1933), was banned by the Nazis, and fearful that his part-Jewish background would be discovered, he fled to Paris. From there, after making one film, *Liliom* (1934), he went to the United States and became an American citizen. Although frequently at odds with the studio system, which discouraged screenwriter directors, Lang was to make a number of great films in

Film director Fritz Lang

Hollywood over a twenty-year period. His first, *Fury* (1936), an indictment of lynch law, was followed by the bitter *You Only Live Once* (1937), in which a man is executed for a crime he did not commit. He made a pair of Westerns, *The Return of Frank James* (1940) and *Western Union* (1941), followed by a series of thrillers, including *Manhunt* (1941), *The Woman in the Window* (1944) and *Scarlet Street* (1945). Lang was constantly interested in the idea of a lone hero seeking vengeance against dark and conspiratorial forces and becoming corrupted in his pursuit, a theme that can be found in films as disparate in setting as the espionage thriller *Ministry of Fear* (1944), the Western *Rancho Notorious* (1952) and the gangster film *The Big Heat* (1953). Lang's last American film, *Beyond a Reasonable Doubt* (1956), with its bold plot twist, is a cynical summing-up of his beliefs, in which fate achieves its ends, however ironically, and the dark side of human nature, given time, inevitably comes to the surface. He was the master of the *film-noir*, and, through the skilled assembly of his images, made the nightmare real.

Stan Laurel (1890–1965) American, ex-British
& Oliver Hardy (1892–1957) American
Comedians

Laurel and Hardy were the greatest comic double act in the history of the cinema. At first they had followed separate careers, though once appearing in a film together in 1917, and it was not until 1926 that they were persuaded to team up for a film at the Hal Roach Studios. They were to go on to make more than a hundred films there, twenty-seven of them feature length.

Hardy was the fat one and Laurel the thin one, but the characterization was far more subtle than

that. Oliver Hardy, a lawyer's son from Georgia, usually wore an air of Southern dignity and courtliness, which would be shattered as a result of the inane actions of Stan Laurel, whose upbringing in Lancashire in England admirably trained him to imitate gormlessness and incompetence. In fact, it was Laurel who was the motivator of the team, and who largely devised their comic interactions. Laurel had learned his art, like Chaplin (*q.v.*), with Fred Karno, and first went to the United States with that troupe. It was he who was the uncredited director of most of the partnership's films at the Roach Studios.

The brilliance of Laurel and Hardy's comedy resided in their self-absorbed stupidity, their willingness to embark on hare-brained projects that even the most witless spectator would see were foredoomed. Olly was the fall guy, the perpetual victim of Stan's bumbling, invariably ending up with the bucket of whitewash on his head or buried in the cream pie. Theirs was a

Advertisement for Laurel and Hardy's Swiss Miss, *1938*

comedy of escalation, in which sometimes entire neighbourhoods would be drawn into disasters, such as the gigantic pie fight in *The Battle of the Century*. Massive destruction was very much a hallmark of the humour, and cars, restaurants and houses were smashed into unrecognizable messes at the climax of many of their escapades.

The partnership began and flourished in the days of silent films, but unlike many other great film comedians before the advent of talkies they had no problems adapting to sound. Olly's genteel, patronizing wheedling and Stan's whining and often hopelessly scrambled articulation complemented each other perfectly. The bowler hats symbolized their pretensions for gentlemanly formality, but succeeded in making them look like a pair of demented valets.

In 1940 the 'boys' went to Twentieth Century Fox, where they lost creative control, and their last few feature films were unremarkable. Their fame today is as great as when they were alive, thanks to the ability of television to transmit their great two-reelers, of which *The Music Box*, *Perfect Day* and *County Hospital* are among the best.

D. H. Lawrence (1885–1930) British
Novelist, poet and essayist

D.H. Lawrence was born in the mining town of Eastwood, Nottinghamshire. His father was a miner, his mother a former schoolmistress, and both parents feature prominently in Lawrence's first major novel, *Sons and Lovers* (1913), a largely autobiographical work written after his mother's death. It deals with Lawrence's boyhood and adolescence, and was acclaimed for its realistic picture of working-class life.

Lawrence left school at sixteen, became an uncertified teacher, and five years later took a course in teaching at the University College, Nottingham, after which he taught in Croydon, Surrey. His home and family background, which mingled working-class independence with an aspiration – derived and encouraged by his mother – both to learn and to teach, led Lawrence to literature and creative writing. His first poems were published in *The English Review* in 1909 and his first novel, *The White Peacock*, in 1911.

Eloping in 1912 with Frieda von Richthofen, the German wife of a Nottingham professor, Lawrence lived mainly abroad for the rest of his life. *Look, We Have Come Through* (1917), a collection of poems about his relationship with Frieda, was followed by a number of novels of great power and originality, such as *The Rainbow* (1915) and *Women in Love* (1921), in which Lawrence explored the tensions between puritanism and sexuality in his own nature as well as in modern society. He was fascinated by the

LEFT *A portrait of D. H. Lawrence by J. Juta, 1920;* BELOW *the first paperback edition of* Lady Chatterley's Lover

Nietzschean idea of the *uebermensch* or superman, the hero whose great strength placed him above conventional ideas of morality, and expressed something of this in *Kangaroo* (1923), written during a visit to Australia, and *The Plumed Serpent* (1926), written in New Mexico. In 1925, after a serious chest illness, Lawrence returned to Europe where he lived mainly in Italy. His last major novel, *Lady Chatterley's Lover*, was written in 1926–7 and privately printed in Florence in 1928. For many years it was suppressed, not because of the frankness with which Lawrence dealt with the subject of sexual attraction, but because of his insistent use of the four-letter word for intercourse which seemingly still has the power to shock.

Lawrence has proved to be an extremely influential writer not so much in his style or technique as in his ideas: his philosophy is that the physical and sexual as well as the emotional and mental aspects of men and women are unified in their relationships with the forces of nature to become a form of religion. Apart from his novels, Lawrence wrote a great many essays, among the most valuable and interesting of which are *Pornography and Obscenity* (1930) and *Fantasia of the Unconscious* (1922).

Lotte Lehmann (1888–1976) German
Opera singer

Lotte Lehmann studied singing in Berlin, and made her debut in 1910 at the Hamburg Opera, where her first great success was as Elsa in Wagner's *Lohengrin*; the production was conducted by Klemperer (*q.v.*) who helped and encouraged the young singer. In 1914 she was engaged by the Vienna Opera, and it was there

Lotte Lehmann

BELOW *Lenin: a strident political poster*

that she found her real artistic home, remaining a leading soprano in Vienna until the outbreak of the Second World War, when she made the United States her home for the rest of her life. For the twenty-five years that she was with the Vienna Opera, Lehmann was one of the most greatly loved and admired sopranos not only with that company – though there she was a particular favourite – but also abroad, especially at the Royal Opera House, Covent Garden, and the New York Metropolitan Opera. Her great roles were in the operas of Wagner, Verdi, Puccini (who spoke warmly of her performances) and as Leonore in Beethoven's *Fidelio*. Above all, however, Lehmann triumphed in the operas of Richard Strauss (*q.v.*) who admired her enormously and wrote a number of roles for her, among them the Composer in *Ariadne auf Naxos*, the Dyer's Wife in *Die Frau ohne Schatten* and Christine in *Intermezzo*. During the two decades in which Lehmann sang the role of the Marschallin in Strauss's *Der Rosenkavalier*, she was generally regarded as the finest, indeed virtually the only, possible exponent of the role.

During the war years 1939–45, Lotte Lehmann confined her appearances to the United States, appearing not only in opera but also in song recitals, for she had become a noted singer of German *Lieder*, especially the songs of Schubert, Schumann and Wolf. As an opera singer she was noted not only for the beauty and warmth of her voice but also for the intelligence and authority of her acting. She retired from opera in 1945, but continued to give concerts until 1951, after which she became a distinguished teacher of singing in California. Singing was not her only talent: she was an accomplished painter, and also wrote a number of books about opera and singing, a novel, an autobiography, and a volume of remarkably accomplished poems somewhat in the manner of Rilke (*q.v.*).

Vladimir Ilyich Lenin (1870–1924)
Russian
Political leader

Well might Lenin's first name be Vladimir – 'conqueror of the world' in Russian – for he turned the Marxist theory of history into a revolutionary doctrine which has spread all over the globe.

Marxist-Leninism is the official creed of Soviet Russia, of China, and of all the communist states. It was Lenin who by relentless intellectual and organizational activity – he was a prolific writer and speaker – made the Bolshevik Party the first Marxist Party to seize power.

Born into a well-to-do family living in Simbirsk, on the Volga, Lenin was a clever and active schoolboy. When he was seventeen his elder brother was hanged for conspiring to murder the dictatorial Tsar. From then on, Vladimir Ilyich was always involved in revolutionary activity. It was a life of dodging the secret police, of imprisonment and exile, first in Siberia and then in western Europe. Lenin concluded that revolution could only be made by full-time agitators obeying orders strictly from the top. He fought this view through the main Marxist Party in Russia, and the majority were with him ('bolshevik' means 'majority'). From then on Lenin edited newspapers (he was a great journalist) and moulded the Bolsheviks into a party following his own ideas of 'democratic centralism', with Lenin, as chairman, at the centre.

Lenin welcomed the First World War. He saw it as the last self-destructive stage of capitalism and imperialism, which would end in the workers of the world uniting against the officers and financiers. It took three years before the incompetent Tsarist regime fell to a massive general strike in the revolution of February 1917. Meanwhile, Lenin had been in exile in Switzerland. He was allowed to cross Germany in a 'sealed' train by the German Government, who thought that Lenin in Russia would hasten the Revolution and consequently result in Russia's withdrawal from the war. Lenin, aided by Trotsky and other able Bolsheviks, overthrew the provisional Government in October 1917 with the slogan 'All power to the Soviets'. A Soviet was a council of workers and soldiers, and the Bolsheviks controlled most of them. Once in power, Lenin quickly made peace with the Germans and concentrated on fighting, with the new Red Army, all the many enemies of his new Government within the country. He was enormously energetic, and imposed the 'dictatorship of the proletariat', which meant that of the Bolshevik Party, on to Russia. Even the old Tsarist secret police system came back to weed out 'enemies'. In 1924 Lenin was cut down by a number of severe strokes, just as he had begun to feel a sense of guilt about the dictatorship he had imposed and the opportunities it would give to Stalin (q.v.) who had gained control of the party during Lenin's illness.

William Hesketh Lever (1851–1925)
British
Manufacturer

Son of a Bolton grocer, Lever started his working life in his father's shop, cutting up and packaging the large bars in which soap was then made. By the age of thirty he had his own shop in Wigan and, with his brother, had bought a small, none too successful factory in nearby Warrington. He clearly had business acumen from the start, selling the shop after five years for £60,000. But the idea that made his name, his vast fortune and Unilever the giant corporation it is today was to

Early products from William Lever's Port Sunlight factory

sell soap in small bars, under a brand name he invented – Sunlight. At a time when branded consumer products were few and far between and when there was no trademark protection, Lever pioneered mass consumer products, backed by heavy advertising.

By 1888, within less than a decade, the Warrington soap factory had grown into Port Sunlight on the bank of the Mersey. With its factories, workers' model homes (still there and lived in today), social clubs, sports' fields, art gallery, docks and rail links, Port Sunlight became *the* company town. 'It was splendid', wrote a contemporary, 'to see him at Port Sunlight sitting in a glass room with a thousand clerks on his right and a thousand on his left.' A Liberal Member of Parliament for a short spell, a Congregationalist and an ardent believer in thrift, Lever was a prototype of the modern, aggressive business tycoon. His soap factories went up around the world and takeovers of competitors (Pears, Prices and Crosfield among them) led to Lever Brothers being dubbed 'the soap trust'. If he could not get the service he wanted, Lever provided it himself, whether it was plantations in Africa and the Pacific or shipping companies. Today, Unilever is one of the biggest transport organizations in Europe because Lever decided he needed his own road haulage company for speedy, prompt delivery.

Made a baronet in 1911, then a peer and finally a viscount, Lever was also mayor of Bolton. People laughed at his costly failure to revive the fishing industry on the Hebridean island of Lewis, but out of it grew Unilever's present-day food business. Shortly before he died, Lever Brothers was producing 252,000 tons of soap a year, had 85,000 employees and was worth around £56 million.

Claude Lévi-Strauss (b. 1908) French
Anthropologist

Before the Second World War, Lévi-Strauss conducted fieldwork among the Indians of Brazil and became Professor of Sociology at São Paulo. He waited out the war years in America, and since then he has taught in Paris.

Lévi-Strauss's professional fame derives originally from a bulky volume published in 1949 called *The Elementary Structures of Kinship*. This was a study of the manner in which primitive peoples utilize the ties of kinship and marriage as a basis for social organization. An elementary structure is one which divides people into those a person can marry and those he or she cannot. In direct opposition to the accepted views of the time, he argued that the circulation or exchange of women between groups was the purpose of these rules of marriage, either within the tribe or outside it, rules that had the effect of bonding the exchanging groups into a cohesive social structure.

Claude Lévi-Strauss

BELOW *Champion of the workers, American trades unionist John L. Lewis*

A number of other works appeared, although these did not extend his fame beyond narrow professional frontiers. But Lévi-Strauss's three-volume work *Mythologiques* (1964–7) rapidly became the subject of intense discussion. It was regarded as the paradigm of a new movement of thought: structuralism. This involves not the structures of kinship, but the structures Lévi-Strauss claimed to detect in all human, mythological and analogical thinking; in particular in patterns of opposition. Black and white, raw and cooked, honey and ashes, these are the sorts of opposite poles around which much human thought – most conspicuously in primitive societies – is organized. It is not that people think their thoughts around these oppositions, but rather that these oppositions are basic to human thought.

John Llewellyn Lewis (1880–1969)
American
Trades unionist

Lewis was one of the most powerful and important figures in the American labour movement. He ran the United Mine Workers' Union as its president for forty years and took a leading role during the 1930s in expanding organized labour into the ranks of the unskilled and semi-skilled workers in manufacturing industries, who had been almost impossible to unionize before.

Often an autocratic and aggressive leader, Lewis gave voice to millions of American workers who had been regarded with contempt by the old craft unions in the American Federation of Labor. At the Federation's 1935 convention, Lewis championed the unskilled and semi-skilled, urging his fellow trade unionists to welcome them into their ranks. 'I have pleaded your cause not in the quavering tones of a mendicant asking for alms but in the thundering voice of the captain of a mighty host, demanding the rights to which free men are entitled', he declared. 'Heed this cry from Macedonia that comes from the hearts of men. Organize the unorganized.'

Lewis was born in Lucas, Iowa, on 12 February 1880. He entered the coal mines at the age of fifteen in the state of Illinois, where he became a formidable fighter for his fellow workers. In 1911 the young Lewis came to the notice of the president of the Federation of Labor, who gave him a job as a field agent for the organization. But nine years later Lewis was elected president of the United Mine Workers' Union, a position he held unchallenged until his retirement in 1960.

Lewis was brought to national prominence by his creation of the Congress of Industrial Organizations (CIO) in 1938 as a breakaway from the Federation, which had refused to open its ranks to the unskilled. As the CIO's first president, he launched an aggressive recruitment campaign in the car factories and steel mills of America to win union recognition from harsh, unsympathetic employers. The battles were often long and bloody, but by 1940 the CIO had over three million members. Lewis was an admirer of President Roosevelt's (*q.v.*) New Deal in the mid-1930s and he gave energetic support to Roosevelt in his 1936 election campaign, although in 1940 Lewis backed the Republican candidate. When Roosevelt was elected president for a third term in 1940, Lewis resigned as CIO president, later taking the United Mine Workers' Union out of the organization. Both during the war years and afterwards he clashed with successive presidents. The militancy of his union made organized labour unpopular with many Americans, though his philosophy of high wages and high productivity strongly appealed to the miners.

David Lloyd George (1863–1945) British
Political leader

Lloyd George took British politics by the scruff of its aristocratic neck and put it firmly into the democratic twentieth century. A Welshman (though born in Manchester), he at first fought Welsh causes – by profession he was a solicitor – and entered Parliament in 1890. In December 1905 he became a member of the Liberal Cabinet as President of the Board of Trade. He was to remain unbrokenly in office, successively as Chancellor of the Exchequer, Minister of Munitions and Prime Minister, until 1922. But he never achieved office after that, though he retained his parliamentary seat until 1945.

In a Cabinet of Liberal gentlemen he was outstanding as an orator, a radical who could draw the crowds with his fierce and bitter political rhetoric. He attacked the aristocracy – a duke, he said, cost as much as a battleship – and imposed taxes on the wealthy classes, who hated him in return. In an era of increased working-class political awareness, which included massive strikes in vital industries and the beginning of the rise of the Labour Party, Lloyd George was a vital asset to his party. His 'War Budget' of 1909 was designed to raise money for a fight against poverty, and his National (Unemployment) Insurance Act of 1911 marked an important stage in the creation of the Welfare State.

When the First World War came, he proved to be among the most energetic and able of ministers, and was chosen to succeed Asquith, the Liberal Party leader, as Prime Minister in the dark days of 1916, at the head of a Government which included many of his former Conservative enemies. The originality of his mind and his powers of leadership were beyond question, and

under him the war effort was properly organized, directed by a small War Cabinet. 'Ll.G.' enjoyed the personal power that his position and wartime conditions gave. Having succeeded in winning the war, he now declared that he wanted to 'win the peace'; a general election was held on 14 December 1918, and all those MPs (the majority were Tories) who had supported his wartime Government were given a 'coupon' in recognition of their loyalty, a seal of approval from Lloyd George which it was essential for an MP to have if he wished to be elected at this time of victory. Allegiance among Liberals was now divided between Lloyd George and Asquith, a split which finished them as a party of government.

Lloyd George was one of the 'big three' involved in drawing up the terms of the Peace Treaty of Versailles in 1919 and showed great statesmanlike qualities. His days as a dynamic national leader ended in 1922, when his Government was overthrown by the withdrawal of its Tory support, though he again became leader of the Liberal Party in 1926 and held that post until 1931.

Frank Lloyd Wright (1869–1959)
American
Architect

'I intend to be the greatest architect of all time', said Frank Lloyd Wright in 1932. Not everyone would agree that he realized his ambition but most would accept that he became the greatest *American* architect of all time.

He entered the profession in 1887 without any formal architectural training although he was a qualified engineer, and his path was smoothed by a mixture of nepotism, arrogance and good luck. Less than a year later he was working for the brilliant Louis Sullivan and making contacts with his first clients. Their commissions ended his association with Sullivan and began his series of remarkable private houses which led ultimately to his famous Prairie Houses of the early 1900s.

Most of the Prairie Houses were nowhere near the prairie – they were in the suburbs of Chicago. Yet they managed, with their emphasis on horizontal lines and their use of internal space, to echo the sweeping plains of the Midwest which Wright loved. The influence of Japanese architecture in these long, low houses was undeniable (even if Wright himself tried to deny it), but the end result was utterly American.

Those houses have had a lasting effect upon American architecture. Two non-residential buildings from the same period – the Larkin building, Buffalo (1904), and the Unity Church, Oak Park, Illinois (1906) – also influenced modern European architecture, via Le Corbusier (*q.v.*) and the German 'Bauhaus' group. Despite his contempt for the European architects, the

LEFT *Lloyd George, Liberal leader, a remarkable orator and a great statesman*

The Guggenheim Museum of Art, New York, designed by Frank Lloyd Wright

association with Europe helped Wright to achieve recognition in America in the 1930s, and commissions followed: for the superb Kaufmann House at Bear Run, Pennsylvania (1936), and the Johnson Wax building, Racine, Wisconsin (1938).

Among his later works, Taliesin West, Arizona (1938–59), was very much a development of the earlier Prairie Houses: long and low, romantically beautiful, it had a wood and canvas roof erected on top of massive blocks made out of rock and cement (Wright called them 'desert concrete'). His later commissions for private houses were also highly successful and widely publicized. But Wright was always something of an eccentric and his beliefs – notably his rejection of the city – put him increasingly out of touch with the twentieth century. He rejected square shapes as alien to human nature, and spent his last years working with circular patterns. His most famous building from this period was a beautifully sculptured spiral structure, the Guggenheim Museum of Art in New York (completed in 1959).

Henry Luce (1898–1967) American
Magazine publisher

Henry Robinson Luce was born in Tengchow, China, where his parents were American Presbyterian missionaries, an unlikely background for a man whose *Time* magazine was to pioneer the lively weekly news magazine format, and who had as much if not more influence on modern journalism than any of his contemporaries.

While at school in America, Luce struck up a close friendship with Briton Haden. It was an attraction of opposites – Haden was a lively young blade with a passion for Homer – but the friendship endured through Yale University, where they edited the college daily, and through their subsequent enlistment for military service. After a spell apart while Luce was at Oxford or working as a Chicago newspaperman, they came together on the *Baltimore News*. Luce's conviction that people must be kept informed, and their

RIGHT *Henry Luce, founder of* Time *and* Life

shared belief that this could best be done through a weekly magazine seemed foolish to some. But in 1923 they scraped together $86,000 from every well-heeled relative and acquaintance they knew, rented a $30-a-week office in an old brewery and printed *Time*'s first issue of 12,000 copies.

Haden died in 1929 but Luce continued to push ahead. In 1930, in the depths of the Depression, he launched the glossy business magazine *Fortune*, at the unprecedented price of $1, and in 1936 he followed it with *Life*, the widely copied founder of photo-journalism. After another great success, *Sports Illustrated*, Time Inc. expanded into book publishing, radio, television, paper manufacture and films, though Luce himself remained very much the journalist, devoting a good deal of his time to editing and developing the distinctive uniform 'Timestyle', with its inverted sentences and compound adjectives.

Luce was a strong patriot and dedicated anti-Communist: his determined support for Chiang Kai-shek influenced America's hostile attitude towards China's rulers for years, and he maintained a firm stance as a progressive. At sixty-eight, to parody *Time*, death came to influential, innovative magazine tycoon Henry Luce.

Dr Thomas Mann, 1947

Thomas Mann (1875–1955) American, ex-German
Novelist

Thomas Mann is considered to be the greatest German novelist of the twentieth century. He was born into a middle-class merchant family in Lübeck and drew upon family history for his first novel, *Buddenbrooks* (1901), a saga which traces the decline brought about by the artistic leanings of successive generations. Mann was always aware of the tension between conflicting sides of his own nature – the solid, bourgeois citizen and the creative artist whose principal concerns were with the spirit. In *Death in Venice* (1912), and indeed in the greater part of his vast output, Mann examines conflict of this kind not only on a personal level but also in society. Just as in private lives art brings with it a certain decadence, so in the public sphere philosophy brings the danger of revolution and violent change.

Mann developed many of these themes in essays and short stories, but did so most successfully in his novels, for he was not only a novelist concerned with ideas but also a creative artist of imaginative genius: an uncommon combination. *Der Zauberberg* (*The Magic Mountain*, 1924) uses its story of patients in a tuberculosis sanatorium in Switzerland to sym-

bolize the moral sickness that had infected Europe. It was this novel that earned Mann the Nobel Prize for Literature in 1929. His elder brother Heinrich, a distinguished novelist of liberal views, urged him to commit himself to political radicalism, but Thomas Mann was too complex a thinker or too pure an artist to do any such thing. However, he was forced into exile by the advent of Hitler in 1933, and by 1939 he had made his way to the United States, becoming an American citizen in 1944. He made unequivocal speeches and broadcasts denouncing Nazi Germany, which were subsequently collected and published, but he never attempted to use his art for propaganda purposes.

His novels are for the most part long and complex, but they are immensely rewarding to the reader. *Lotte in Weimar* (1939) beautifully conjures up the personality of Goethe, while for *Joseph und seine Brüder* (*Joseph and his Brethren*, 1933–43), a tetralogy of novels, Mann went back to the biblical story of Joseph, whose life he fictionally clarifies for modern readers. *Doctor Faustus* appeared in 1947, the same year as Mann returned to Switzerland, where he was welcomed by both West and East Germany; the novel is considered by many to be Mann's masterpiece.

Mao Tse-tung (1893–1976) Chinese
Political leader

Mao was almost eighteen when the imperial administration of China, which seemingly had existed for ever, was overthrown by revolution. But after the revolution China seemed worse off than it was before, and Mao determined that one day China would be strong. From his earliest days in politics he advocated physical culture and

在毛澤東的旗幟下勝利前進

Chairman Mao: a propaganda poster

native province of Hunan. The communists were overwhelmed, but Mao led the remnants of the force into the mountains, and then, after years of fighting, to Yenan in the north of China by the celebrated Long March. It was thousands of miles, and tens of thousands of people died. After it, however, Mao was in clear control of the Chinese Communist Party (1935).

Mao now had to watch for enemies from three directions. He fought both the Kuomintang and the Japanese. There was also Stalin (*q.v.*) in Moscow, who might try to order policy and doctrine within the Chinese Communist Party. Mao sought consolation in military and political writing and in poetry (his poems, and his calligraphy, are acknowledged to be of fine quality). His aim as a Chinese nationalist was to completely colour Marxism, as he said, with a Chinese tint, to make Marxism Chinese by frequent allusion to Chinese classical literature and history.

Power, he said, grew out of the barrel of a gun, and in 1946–9 he enhanced his high reputation as a military leader by driving the Kuomintang out of mainland China and over the sea to Taiwan. By doing so he was able to proclaim the People's Republic of China in 1949 with himself as Chairman.

Mao's complex personality and ruthlessness now had opportunity for full expression. He wished for a direct link between himself and the masses, thus fostering the cult of Mao-worship. He called on the peasants to kill the landlords and then the counter-revolutionaries. The toll must have been over two million dead. Then there was 'thought reform', self-criticism, the destruction of a person's previous identity so that he could be moulded to the correct image. Above it all loomed giant pictures of Mao, the cult of his personality, and the Little Red Book of his sayings which everyone possessed. Mao said that the human will could triumph over any material obstacle. He proclaimed the Great Leap Forward, by which people were to work in labour-intensive communes. He called for the Cultural Revolution (1966–9) to eliminate any remaining liberalism. This saw sensitive men and women sent to perform degrading menial tasks and officials bullied and beaten by young Red Guard thugs, while the worship of Mao reigned supreme.

Mao 'retired' from government in 1959 by resigning as Chairman of the Republic but remaining leader of the Communist Party. At his death in 1976 the more pragmatic communists breathed a sigh of relief and started to put China's Government on a more realistic basis. The cult of Mao is now a thing of the past and he is regarded as a man like any other, but in his time his influence and power over the people of China – around 900,000,000 of them – seemed infinite.

military training, all in the service of nationalism. He also became a communist.

Though at first the communists collaborated with the Kuomintang ('nationalists') – the revolutionary party – under the leadership of Chiang Kai-shek, the Kuomintang turned on the communists in 1927, shooting down workers in Shanghai and capturing and strangling many Communist Party officials.

Mao, born of a peasant family, had become a member of the Central Committee of the Communist Party in 1923. Now, in 1927, he was to be the leading figure of the Autumn Harvest Uprising against Chiang Kai-shek in his own

Guglielmo Marconi (1874–1937) Italian
Inventor

In 1894, the year that Heinrich Hertz died, a young Italian, Guglielmo Marconi, read about Hertz's research on electrical waves. Hertz had discovered that a spark generates electrical waves, and Marconi, who was then twenty years old, realized that the waves could be used for 'wireless' communication.

Marconi was born in Bologna and started his first experiments at the family country house just outside the town. After a year he was sending morse messages over a distance of a mile. The essential part of his receiver for these early radio transmissions was a 'coherer', a tube containing iron filings with electrical connections top and bottom. When wireless waves struck the tube, the filings arranged themselves so that a current would pass and operate a meter or buzzer. The tube had to be continuously tapped to break the current until the next burst of radio waves arrived.

In 1896 Marconi took out a patent in Britain and in the next year he showed that radio could be used from ship to shore. He gradually improved his aerials, transmitters and receivers, and on 12 December 1901, he achieved his great triumph, sending a message across the Atlantic from Cornwall to Newfoundland. Electromagnetic waves – radio waves are one kind of electromagnetic wave – travel in straight lines and therefore should be useless for long-distance communications on the spherical Earth. But Marconi suspected that the waves followed the curvature of the Earth, and his trans-Atlantic transmission confirmed this idea. The first person to succeed in sending a wireless signal across the Atlantic, Marconi received the Nobel Prize in 1909. In 1920 his company opened the first public broadcasting station in Britain.

Marx Brothers American
Chico (Leonard) (1887–1961)
Harpo (Adolph Arthur) (1888–1964)
Groucho (Julius Henry) (1890–1977)
Zeppo (Herbert) (b. 1901)
Film comedians

Minnie Marx of New York was determined that her sons made their way in vaudeville, and years before they first appeared in films they had gained hard experience from touring. They were playing by night on Broadway in *Animal Crackers* when they made their screen debut in *The Cocoanuts* (1929). Their anarchic brilliance and zany originality transcended the short-comings of this poorly constructed film, and they went on to make *Animal Crackers* (1930), followed by *Monkey Business* (1931), *Horse Feathers* (1932) and the best of their early films, *Duck Soup* (1933). After its relative failure they changed studios, from Paramount to MGM, and their later films, which include *A Night at the Opera* (1935) and *A Day at the Races* (1937), were enhanced by romantic sub-plots, musical interludes and elaborate setpieces, to the detriment of the flow of gags and comedy routines.

The Marx Brothers were an ill-assorted group. Chico looked and spoke like a demented Italian organ-grinder; Harpo said nothing, but mimed lascivious expressions with his rubber face, surmounted by a garish curly wig; Groucho, disguised behind glasses and a greasepaint

The Marx Brothers, 1935: (left to right) Chico, Groucho and Harpo

moustache, paced restlessly in his dark frock-coat; Zeppo looked relatively normal and was the romantic lead in the first films before he dropped out of the partnership. It was Groucho who was the kingpin and whose presence made the team work. He always played an obvious confidence trickster, possessed of enough hypnotic power to bamboozle the most pompous of dupes, the best remembered of whom was the incomparable actress Margaret Dumont, a matronly lady who invariably played some society hostess ear-marked for Groucho's absurd romantic onslaughts laced with insults. He was the most successful of the brothers, and when the films faded out after *Love Happy* (1950) he followed an entirely new career as a television quizmaster, handing out insults to the contestants in *You Bet Your Life*.

The Marx Brothers stood out in an increasingly conventional world, living proof that madmen could take over and turn life on its head. Significantly, their greatest success sprang from the years of the Depression – when it seemed that they filled the need for irreverence and laughter.

Thomas Masaryk (1850–1937)
Czechoslovakian, ex-Austro-Hungarian
Political leader

This son of a country coachman buried the mighty empire of the Hapsburg monarchs. At the end of the nineteenth century, the ramshackle Austro-Hungarian Empire ruled over a score of diverse racial groups in south-central Europe from the capital, Vienna, and also from Prague. It was by no means a totalitarian state, but many of the nationalities felt stifled and frustrated by its army and its bureaucracy, in which the top positions were usually occupied only by

Austrians or Hungarians, often aristocrats.

Masaryk became a university lecturer in philosophy at Vienna in 1879 and later Professor of Philosophy at Prague. He had advanced ideas; his first academic work was a study of suicide in modern mass society. He was a great seeker after truth and often exposed those who, even for causes with which he sympathized, put forward falsehoods. From 1889 he became interested in politics, taking his seat in the Austrian Parliament in 1891. At first he was among those who dreamed of transforming Austria-Hungary into a democratic federation of free peoples, clustered around the Danube waterway. This would have had huge economic advantages.

But the Hapsburgs were drawn into an entangling alliance with Germany, and together the two powers embarked upon an expansionist policy in the Balkans. Serbia, a small nation of Slavs, stood in the way. Masaryk, a devotee of Slav culture, defended the Serbs in the Austrian Parliament, as well as other Slav nations unfairly treated by the Hungarian or Austrian Governments. He bitterly opposed the German alliance. When the First World War broke out he made his way in 1915 to London. There he worked for the independence of his native Czech motherland, seeing that it would make a viable state if joined with neighbouring Slovakia.

This policy was accepted by the British and the French, as Masaryk was able to find powerful friends to urge the case. In 1917 he was in Russia, organizing former Czech prisoners of war into a Legion for the Allies. In the following year he saw President Wilson (*q.v.*) in the United States and got American backing (there were large numbers of Czechs in America, and Chicago was said to be the second Czech city in the world). On 3 June 1918, Czechoslovakia was recognized as an allied power. When the Hapsburg Empire collapsed that October, the new state was proclaimed and Masaryk became its first president. He resigned his presidency in 1935, dying two years later. He was certainly the father of his country, respected by all, and the Czechs and the Slovaks, when they disagreed, trusted him to settle their disputes. However, his policy of persuading the powers to allow a large number of small national states to succeed the Hapsburg Empire left a power vacuum in the area. Hitler (*q.v.*), whose rise filled Masaryk with foreboding, was quick to exploit this, and nearly all of those states now form part of the Soviet Empire.

Henri Matisse (1869–1954) French
Painter

Matisse, the oldest of the great masters of twentieth-century painting, began his career in 1891. His first important work was the 1904–5 *Luxe, Calme et Volupté*, a large figure composition in which he uses complementary colour contrasts, but it was *Woman with the Hat*, shown in 1905, which established him as one of the leaders of Paris avant-garde painters. His use of brilliant, pure, non-naturalistic colour earned Matisse and some other painters the name *Les Fauves*, the wild beasts. *Joy of Life* (1905–6), a large composition of nude figures in a landscape, was, in the liberties taken with scale, perspective, anatomy and colour, more daring than anything his contemporaries had painted.

During the following ten years Matisse produced a group of brilliant masterpieces. Among them are *La Danse* and *La Musique* (both 1910), works of great originality. Few paintings better illustrate the boldness of Matisse's art of this period than *Red Studio* (1911), in which still-life objects, paintings and sculpture are set against a monochrome red with a deceptive simplicity. His sculptures number some seventy works and include the four magnificent reliefs of the female back, made between 1909 and 1930.

In 1916 Matisse settled in the south of France, where he lived for the rest of his life. His art became more relaxed and less daring and original in composition. For the next twenty-five years he painted and drew nudes and odalisques, still-lifes, portraits and interiors, which in their sensuality and brilliant use of colour are among the most appealing paintings of the twentieth century. He had created, as he had written in 1908, 'an art of balance, of purity and serenity, devoid of any troubling subject-matter ... as relaxing as a comfortable armchair'.

From 1947 to 1951 he worked on the decoration for the Chapel of the Rosary at Vence in the Alpes Maritimes. The blue, yellow and green

stained-glass windows remind us that Matisse was the greatest colourist of his time. In the stark simplicity of the murals (black lines on white ceramic tiles) he produced what is probably the most successful religious work of the modern era. During the last twenty years of his life Matisse explored a new medium and technique: paper cut-outs, linking, as he said, 'drawing and colour in a single movement'. In this last burst of activity Matisse recaptured and extended the boldness of design and expressive purity of colour that characterize his greatest work.

Golda Meir (1898–1978) Israeli, ex-Russian
Political leader

The woman who became Prime Minister of Israel was born in Kiev, capital of the Ukraine, a city noted for its anti-Semitism. Her family was extremely poor, but managed to leave the country illegally, travelling first to Quebec and eventually settling in Milwaukee, Wisconsin. There she was to join the Labour Zionist Party, and at eighteen she went around the United States to spread the Zionist cause of a national homeland for the Jews in Palestine. In 1917 she married Morris Myerson, having persuaded him to accompany her to Palestine after the First World War (she subsequently hebraicized the name to Meir). In Palestine she was offered a job with the Women's Labour Council, and then

with the Jewish Agency to represent the Jewish point of view abroad.

Meir became a member of the executive committee of the Histadrut Party, and was later elected to the secretariat. When the leader of Histadrut was arrested in 1946 she took his place, representing all Jewish Palestine in political negotiation with the British. In November 1947, when the Jewish state was created, the Arabs began pouring over the border from Syria. Preparing for full-scale war, Meir went to the United States and raised over fifty million dollars for arms. Israel's independence was proclaimed in 1948 and the Arab-Israeli war started the day after. Meir was appointed the first Israeli Ambassador to Soviet Russia, and when Ben-Gurion (q.v.) announced his Cabinet appointments Meir became the first Minister of Labour and Development. It is a measure of her success that at the end of her seven years in the appointment not one immigrant family in Israel was still living in a tent.

In 1956 she became Foreign Minister, by which time she was called Golda Meir, in accordance with Ben-Gurion's wish that Israelis should adopt Hebrew names. She tried to retire twice in her life, at sixty-seven, when she was persuaded to return and form a powerful Coalition Government, and at seventy, when she became Prime Minister instead. Although the job filled her with 'terror', and in spite of the constant crises of war, she proved to be a strong and decisive leader. She could never divorce herself from 'the larger social life' and was loved everywhere for her genuine simplicity and faithful service. She maintained throughout her career that unless Israel was strong there would be no peace. She resigned in May 1974 after concluding the armistice agreements with Egypt and Syria, and died four years later.

Yehudi Menuhin (b. 1916) American
Violinist

Yehudi Menuhin was born in New York City of Russian-Jewish parents. Shortly afterwards the family moved to San Francisco where Menuhin had his first violin lessons at the age of four. A child prodigy, he began to give concerts when he was eight and then went to Europe for further study. His performance of the Beethoven Violin Concerto at the age of eleven astonished its hearers with the young musician's maturity and musicianship as well as the ease of his technique. For the next nine years Menuhin travelled the world, acclaimed everywhere not simply as a virtuoso but as a serious musician. The sixteen-year-old Menuhin's performance of Elgar's Violin Concerto was much admired by the composer, who conducted Menuhin's recording of it.

LEFT *Golda Meir, a decisive leader and a strong fighter for a new Israel*

When he was twenty Menuhin retired from concert-giving for a year to ease the transition from adolescence to maturity. When he reappeared, the earlier charm had given way to a deeper sensitivity which lifted his performances of Bach, Mozart and Beethoven on to an even higher level. He frequently appeared in recitals with his sister Hephzibah as pianist, but he achieved his greatest popularity with the great classical concertos, especially the Beethoven Violin Concerto to which he brought, and still brings, a confidence and nobility in the opening movement and a rare spiritual quality in the slow movement. He was also closely associated with the music of the contemporary Hungarian composer Bartók, who composed his Sonata for Solo Violin for Menuhin.

Menuhin is one of those few musicians whose fame has reached beyond the classical music public, wide though that is, to become a household name. This has been due not only to his willingness in his younger days to play and record popular music, but much more to his involvement in a number of humane and charitable causes. In recent years, while he has continued to delight and to move his audiences with Bach, Beethoven and Brahms, Menuhin has widened his interests to include Indian music and jazz.

Arthur Miller (b. 1915) American
Playwright

With O'Neill (*q.v.*) and Williams (*q.v.*), Miller is unquestionably one of the three greatest American dramatists of the twentieth century. The son of a small-time manufacturer, he was born in New York. He started writing plays at university in the mid-1930s and first made his name with a highly charged emotional denunciation of wartime profiteering, *All My Sons* (1947).

It was a year later, with *Death of a Salesman*, that Miller first achieved greatness: a play about a travelling salesman (for what product we are never told), living on a smile and a shoeshine. It was one of the very first plays to question the success-orientated aspects of the American dream. Willy Loman, its central figure, is a tragic hero brought down by his own desperate need to be loved both privately and publicly, and the play was seen as a massive indictment of the rules by which most of Miller's fellow-Americans then lived.

In 1953 came *The Crucible*, ostensibly about witch-hunting in seventeenth-century Massachusetts but in fact about the witch-hunting then being practised in Hollywood and elsewhere by the anti-communist tribunals, one of which was later to indict Miller himself. Two years later

came *A View From The Bridge* and then a screenplay for his then wife Marilyn Monroe (*The Misfits*). After her death, Monroe turned up as a principal character in Miller's semi-autobiographical *After The Fall*; and since then his plays have included *Incident at Vichy* (1964) and *The Price* (1968).

A sparse and disciplined writer who will often leave five-year gaps between plays, Miller is a moralist with a strong sense of family and the declining authority of fatherhood (a regular theme). His plays have almost all been rooted in some aspect of his own domestic experience, and they stand as powerful slices of post-war American life.

Joan Miró (b. 1893) Spanish
Painter

Twelve years younger than Picasso (*q.v.*), Miró was the second great Spanish painter of this century. He was born in Barcelona and in 1912, after a serious illness, was finally allowed by his reluctant father to study painting. He visited Paris for the first time in 1919. Many of Miró's first mature paintings, such as *The Farm* (1921–2), are evocative landscapes of the Catalonian countryside which he loved, and in their detailed and often dream-like realism anticipate his later work.

Between 1923 and 1926 Miró produced, in works such as *The Hunter* and *Carnival of Harlequin*, his first Surrealist paintings, surreal in that these densely populated canvases represent the world of the imagination and the subconscious, setting incongruous objects in an unexpected context, and treating them with a clarity and heightened finish that makes them

disconcertingly convincing. *The Birth of the World* (1925), with its free association of images and accidental effects, is one of the first major works of pictorial Surrealism. Miró introduced words and phrases into his work, some witty and whimsical, others foreboding. In *Person Throwing a Stone at a Bird* (1926) the distorted shape of the figure has much in common with the imagery of other Surrealists like Dali (*q.v.*) and Picasso; one of their group described Miró as 'the most Surrealist of us all'.

The gaiety, humour and childlike quality of much of Miró's work were from time to time replaced by images of terror, as in the grotesque and terrifying *Woman's Head* (1938) which, like Picasso's *Guernica*, reflects the artist's personal anguish at the atrocities of the Spanish Civil War.

During the Second World War Miró returned to Spain, where he produced his first important set of lithographs. A number of reliefs and constructions date from the 1930s, and since

Carnival of Harlequin *by Joan Miró, 1924–5*

1945 he has made ceramics, murals and large bronze sculptures. In his paintings of the last twenty years, Miró has sustained much of the imagery, power and inventiveness that characterized his work of the 1920s and 1930s. As always, he borrowed and assimilated the art of the past as well as current developments. He will be remembered as one of the greatest colourists of the age.

Piet Mondrian (1872–1944) Dutch
Painter

Mondrian was born in Amersfoort, Holland, the son of the headmaster of a Calvinist primary school. In 1892 he moved to Amsterdam and enrolled in the Academy of Fine Art. Throughout his life Mondrian was deeply interested in religion and philosophy and in 1909 joined the Theosophical Society.

Up to 1908 his work belongs to the landscape tradition of nineteenth-century Dutch painting, but a significant change occurred that year with his introduction of bright colours and Pointillist brushwork (in which the paint is applied in small dots). *Red Tree* (1908) is one of his finest works of this period. Gradually during the next three years, in his paintings and drawings of church façades, lonely landscapes, sand-dunes and seascapes, the forms are simplified and abstracted from nature.

Mondrian saw Cubist works by Braque (*q.v.*) and Picasso (*q.v.*) in Amsterdam in the late autumn of 1911 and began his first Cubist-inspired compositions before leaving for Paris in 1912. In Paris the Cubism of Braque and Picasso had a profound impact on Mondrian. Continuing to base his work on the world around him – flowers, trees and buildings – his subject-matter became less recognizable amid linear patterns.

Composition with Grey, Red, Yellow and Blue *by Piet Mondrian, 1920*

Gradually Mondrian came to eliminate any references to the real world and created pure abstractions. In this he was much influenced by the mysticism offered by theosophy. His horizontal and vertical lines to him represented the opposites of male and female, active and passive, and his use of only the three primary colours – yellow, blue and red – suggested to Mondrian that abstract art, far from being merely decorative, could have a spiritual significance and purity.

Like Kandinsky (*q.v.*), Mondrian wrote papers to explain and justify his neo-plasticism, the term he applied to his abstract art. In his work of the early 1920s rectangles in the three primary colours, linked by a grid of horizontal and vertical black lines, are suspended in a white ground. Form is conceived *as* space, not *in* space. Art, he felt, was not isolated from life but 'should lead to a new society . . . a society of harmonious proportions'.

In 1938 Mondrian moved to London and in 1940 he sailed for New York, where he spent the remainder of his life. In the great works of his last years, such as *Broadway Boogie-Woogie* (1942–3), he responded to the urban environment of New York: colour blocks replace the earlier system of black grid lines and create a pulsating rhythm with musical associations. In the purity and originality of his work Mondrian was among the most influential painters of the twentieth century.

Jean Monnet (1888–1979) French
Politician

Possibly the most important 'back-room boy' in twentieth-century politics, someone who was never in the political spotlight, Jean Monnet was born in Cognac, the brandy-distilling area of France, and his first job was as a salesman for the family brandy firm.

He was brought up partly in the United States, spoke perfect English, and though a good French patriot (how otherwise could he have been a confidant of General De Gaulle [*q.v.*]?) he was enthusiastically and warmly devoted to the ideal of international and, above all, in the closing stages of his life, European unity.

During the First World War he worked as an active supporter of a joint effort and pooling of economic resources on the part of the Allies in the fight against Germany. From 1916 this system was introduced, and the young Monnet became the coordinator and driving force behind it, playing a large part in the eventual victory. At the formation of the League of Nations in 1920 he became the Deputy Secretary-General, working for peace in Europe. He was convinced that any potential enemies must come together and recognize their common interests.

As France neared collapse under Germany's power early in the Second World War, it was Monnet who suggested to Churchill (*q.v.*) a Franco-British union, with joint citizenship, cabinet and parliament. But the French rejected it. Monnet fled to London and from there, with a British passport, went to Washington to work for Britain on economic matters. In 1945 he met De Gaulle in Washington and persuaded him of the importance of a National Plan for France. In 1946, the war now over, the first five-year Plan was approved, and Monnet was placed in charge of it. His own dynamism, charm and enthusiasm radiated confidence in the devoted group he assembled around him. Through the political chaos of those years the Plan was like a beacon, laying the foundations for the tremendous economic leap forward by which France was to be transformed, overtaking Britain as an economic power. But Monnet did not plan only for France with his small, clever band of men. He planned for Europe too, and in 1950 the first European economic institution, the Coal and Steel Community (the Schuman Plan) was masterminded by him. In 1956 he resigned from the French Plan to forward his campaign for a United States of Europe, and from that time on he lobbied ceaselessly for European union. The Treaty of Rome and the structure of the Common Market today owe much to him, but to this Father of Europe they were merely a rather unsatisfactory beginning to the great democratic union he was certain would one day come about.

Marilyn Monroe (1926–1962) American Actress

To some extent Marilyn Monroe embodied the American dream – the girl from Poverty Row who could scale the heights and become a legend. She was the only female film star to equal Garbo (*q.v.*) in her ability to fascinate the public. More has been written about her than any other postwar cinema figure, but she was – and remains – in many respects a mystery even to those who knew her well.

Norma Jean Baker was born in Los Angeles in 1926, to a woman who had serious mental problems. Her childhood was spent in orphanages and with foster parents, and at fifteen she married, to escape further life in an institution. Inevitably the marriage broke up. She worked in wartime aircraft factories and attracted photographic attention, and, when peace came, enrolled in a model agency.

She was later given a contract by Twentieth Century Fox, and a new name, but after minor appearances she was dropped. She also worked at Columbia, who failed to realize her talent. An agent, Johnny Hyde, persuaded John Huston to cast her in a small part in *The Asphalt Jungle*

(1950), which attracted critical acclaim, and Twentieth Century Fox re-signed her, featuring her in *All About Eve*. During her hungry period she had posed for a calendar in the nude; it now became a collectors' item, helping to bolster the Monroe legend. She was rushed into a number of unremarkable films, the first to capitalize on her personality being *Niagara* (1953). But it was a musical, *Gentleman Prefer Blondes*, in the same year which saw the crystallizing of her ability to project sexuality with a humorous innocence. She soon became the leading box-office star, and married America's leading baseball player, Joe DiMaggio, and then America's leading playwright, Arthur Miller (*q.v.*). She took acting seriously, and she was instinctively a magnetic star, possessed with the power to enchant the camera.

Jean Monnet

Marilyn Monroe

Monroe's finest film role was in Billy Wilder's *Some Like It Hot* (1959), although the universally remembered image of her comes from the same director's earlier film, *The Seven Year Itch* (1955), in which she stands, legs apart, over a subway grating, her skirts billowing around her. Her last film was *The Misfits* (1961), coincidentally also Clark Gable's last movie. Her instability and depression became acute, and her unreliability a byword in the industry. After attempts to start a new film with her failed, the studio ignominiously fired her. Two months later she was found dead from a drug overdose; whether it was accidental or deliberate has never been established.

Maria Montessori (1870–1952) Italian
Educationalist

The 'Montessori method' is based on the principle that young children want to learn and enjoy learning, but that strictly disciplined, formal methods of teaching hamper their development. The Montessori teacher is not an instructor, but a friendly, unobtrusive guide, who remains largely in the background while the children teach themselves. Child-sized equipment and furniture is provided and the children use arrangements of beads to start learning arithmetic, three-dimensional puzzles for geometry, sandpaper letters for reading and writing, and so on. Each child goes at his or her own pace and the emphasis is on individual initiative and creativity rather than group activities. The method is intended to encourage self-discipline and self-confidence.

Dr Maria Montessori, founder of the Association Montessori Nationale

Dr Montessori was strongly influenced by the German educationalist Friedrich Froebel (1782–1852), founder of the kindergarten system, in which children learned through play, and by other pioneers of 'child-centred education', which has been adopted in many nursery and elementary schools.

Born at Chiaravalle, near Ancona, Maria Montessori was the first woman doctor in Italy, taking her medical degree at Rome University. She then worked with mentally retarded children at the university's psychiatric clinic and it was with them that she first developed her method. In 1907 she opened her first Children's House (Casa dei Bambini), a school for children aged three to six, in a slum district of Rome. More schools were opened not only in Italy but in Switzerland, England and the United States, and Dr Montessori travelled extensively, lecturing and organizing teacher-training courses. In 1922 the Italian Government appointed her inspector of schools, but she left Fascist Italy in 1934. She subsequently lived in Spain, India and Sri Lanka, and finally in Holland. Her books include *The Montessori Method* (1912), *The Secret of Childhood* (1936), *To Educate the Human Potential* (1948) and *The Absorbent Mind* (1949).

Henry Moore (b. 1898) British
Sculptor

Born in Castleford, Yorkshire, the seventh child of a miner, Moore by the age of ten or eleven had decided that he wanted to become a sculptor. He studied at the Leeds School of Art and the Royal College of Art, London. During the 1920s his carvings were influenced by non-European sources, in particular Pre-Colombian stone carving, as can be seen in the two massive Hornton stone reclining figures of 1929 and 1930 (in Leeds and Ottawa).

During the 1920s and 1930s Moore devoted much of his time to life drawing, and also to making studies for sculpture on which almost all his three-dimensional work was based from 1921 to the early 1950s. Moore's first two- and three-piece compositions date from 1934 and have remained an important theme in his sculpture. His work of the late 1930s includes *Recumbent Figure* (1938), which uses the female figure as a metaphor for landscape, and a number of sculptures with strings. He and his wife moved to Much Hadham, Hertfordshire, in 1940 and have lived there ever since. Between 1940 and 1942 Moore was an official war artist, devoting all his time to drawing. Scenes of coal-miners and of Londoners sheltering in underground stations during the Blitz are among his most admired drawings. In 1943–4 he carved the well-known *Madonna and Child* for St Matthew's Church, Northampton. The first retrospective exhibition of Moore's work was held at the Museum of Modern Art, New York, in 1946; two years later he won the prize for sculpture at the Venice Biennale, which established his international reputation.

Although Moore's interest in carving has continued to the present day, many of his best-known post-war sculptures – *Family Group* (1948–9), *King and Queen* (1952–3), *Locking Piece* (1963–4) – were made in plaster and cast in bronze. From 1959 to 1962 he again made the two- and three-piece sculptures, using landscape forms – rocks, cliffs and caves – to suggest the female figure. As his sculpture became more fully three-dimensional, it came to have a total completeness from every point of view.

Moore has been largely responsible for the revival of sculpture in England and, with fellow sculptor Barbara Hepworth, for the emergence of British sculpture from provincialism into the international stream of modern art. With many of his large bronzes in urban and rural settings around the world, he has probably had more public exposure than any other sculptor in history, and undoubtedly has a place among the greatest sculptors in western art.

Akio Morita (b. 1921) Japanese
Radio and television manufacturer

Born in Nagoya, Morita was destined for his father's generations-old sake-brewing and soya sauce company, but the primitive magnetic recorder he built at school was a pointer to his real interests, which have turned his company, Sony, into a globally recognized name for high-quality consumer electronics.

After, surprisingly, failing the employee entrance examination for the Tokyo-Shibaura Electric Company, Morita worked for a film production and processing company before entering university and graduating in physics. During his one year in the wartime Japanese navy, Morita met his first partner, Masaru Ibuka, but their work developing a heat-seeking bomb was overtaken by the end of the war. In war-torn Tokyo, Ibuka started repairing damaged radio sets and Morita joined him full-time in their newly founded Tokyo Telecommunications Engineering Company. Together they launched Japan's first tape recorders in 1949. It was a tremendous struggle, developing the product, manufacturing tapes with next to no

Henry Moore in his studio at Much Hadham, Hertfordshire

Akio Morita with Sony's latest innovation, the revolutionary combination video-camera and video-cassette recorder

Mother Teresa

Sony produced the first Japanese transistor radio in 1955. It was this development of the use of transistors in domestic electronic machines that led to Morita being called 'Mr Transistor'. The radios were immensely successful and were followed by the world's first transistorized televisions, launched in Japan in 1960 and in America the following year.

The first Japanese businessman to buy an executive jet, Morita, in his endeavours to create a truly international company established a world-wide marketing organization, becoming a pacesetter among Japanese firms in opening up overseas manufacture on a large scale. More than any single company Sony has smashed the image of Japanese goods as cheap, trashy imitations, and the company thrives on its technical innovation and excellence. After its Trinitron colour televisions established new yardsticks for picture quality, Sony then pushed ahead selling video-cassette technology in consumer markets.

Mother Teresa (b. 1910) Indian, ex-Albanian
Nun

Mother Teresa was born Agnes Gonxha Bojaxhiu, the daughter of a grocer, at Skopje in Serbia (now in Yugoslavia). Determined to be a missionary, she went to Ireland for training with the Congregation of the Loreto Nuns in Dublin. There she learned English, and in 1929 she arrived in India as a teacher. In 1948 she founded the Order of the Missionaries of Charity, dedicated to the relief of poverty and suffering. The Order now has numerous centres in India as well as in other countries, including Great Britain, Australia, Venezuela, Tanzania, Jordan, Yemen and Sri Lanka. The centres serve the destitute, the dying, the blind, the crippled and the old, orphans and abandoned children, and the Order runs the leper colony of Shanti Nagar (Town of Peace), near Asansol, north-west of Calcutta.

It was in Calcutta itself that Mother Teresa began her relief work and she is famous for her years among the poor there, in some of the world's most atrocious slums. She became an Indian citizen, and she and her nuns wear the Indian sari instead of the conventional nun's habit. The Indian Government honoured her in 1963 with the Padmashri Award for her services to the Indian people. In 1971 she was the first winner of the Peace Prize instituted in memory of Pope John XXIII (*q.v.*), and she also received the John F. Kennedy (*q.v.*) International Award. In 1979 she won the Nobel Prize for Peace, and announced that she would devote the prize money, of close to £100,000, to her charitable work.

raw materials, and finally convincing the Japanese, who had never even seen tape recorders, that they needed them. But the recorders soon grew into a profitable business.

Morita's big break came in 1953, when he signed an agreement to use the transistor technology Western Electric had invented in America. Not even the brightest American companies had managed to apply transistors to radios, but battling against many problems,

Benito Mussolini (1883–1945) Italian
Dictator

The first of the Fascist dictators, Mussolini was to provide a model for other European dictators. But Italian Fascism had something essentially Latin about it, which is perhaps why a number of South American regimes today are still faintly reminiscent of Mussolini's Italy.

Mussolini was born of lower middle-class parentage in northern Italy. He was a voracious reader as a youth, and became first a schoolmaster, then a journalist and a socialist agitator, advocating revolution. He was of unsystematic temperament and amorous by nature. He was also a strong nationalist, and was thrown out of the Socialist Party he belonged to because of his wish that Italy should fight against Germany and Austria when the First World War broke out. (Austria occupied territory that Italy claimed as her own.) When Italy entered the war in 1915, Mussolini fought with some distinction.

For some years Italy, which had only comparatively recently been made a unified nation, had suffered from weak and indifferent government. There were many patriotic Italians who detested the corrupt party politicians. Italy, they remembered, had once been the heartland of the Roman Empire. In 1919 Mussolini called on Italians to show unity and not division. His symbol was the Roman fasces, a bundle of rods and an axe bound together, showing power, strength and authority. He advocated a mixture of nationalism and socialism, and also the corporate state, in which institutions were devised so that workers and employers could achieve the common good. In 1921 he was elected to Parliament. Astonishingly, he was called to power by the king in 1922, who appointed him Prime Minister, after the notorious march on Rome of Mussolini's Blackshirts, who congregated in the city to show the strength of the party.

The 'Duce' ('leader') then brutally used his Blackshirts to intimidate his opponents. They generally stopped short of murder, but were generous with beatings-up and forced people to swallow enormous doses of castor oil.

Only one party, the Fascist Party, was now allowed; criticism was not permitted, and military training and uniforms were forced on the youth of Italy. Grandiose monuments and public buildings arose and the sloppiness of old official Italy was replaced by a certain efficiency – the trains really did run on time.

Alas, the 'Duce' craved military glory. He invaded Abyssinia, and exposed the weakness of the League of Nations which remained helpless even after denouncing Italy's aggression. At first Mussolini was neutral when the Second World War broke out in 1939 (he did not really care for Hitler), but as France collapsed he hastened to

Benito Mussolini

share in the spoils, and Italy entered the war in 1940. Her armed forces proved only too easy to defeat, even by little Greece, and her fine navy was soundly thrashed by Britain's Mediterranean fleet.

Mussolini was dismissed by the Fascist Grand Council and the king in 1943. Rescued by Hitler, he was installed in a German-controlled puppet state in northern Italy, but in Como in 1945, he was eventually shot, together with his faithful mistress, and their bodies were exposed to public derision in Como and Milan.

N

Vladimir Nabokov (1899–1977)
American, ex-Russian
Novelist

Nabokov is best known for his English-language novels, particularly *Lolita* (US 1955, UK 1959), although his first works were written in his native Russian. Born into an aristocratic Russian family in St Petersburg (now Leningrad) in 1899, Nabokov left Russia after the communist Revolution of 1917 and studied at Cambridge, where he began to write poetry. He later lived in Berlin, Paris and London, before going to the United States in 1940 and becoming an American citizen in 1945. His first novels (in Russian) were published in the 1920s and 1930s, but it is as an English-language writer in America that he first made his reputation. *The Real Life of Sebastian Knight* (1941), and *Bend Sinister* (1947) were merely steps towards his most successful novel, *Lolita*.

Lolita brought Nabokov both literary fame and popular notoriety, for his subject was the

Some of the published works of Vladimir Nabokov

passion of a middle-aged professor for a pre-cociously nubile twelve-year-old. The novel also reached the screen, though in a somewhat expurgated Hollywood version. *Lolita* is not a study in sexuality but a satire on modern society's hypocritical attitude to sex and romantic love.

Although Nabokov's reputation as a literary stylist continued to grow, none of his later novels achieved the popular success of *Lolita*. His earlier European writings suffer from a certain coldness of manner, but from *Lolita* onwards he found a perfect unity of style and subject, and was at his best in describing the contemporary American scene with an ironic but not unsympathetic European eye. *Pale Fire* (1962) was acclaimed as an original and highly imaginative work; *The Gift* (1963) was an English translation of a novel Nabokov had written in Russian in the thirties. Two of his finest later works appeared in 1973: *Transparent Things* and a collection of short stories, *A Russian Beauty*.

In his last years, Nabokov and his wife returned to Europe to live in a hotel in Montreux, Switzerland, where Nabokov, in addition to writing, found time to pursue his hobby; he was an expert on rare butterflies.

Jawaharlal Nehru (1889–1964) Indian Political leader

Born into a wealthy high-caste family of Kashmiri origin, the young Nehru was brought up in Allahabad like a small English boy of the time, wearing sailor suits, Eton collars and even the kilt. His father was a rich and highly westernized lawyer, with a huge house, and Nehru's early education left him thinking in English for the rest of his life. He came to England and was educated at Harrow and Trinity College, Cambridge, and

RIGHT *Jawaharlal Nehru*

then qualified as a barrister at the Inner Temple. He was, he said, 'a queer mixture of East and West, out of place everywhere, at home nowhere'.

Back in India by 1912, Nehru drifted towards nationalism, and met Gandhi (*q.v.*), whose views on non-violent non-cooperation he shared. In 1919 came the Amritsar massacre, when British troops fired into a crowd, killing 379 and wounding 1,200. Nehru's father, formerly so pro-British, now turned passionately against them, later becoming President of the All-India Congress. In 1921 both Nehrus, now wearing traditional Indian clothes, were imprisoned for political agitation, together with 30,000 others. Nehru had married in 1916 but he was to neglect his wife for politics; they had one child, Indira, the future Prime Minister, born in 1917.

Nehru agitated from 1929 for complete Indian independence from British rule. All through the 1920s and 1930 he was constantly in and out of prison, and was a leading figure in the Congress's activity both in India and abroad. In 1942 he called on the British to 'quit India'. He was jailed until 1945. Following the Labour Party's victory in Britain after the war, Nehru was released, as Labour's policy included giving dominion status to India. The situation in India now became highly unstable: there was a naval mutiny and rioting, arson and looting spread. This communal violence continued until the general election of 1947 when the Moslems, led by Jinnah, insisted on partitition. Amid great bloodshed, partition took place, presided over by Lord Mountbatten who led the interim Government overseeing the transition to independence. Nehru was appointed vice-president, and on independence he became India's first Prime Minister. He wished to see his vast, poor and undeveloped country become a welfare state and

Pier Luigi Nervi's Exhibition Hall at Turin, 1948–9

was the first Hindu leader to approve of birth control. He became the apostle of non-alignment and peaceful co-existence. He was, however, more eager to condemn the West than the East (he kept silent over the Russian invasion of Hungary); and his sudden occupation of Goa by armed force, and his preparations for India's own atomic bomb, hardly seemed to conform with his doctrines of neutrality. He was quite taken aback when China, whose friendship he had cultivated, showed its teeth in a sharp border clash. Inconsistent, intolerant of criticism – he surrounded himself with 'yes-men' – Nehru at least was content with the freedom of expression he found in India, the world's largest free democracy to the birth of which he had contributed so much.

Pier Luigi Nervi (1891–1979) Italian
Architect

Twentieth-century architecture has been dominated by the International Style, a style based upon the belief that 'form follows function' and on the rejection of ornamentation. So perhaps it shouldn't be surprising that Pier Luigi Nervi, an engineer, is recognized by architects as one of the foremost builders of his age. He described himself as a 'creative engineer', a believer in 'the inherent aesthetic force of a good structural solution'. He was, simply, the world's greatest designer of concrete structures.

By the time Nervi graduated from civil engineering school in Bologna in 1913, the earliest signs of the International Style had

already appeared and engineers had begun to explore the possibilities of reinforced concrete. Initially, the advantages of concrete, its cheapness and its ability to span large areas without the need for supporting columns, were exploited most fully in 'pure' civil engineering projects: bridges, exhibition halls, railway stations. Nervi's early structures included a sports' stadium in Florence (1930–2), which has beautiful, soaring and apparently unsupported spiral staircases, and a series of aircraft hangars (1935–41).

After the Second World War reinforced concrete began to be far more widely used, and Nervi, particularly after his Turin Exhibition Halls (beginning 1948) were built, became established as its greatest exponent. He continued to work in Italy on civil engineering projects: Naples Central Station (1954), the Olympic stadia in Rome (1960), a paper factory at Mantua (1960–2). He also received commissions from all over the world for all forms of public buildings: the UNESCO building in Paris (1953–6), the Pirelli building in Milan (1955–9), and the Victoria Place Tower in Montreal (1962–5).

On these buildings, and for the superb exhibition hall at La Défense in Paris (1958), Nervi worked merely as an engineer for the architects. As a result, the structural purity and the individuality of his own 'architecture' were often submerged – to the dismay of Nervi's followers, who now look back to the Florence stadium and the aircraft hangars at Orvieto (1935) for his greatest work.

in *Scheherazade*, the Spirit in *Le Spectre de la Rose* and that of the poor frustrated puppet Petrouchka in the ballet of that name.

As early as 1910 Nijinsky's thoughts were preoccupied with devising a new form of choreography, and it was a sign of his true genius that when he created his first ballet, *L'Après Midi d'un Faune*, it was in a two-dimensional style, the dancers looking as though a Greek frieze had been set in motion, a style of dancing which was far removed from his own. Premiered in 1912, this ballet was soon followed by *Jeux* in May 1913 which again broke new ground. Set as a tennis match at a weekend houseparty, it was the first modern classical ballet to be danced in everyday clothes. In that same month he also unveiled perhaps his greatest monument, *Le Sacre du Printemps*, though but a few fragments recreated by some of the original dancers remain. To Stravinsky's (*q.v.*) pulsating score, Nijinsky recreated the world of primitive, peasant Russia, in which the dancers had to cope with complex rhythms and intense, pounding steps. It caused a sensation, indeed a riot, when first seen in Paris in 1913, and is now regarded as the real breakthrough to modern ballet. Soon afterwards Nijinsky broke with Diaghilev, and though outside pressures occasionally brought them together they were never to establish good relations again. Within five years of the great creative days of *Sacre*, Nijinsky's mental instability had become incurable. He was to live for another thirty years, dying in London in 1950.

Kwame Nkrumah (1909–72) Ghanaian
Political leader

The first black African colony to become an independent nation was Ghana, under Kwame Nkrumah's leadership. As a British colony the country had been called the Gold Coast, but in March 1957, on independence, Nkrumah renamed it. Significantly, Ghana had been the name of a great empire. It was symbolic of Nkrumah's dream of a new, united Africa under his own leadership. He had a vision of Pan-Africanism, a United States of Africa, which he was pretentiously to develop using the services of a number of black intellectuals from Africa, North America and the Caribbean. Nkrumah also set up an Ideological Institute in Ghana to propagate his ideas.

These ideas had one simple foundation: Africa for the Africans. Nkrumah had left his country in the 1930s, and studied in London and in the United States (he always called himself Dr Nkrumah, although he never earned his doctorate – it was merely an honorary title). He spent much of his time on 'progressive' and anti-colonialist activities, and he became aware of the plight of those blacks who lived outside Africa

Vaslav Nijinsky dancing in Paris with Diaghilev's Ballets Russes

Vaslav Nijinsky (1888–1950) Russian
Ballet dancer and choreographer

Nijinsky was marked out as a unique talent almost from the day he entered the Imperial Ballet School in St Petersburg. His looks and his prodigious technique ensured that by the time of his early graduation he was chosen to partner the foremost ballerinas. Diaghilev (*q.v.*) came into Nijinsky's life in 1908 and immediately recognized not only the outstanding performer that he was, but also his possibilities as a creator of dance. After the impact he made in Diaghilev's first Paris season in 1909 and his subsequent dismissal by the Imperial Ballet (an affair in which Diaghilev was not totally without interest), Nijinsky became the permanent star of Diaghilev's company, the Ballets Russes, dancing such spectacular roles as the Golden Slave

and were oppressed in their own countries, particularly the United States. To these, the descendants for the most part of slaves, the Africa he saw was to be a spiritual home.

His homeland, the Gold Coast, which had had contact with Europe since the Middle Ages, was among the most developed of African colonies. There was a strong, educated middle class (to which Nkrumah did not belong, and which was snobbishly to chide him for this); there were good schools and reasonable communications and economic development. Indeed, by the standards of its neighbours, the Gold Coast was rich. It had gold, timber and, above all, for over fifty years it had grown cocoa, a peasant crop. On independence, the colonial Government handed over to Nkrumah a handsome surplus in the treasury. Independence had taken Nkrumah ten years, building up a mass organization, the Convention People's Party, a short term of imprisonment for political agitation – from which he was released in 1951 to head the Government – and then a few years of guardianship under a British governor before Britain granted complete independence.

Nkrumah's example, and his direct efforts, led to the independence movement speeding up throughout Africa. His achievement also gave a great psychological boost to the civil rights movement in the United States. But his actual administration was wasteful, unrealistic and corrupt. He persecuted and jailed his political opponents and put down all attempts at free speech. He demanded a fawning worship from a very democratically minded people. They responded with a military coup in February 1966, overthrowing Nkrumah's regime when he was abroad on a state visit. He died in exile in 1972, but his body was brought back later that year and buried with some honour in Ghana.

Rudolf Nureyev (b. 1938) French, ex-Russian
Ballet dancer

Nureyev has made two important contributions to the world of ballet over and above his brilliance as a dancer: he was a prime force both in revitalizing male dancing in the West after his defection from Russia in 1961 and in introducing important elements of Russian ballets into the western repertoire. While still a young dancer at the Kirov Theatre in Leningrad, he already had confidence enough to amend elements of choreography in major classical ballets, and so polished were they that his changes were generally accepted.

For Nureyev, born in Ufa, capital of the remote province of Bashkir, in the difficult war

Kwame Nkrumah

Rudolf Nureyev in the Royal Ballet's production of Apollo, *1971*

undoubtedly merited. An early invitation to dance with Margot Fonteyn (*q.v.*) not only gave her an incentive at precisely the time that she needed it, but also started a special partnership that caught the imagination of a public much wider than the regular ballet audience. From recreating Russian classics, Nureyev soon moved to doing his own highly personal versions of them, bringing the male dancer to the centre of the stage. A difficult and demanding person to work with, he is constantly looking for new ways in which to expand the horizons of classical productions, or of works by the great modern dance choreographers such as Martha Graham (*q.v.*). Whatever the style of the work, Nureyev dances with a seemingly inexhaustible dynamism and theatrical magic, bringing an ever wider audience to the enjoyment of ballet.

Paavo Nurmi (1897–1973) Finnish Athlete

No Olympic stadium has experienced a greater roar of acclaim than that accorded in Helsinki in 1952 as a spare, balding fifty-five year old – the greatest legend from the legendary age of Finnish distance running – circled the track, torch held high, to light the Olympic flame.

It was the first the world had seen of Paavo Nurmi for twenty years, when amid bitterness and controversy he had been disqualified from Olympic competition (for contravening the rules on amateurism) on the eve of the Los Angeles Games, hot favourite to walk away with the

years, to enter the Kirov had been a struggle. Surprisingly, he started as a folk dancer (and to help pay for his studies gave folk dance lessons at a very early age at the local workers' collective) and it was with a folk troupe that he first went to Moscow and determined to join the Bolshoi School there. Offered a place, he ultimately refused it on practical grounds (he would have to have found his own accommodation there) and went to Leningrad. He was eventually offered a place, but at a grade that would have meant him having to do military service, effectively ruining the chances of a good career. His insistence on joining a higher grade was accepted, but he was also marked out as a troublemaker. Such single-mindedness and obsession with ballet has lasted throughout his career.

Although his career with the Kirov was highly successful and allowed him to dance most of the major classical roles, he realized the limitations of the company while on tour in Paris. Suddenly ordered back to Moscow, instead he made a 'leap to freedom' at Paris airport which ensured him publicity on a major scale, publicity which first his dancing and later his choreographic genius

marathon and bring his tally of Olympic gold medals to an astonishing ten.

As it is, his collection of nine Olympic golds, not to mention an extra three silver and thirty-one world records set between 1920 and 1932, is a unique achievement among athletes. Nurmi remains the greatest in an awesome tradition of long distance running in Finland that began with Kohlemainen (Nurmi's idol as a schoolboy) in 1912, and built up to world dominance in the 1920s and 1930s with Nurmi himself and many others, a tradition that was to be revived with such acclaim in the 1970s by the remarkable Lasse Viren.

Nurmi was a runner a full generation ahead of his time. Uniquely for the 1920s, he followed a training regime very close to that of champions fifty years later: a punishing schedule of training runs, strict diet, harsh self-discipline and a fierce ambition, quite apart from a keen and deep analysis of his own running – invariably he ran, even in championships, with a stop-watch in his hand.

His greatest day came in Paris in the 1924 Olympic Games when the organizers – some said in an attempt to curb Nurmi's invincibility – had scheduled the finals of the 1,500 metres and the 5,000 metres just an hour and a quarter apart. Quite undaunted, Nurmi took on both. He won the 1,500 metres by a lordly ten metres and the 5,000 metres in comfort from his fellow-countryman and great rival, Ville Ritola. It was hardly unexpected: with typical care Nurmi had arranged a trial for himself in Finland a week or so before the Games, in which he ran the two distances a mere sixty minutes apart – and he had broken the world record in both.

Laurence Olivier (b. 1907) British
Actor

Unrivalled among contemporaries as Britain's leading stage actor, Olivier was born in Dorking, the son of a clergyman. His career started in relatively undistinguished short-lived West End stage runs and minor British films, though he had served a classical Shakespearean apprenticeship at the Birmingham Repertory Theatre (1926–8).

One of his first real successes was as the romantic Captain Stanhope in *Journey's End*, a role he abandoned in favour of a catastrophic *Beau Geste*. From this he was rescued by Noël Coward (*q.v.*), and in 1930 they played opposite each other in Coward's *Private Lives*. After triumphant West End and Broadway seasons with Coward, Olivier made his first foray into Hollywood movies, only to be abruptly dismissed from *Queen Christina* by his co-star, Greta Garbo.

Lord Olivier

Back in the London theatre he scored successes in *The Rats of Norway* and *Theatre Royal*, but it wasn't until the famous 1935 *Romeo and Juliet*, in which he and his fellow actor John Gielgud (*q.v.*) alternated Romeo and Mercutio, that he finally came into his own as a leading classical actor. In 1937, at the Old Vic, he played the roles of Hamlet, Henry v and Macbeth, and the following year Iago and Coriolanus.

His film career also began to take off in the late 1930s, thanks largely to *Fire Over England* (in which he played for the first time opposite Vivien Leigh, whom he was later to marry) and then *Wuthering Heights* (1939) in which his performance as Heathcliff would have assured him a prosperous Hollywood screen career had not the outbreak of war brought him back to England and the Royal Navy's Fleet Air Arm.

By 1944 he was back at the Old Vic for *Richard III*, *Peer Gynt* and *Uncle Vanya*, and this was also the year of his first Shakespearean film, *Henry V*. The post-war years brought him to the screen in his own productions of *Hamlet* and *Richard III* (as well as thirty-four other films) but the stage had always been his first home and would remain so until ill health forced a sort of retirement in the 1970s. By then he had spent the best part of a decade as the first director of Britain's National Theatre, and as an actor he had set up landmarks as Othello, as the failed music-hall comic Archie Rice in John Osborne's (*q.v.*) *The Entertainer*, and as Coriolanus, Macbeth and Titus Andronicus. In 1960 Olivier and Vivien Leigh were divorced and in 1961 he married the stage actress Joan Plowright.

Though his departure from the National Theatre in 1973 was also effectively to mean his departure as an actor from any kind of theatre, he continued to direct both in London and on Broadway. Olivier has also starred in a series of classic dramas on television and involved himself in a number of film roles, not all of which have done him credit.

It would sometimes be argued that vocally if not physically John Gielgud had the Shakespearean edge, but undoubtedly Laurence Olivier has now joined the great actors Garrick, Kean and Irving among the theatrical giants. Knighted in 1947, in 1970 Olivier was awarded the first peerage ever given to an actor.

Eugene O'Neill (1888–1953) American
Playwright

O'Neill is arguably the greatest playwright of the century. The son of an actor (James O'Neill, famous for his role in *The Count of Monte Cristo*), O'Neill spent much of his childhood on tour with his father, until he went to Princeton University from which he was dismissed after a year for 'hell-raising'.

After a short-lived marriage he went to sea in the merchant navy, prospected for gold in Honduras, stage-managed for his father, and finally collapsed into a sanatorium suffering from tuberculosis.

Emerging in 1912, and by now determined to be a playwright, O'Neill began to write one-act plays based on his seafaring days; these were eventually grouped together as *The Long Voyage Home*. In 1920 he won a Pulitzer Prize for a realistic rural drama (*Beyond the Horizon*) and for the next fourteen years he wrote a succession of masterly scripts, among them *The Emperor Jones* (1920), about a self-appointed negro leader, *Anna Christie* (1921), about the redemption by love of a prostitute, *All God's Chillun Got Wings* and *Desire Under The Elms* (both 1924 and both marital dramas), *The Great God Brown* (1926), and then *Strange Interlude* (1928), a sprawling nine-act emotional drama.

After that came *Mourning Becomes Electra*, which is an updating of a Greek tragedy and takes place in New England after the Civil War, and a comedy, *Ah, Wilderness* (1933), but then, despite a Nobel Prize for Literature (the first American playwright to receive it), he disappeared from the theatre until 1946 when he allowed a production of his five-hour bar-room epic *The Iceman Cometh* to be produced. This, and the 1954 *Moon For The Misbegotten*, were at least in part based on his own family history of alcoholism and despair. In the same autobiographical series came *A Touch of the Poet* and *More Stately Mansions*, but it wasn't until 1956, three years after his death, that the world was allowed to see O'Neill's greatest autobiographical masterpiece, the play about himself, his brother and his parents that he called *Long Day's Journey Into Night*. It was the most powerful obituary for the most powerful of all American dramatists.

Harry Oppenheimer (b. 1908) South African
Financier

Oppenheimer, chairman of the giant Anglo American Corporation and of De Beers, has been involved in mining and in the social and political challenges facing business world-wide – but particularly in southern Africa – since the 1930s, first as lieutenant to his pioneering father, the late Sir Ernest Oppenheimer, and, since the Second World War, mainly on his own.

His elevation to the managing directorship of Anglo American in 1945 coincided with sensational expansion: the opening of seven mines in the Orange Free States goldfields of South Africa (with the help of Western European capital), and expansion of copper mines in Northern Rhodesia (now Zambia). He insisted that Welkom, the new town for the Orange Free States mines, should have the best possible town planning, working conditions, amenities and social services, and should serve as a model for this kind of development. He also attempted to break the traditional migratory system by housing all black married workers and their families on the mines, though in this he was thwarted by the Nationalist Government.

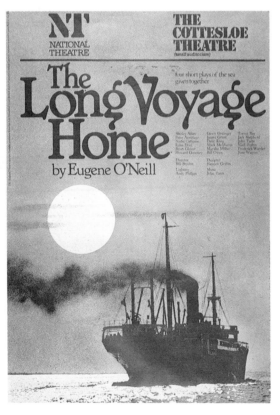

ABOVE *Eugene O'Neill;* RIGHT *poster for the 1979–80 National Theatre production of O'Neill's* The Long Voyage Home, *directed by Bill Bryden*

His concern for people is reflected generally in his business leadership; allied to it is his belief that 'the process which above all others can improve the conditions of low-paid workers is economic growth'.

Oppenheimer entered the South African Parliament in 1948 as a member of the United Party, then led by Field Marshal Smuts (*q.v.*), in opposition to the Nationalist Government which gained power at that election. The removal of mixed race voters from the common roll in 1955 led him to accuse the Government of breaking solemn pledges.

He quit politics in 1957 to concentrate on business, but he remains an influential and active backer of the Progressive Federal Party in South Africa which seeks an equitable distribution of power, opportunity and rights in the country for all races living there. He has long maintained a friendly contact with leaders of southern and central black African states, a facility denied most South African politicians. He says of this relationship: 'We in the Anglo American Corporation Group have long had important interests in virtually every country in this vast area and are therefore perhaps more conscious than most of the high cost of division and strife, and of the benefits which would flow to all its peoples from a relaxation of tension and co-operation on a regional basis.'

Through Anglo American, Oppenheimer is involved in new mining and general development in Britain, Canada, the United States, Brazil and Australasia; the company itself had a total market value in March 1980 of eleven thousand million rands (around six thousand million pounds sterling).

George Orwell (1903–50) British
Novelist and essayist

George Orwell, whose real name was Eric Blair, was born in India, the son of a civil servant, and educated at Eton. After leaving school he joined the Imperial Police in Burma, where he remained from 1922 to 1927, and it was that experience which gave him material for an attack on British imperialism in his novel *Burmese Days* (1934). By the time of its publication Orwell had spent a number of years as a hobo, and had developed a social conscience that led him to embrace socialism as a cure for social ills. His years of near-destitution are described graphically in *Down and Out in Paris and London* (1933). His commitment not to any one political party but to the cause of the working class led Orwell to concentrate for a time on journalistic writing at the expense of his novels: *The Road to Wigan Pier* (1937) investigates unemployment in the north of England and is written with considerably more passion and conviction than his novels

of this period, *Keep the Aspidistra Flying* (1936) and *Coming up for Air* (1939).

Orwell went to Spain in 1936 to report on the Spanish Civil War as a journalist, and in *Homage to Catalonia* (1938) expressed his disillusionment with communism, though in his articles and essays written during the war years he was still preaching and apparently believing in the imminence of a revolution in Britain. It was only in the last years of his life that Orwell was able successfully to inject his feeling for politics into fictional form and create novels that were artistically satisfying – the allegorical satire *Animal Farm* (1945) and his best-known novel, *1984* (1949), a denunciation of totalitarianism, whether of the right or of the left. In it Orwell presents a society in which even the thoughts of its citizens are controlled by the state. It was with these two novels that he finally achieved popularity with a wide public.

Harry Oppenheimer, chairman of Anglo American and De Beers

George Orwell; BELOW *Orwell novels in paperback*

John Osborne

BELOW *1936 Olympics: Jesse Owens at the start of the 200-metre race that he won in the record time of 20.7 seconds*

John Osborne (b. 1929) British
Playwright

An actor turned playwright, John Osborne is best known for his play *Look Back in Anger*, which in 1956 established both a Royal Court Theatre revival of British drama and the journalistic cliché of the 'angry young man'.

In fact a more conservative and even reactionary play than was at first understood, *Look Back in Anger* nevertheless established the fortunes of both Osborne and the Royal Court and provided, wrote one critic, 'a focus for the manifold frustrations of post-war Britain'. Osborne had already written other plays in collaboration with Anthony Creighton, but his next solo effort was *The Entertainer* (1957) which paralleled the collapse of Britain with the collapse of an aged end-of-the-pier comic called Archie Rice. This central role gave Laurence Olivier (*q.v.*) one of the greatest opportunities of his distinguished career, and brought him for the first time into the forefront of modern British theatre.

Since then Osborne has written one failed musical about a gossip-columnist (*The World of Paul Slickey*, 1959), an epic historical pageant (*Luther,* 1961), a masterly account of the crack-up of a London solicitor (*Inadmissible Evidence*, 1964), another historical pageant (*A Patriot For Me*, about the pre-First World War Austrian spy Redl) and some savage attacks on England past and present, of which the best is perhaps *West of Suez* (1971).

A prolific and depressive dramatist, often better at creating great characters than great plays, Osborne will perhaps be best remembered for writing about contemporary situations and issues. Starting as the social and stylistic enemy of Noël Coward (*q.v.*) and Terence Rattigan, he has ironically ended up more conservative than them, and appears now a somewhat reactionary figure firing off the occasional tirade to the newspapers from a home counties address. A prolific screenwriter too, he is the author of several television plays and the script for the film *Tom Jones*, directed by the man who first directed much of Osborne's work at the Royal Court, Tony Richardson. An occasional actor, Osborne has been married to three actresses, among them Jill Bennett, and two writers. His own family background, he once noted, was that of 'brawling, laughing, drinking, moaning failed innkeepers'.

Jesse Owens (1913–80) American
Athlete

Owens's supremacy as a sprinter and long-jumper would guarantee him a place in any sporting Hall of Fame, but it was the manner and the setting of his most spectacular triumphs that added to the legend. In the 1930s he became a living symbol in the propaganda fight against Fascism, and he remains the best known and best loved of all the hundreds of world-beating black American athletes.

His greatest feat, purely in athletic terms, occupied a single afternoon (actually a single hour of a single afternoon) at Ann Arbor, Michigan, in May 1935, when he equalled the world 100 yards record, broke the world records for 220 yards and 220 yards hurdles (and by so doing broke the slightly shorter distance 200 metres and 200 metres hurdles world records) and, with a single leap, set a new long-jump world mark that was to stand for twenty-five years.

But if that was Owens's finest performance, his finest moment came a year later in Berlin's Olympic stadium. Whether or not Hitler (*q.v.*) actually walked out of the stadium in disgust at Owens's masterly long-jump victory over the German Luz Long is still a matter of controversy; the likelihood is that Hitler was leaving anyway, and had lingered only because the long-jump competition was such a thriller. But the fact remains that Owens did more in a few days of Olympic competition (four gold medals won in impeccably smooth style and received with a modest and infectious grin) than anyone else in the world had done by any other means to make the Nazi tenets of racial purity look ridiculous.

The Berlin crowds adored him. Leni Riefenstahl, director of the Nazi Government's official Olympic film, dwelt lovingly upon – and captured superbly – the incomparable grace of his running; and, to prove that even such heroics as these are subject to the pettiness of the world, Owens arrived home in the American South to find that he was still required to sit in the less-favoured seats on buses, segregated from his white 'superiors'.

P

Emmeline Pankhurst (1858–1928)
British
Suffragette

The militant leader of the votes-for-women movement was born Emmeline Goulden, one of the ten children of a prosperous Manchester cotton-printer. The city was at that time the centre of the emancipation cause. In 1879 she

Mrs Pankhurst, arrested after the suffragettes' attack on Buckingham Palace, May 1914

RIGHT *Linus Pauling, advocate of vitamin C, takes his own medicine*

married Dr Richard Pankhurst, one of the founders of the Suffrage Committee, a barrister and later a radical Liberal candidate. They had four children, of whom Christabel, Sylvia and Adela were to become Emmeline's greatest supporters. After her husband's death in 1898, Mrs Pankhurst became the registrar of births and deaths for the city of Manchester. A great beauty with violet eyes and black hair, she soon developed a mellow, effortless public speaking voice which carried clearly through the shouts and jeers of her audiences.

In 1889 a group of women met at Mrs Pankhurst's home to form the Women's Franchise League, which worked for equality for women in divorce and inheritance, and in custody and guardianship of their children. More militant than her contemporaries, Mrs Pankhurst gave suffrage a vivid new image. In October 1903 she formed a new organization, the Women's Social and Political Union, which had the battle-cry 'Votes for women!' At that time the suffrage movement seemed a hopeless cause, but Mrs Pankhurst stepped up the militancy of her tactics. Suffragettes were arrested and fined for heckling Cabinet ministers, interrupting political meetings to demand answers on votes for women, smashing windows and causing an uproar in the House of Commons. Public meetings became more violent; suffragette speakers were pelted with rotten eggs and physically attacked. Mrs Pankhurst, frequently imprisoned, was subjected to forcible feeding when she and other suffragettes went on hunger strike. By 1912, an entire wing of Holloway prison was occupied by suffragette prisoners. The WSPU tactics culminated in its leaders being charged with conspiracy, and in 1913 Mrs Pankhurst was sentenced to three years. Released within a year, she now rebelled against a 'Cat and Mouse' Act that allowed hunger-strikers to be released and then imprisoned again. With the outbreak of the First World War, Mrs Pankhurst called off her campaign and the Government released all suffragette prisoners. The Representation of the People Act was passed in 1918, giving the vote to women over thirty, a crucial first step in their fight for equality and one for which Mrs Pankhurst's determination and courage was largely responsible.

Linus Pauling (b. 1901) American
Biochemist

Every atom has a small, dense nucleus surrounded by electrons, and we know that when atoms link together to form compounds, the outer electrons form links between the atoms. We know that particular compounds have definite shapes, but we also know that the electrons that form the links between the atoms

cannot be in fixed positions. They must really be whirling around the atoms. It was Linus Pauling who showed the way out of this paradox, a triumph that earned him a Nobel Prize in 1954.

His ideas are deeply mathematical, but the basis is simple. He worked out the energy of the various electrons both on separated atoms and when the atoms had combined. He found that they had less energy in the combined state. This fits in with two known facts – that atoms give out energy when they combine, and that energy has to be put into a compound to break it up into its elements.

Pauling applied his theories to the structure of proteins and suggested that the giant molecules of a protein must be arranged in a helical shape. He also showed that some kinds of inherited illness could be the result of the formation of a slightly altered form of haemoglobin – the chemical that carries oxygen in the blood – resulting from a gene inherited from a parent and causing a disease with recognized symptoms.

Only three people have won two Nobel Prizes, among them Pauling who won his second one, a Nobel Prize for Peace, in 1963, in recognition of his efforts towards nuclear disarmament.

He entered another controversial area with his studies of vitamin C. He holds that we have been misled by nutritionists, whose recommended daily dose of vitamin C is really, he says, only the minimum dose needed to prevent the signs of a vitamin deficiency disease. For positive health, Pauling reckons, we need much more, roughly twenty times the recommended minimum.

Pele (b. 1940) Brazilian
Footballer

He was christened Edson Arantes do Nascimento (the family called him Dico) but to the boys in the small up-country town of Tres Coracoes he was, unaccountably, Pele – and the name stuck. By the time he left football in 1977, in a welter of sentimentality totally at odds with Pele's attitude and nature, he had become synonymous with football, not only in Brazil where he was revered almost as a god, but everywhere in the world where football is played and a good deal of places where it is not.

Pele's silky speed, his two-footed control, his balance, his mesmerizing ball-skills and the beginnings of his blistering right-footed shot were all instilled early in his childhood by his father and his young companions. From then on it was only a question of channelling this rare combination of skills to the needs of the Santos club of São Paulo and the Brazilian national squads, for success to be inevitable.

As a precocious seventeen year old Pele scored two magical goals in the 1958 World Cup final in Stockholm; twelve years later, a mature player with a masterly tactical awareness, he led Brazil to the most impressive of World Cup victories in Mexico City. In between, he had missed the 1962 final through injury, and in the 1966 tournament had, with his team, been mercilessly and disgracefully kicked into submission.

Even without the World Cup triumphs, the feats are legendary; 1,280 goals in a career of 1,362 matches; an automatic choice for Brazil for fifteen years; a growing adulation that brought him to the presence of two popes, ten kings, five emperors, seventy presidents and forty heads of state.

But, it might be argued, it was after his retirement from Santos and Brazil in the mid-1970s that Pele's greatest contribution to the future of the game was forged, when he went to New York and graced the Cosmos line-up for a season or two. By doing so he stirred in North America the beginnings of a soccer interest that could, in time, shift the whole balance of power in world football.

Jean Piaget (1896–1980) Swiss
Psychologist

Born in Neuchâtel, Piaget was a youthful prodigy as a zoologist and later turned to psychology, holding professorships at Geneva and Lausanne Universities. He founded the International Centre for Genetic Epistemology at Geneva in 1955.

'Genetic epistemology' is Piaget's theory of mental growth in children. It is extremely complicated but, briefly, there are three main

stages. First, in the sensorimotor period (on average from birth to age one and a half), children learn to distinguish themselves from the rest of the world and the objects it contains. Second, in the concrete operational period (on average from one and a half to eleven), they become able to think logically about objects, separately from the objects themselves. Third, in the formal operational period (on average from eleven to fifteen), they can think about abstract ideas, as distinct from concrete objects.

Piaget made extensive notes on his own children's progress. He set out to establish the 'normal' course of development by observing children and setting them tests. His 'conservation' tests have been employed all over the world. A typical example is to show a child two balls of clay of equal size, mould one of the balls into a sausage-shape, and then find out whether the child understands that the two pieces of clay are still of equal size. Piaget did not expect a child to understand this until about the age of seven.

The incomparable Pele playing for the USA against England in 1976

Professor Jean Piaget

Piaget's numerous books include *The Origin of Intelligence in the Child* (1953), *The Early Growth of Logic in the Child* (1954), *The Psychology of the Child* (1969) and *The Principles of Genetic Epistemology* (1972). His theories and methods have influenced psychologists, educationalists and schools since the 1950s. A more critical attitude to his work has recently developed, however, and he has been attacked for seriously underestimating the intelligence of young children and the speed with which their rational powers can and should develop.

Pablo Picasso (1881–1973) Spanish
Painter

Picasso, born in Malaga, the son of an art teacher, showed exceptional talent from an early age and achieved a success in his lifetime that no other artist has equalled. He visited Paris for the first time in 1900 and settled there permanently in 1904, and it was during these early years that he produced some of his most lastingly popular work – paintings of the poor and of social outcasts, which came to be known as his Blue Period, soon to give way to the tender and often wistful Rose or Circus Period (1904–5).

Les Demoiselles d'Avignon of 1907 heralded the beginning of Cubism (in which several facets of a three-dimensional object are depicted in a combination of geometric shapes), probably the most influential art movement of the century. Because of this, and its violence and abandonment of accepted perspective, the painting represents a pictorial revolution in the history of western art.

Late in 1907 Picasso met Braque (*q.v.*) and for the next seven years they were to work closely together on the development of Cubism. By 1910–11 Picasso's Cubist painting had become almost completely abstract, with only a few clues, like a pipe, a bottle or a moustache, to suggest the subject emerging from the fragmented forms. Like Braque, Picasso introduced lettering and words into his work.

Picasso's art from 1914 to the mid-1920s swung from Cubist compositions to drawings and paintings of extraordinary realism, to stage sets and costumes and to the classically inspired figure compositions of the early 1920s. The distorted body forms and the aggressive sexual imagery of his figure paintings of the late 1920s and 1930s have much in common with the work of the Surrealists. In 1937 Picasso painted his monumental *Guernica* to commemorate the bombing of the Basque capital during the Spanish Civil War. It is probably the most powerful visual statement and protest in the century against the horrors of war and the suffering of a civilian population.

During the Second World War Picasso continued to live in Paris and in 1945 settled in the south of France, where he remained for the rest of his life. His enormous vitality was unabated, and in paintings, drawings, sculpture, prints and ceramics his prodigious output continued. Picasso's earliest sculptures had been made in the first decade of the century and his extraordinarily varied images in wood, bronze and found objects number more than 650 works. Portraits of friends and family, re-creations of classical paintings, and erotic fantasies are the subjects of his late work. Undoubtedly his greatest contributions to the history of art were his Cubist paintings and constructions, but he will be remembered in a broader context as this century's most creative artist, whose variety of styles and whose invention and genius in so many media are without parallel.

Les Demoiselles d'Avignon *by Pablo Picasso, 1907*

Mary Pickford (1893–1979) American, ex-Canadian
Actress

Born Gladys Smith in Toronto, Pickford went on stage at an early age. In 1909 she entered films with the director D.W. Griffith at his Biograph Studios in New York. Within a short time she was to become the most popular star in film history, known everywhere as 'the world's sweetheart', a position she occupied for the best part of two decades.

Pickford's fame was to some extent accidental, the result of being in the right place at the right time. She was never a major actress, and even at the height of her popularity there were other stars who were much more accomplished screen performers. Her diminutive build allowed her to play child roles long into mature adulthood, and the dimples and dangling gold curls were her trademark. The roles for which she was famous were those such as *Pollyanna*, *Tess of the Storm Country*, *Rebecca of Sunnybrook Farm* and even *Little Lord Fauntleroy*.

Pickford was also a shrewd businesswoman, and was one of the founders of United Artists, alongside Douglas Fairbanks, who became her husband in the same year (1919). They lived in a Beverly Hills mansion called Pickfair – she was to die there nearly sixty years later – and were the reigning royal family of Hollywood.

Eventually tastes changed and the kiss curls were shorn off in 1928. The coming of sound was a disaster for Pickford, and her four talkies not only demonstrated her dramatic limitations but proved that the new Mary Pickford was unacceptable to a public that had been conditioned for so many years to the 'Little Mary' image. In 1935 her marriage to Fairbanks broke up and she married former co-star, Charles 'Buddy' Rogers. Retirement from the screen left her free to pursue business interests, which embraced not only United Artists but later a cosmetics company. In her last years she seldom ventured from her bedroom at Pickfair. She donated fifty of her Biograph films to the American Film Institute, a gesture that was instrumental in securing her a special Academy Award in 1975 for her outstanding contribution to the cinema.

Gregory Pincus (1903–67) American Biologist

The work of Pincus has affected the lives of millions of twentieth-century women. In the 1940s and early 1950s he developed what could be the most important pharmaceutical invention of the century, the contraceptive pill.

Pincus took his first degree at Cornell University in 1924, and after research both at Harvard and abroad he became Professor of Physiology at Tufts University in 1944 and a research professor of biology at Boston University in 1951.

Most of Pincus's research was in various aspects of reproduction, but a crucial development occurred in the 1940s when he showed that pregnant women produce large amounts of a hormone called progesterone which prevents ovulation during pregnancy. In this way the body protects women from a double pregnancy. Pincus realized that the function of this hormone

could be extended to prevent pregnancy generally.

It was at this point that he met Margaret Sanger, the American pioneer of birth control, and when she deplored the lack of a reliable contraceptive he realized that progesterone could be the answer. Unfortunately, human progesterone is too rare to be useful as a general medicament; what was needed were synthetic progesterones, or similar compounds produced more abundantly in nature. A natural compound was extracted, with great difficulty, from the

Silent screen star Mary Pickford

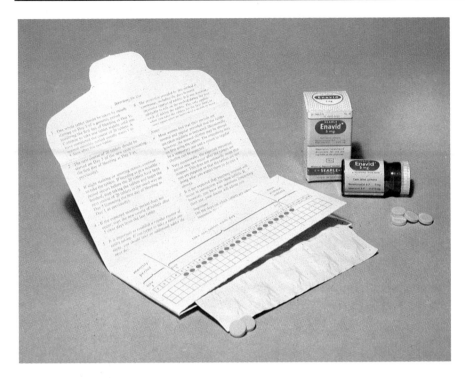

Conovid and Enavid, two of the first contraceptive pills resulting from the research of Gregory Pincus

realized was that this could be explained if energy travelled in 'packets', atoms of energy called quanta. High-frequency radiation, such as violet light, would be composed of quanta of high energy, and these would be produced in a large quantity only if the radiating object were very hot. The idea of quanta of energy is simple but unexpected. It explains very easily much of what happens in the world of physics, which is why both Einstein and Bohr found the idea of such value.

Planck was a famous scientist in his lifetime, and the premier German scientific research centre was named the Max Planck Institute in his honour.

roots of a Mexican vine and synthetic chemistry produced alternatives. Pincus and his colleagues tried some two hundred compounds before finding three that seemed suitable for human use. The first clinical trials took place in 1954, and their success provided the first ever method of contraception that was virtually certain; the odds against a woman on the pill becoming pregnant during the whole of her life are only between five hundred to one and five thousand to one.

Max Planck (1858–1947) German
Physicist

Modern physics can be said to date from the announcement of Planck's quantum theory at the turn of the century. It earned him a Nobel Prize in 1918, and applications of the theory were to win Nobel Prizes for Albert Einstein (*q.v.*) and Niels Bohr (*q.v.*).

Max Planck was born in Kiel, Germany, and educated first in Munich and then at the University of Berlin, where he became Professor of Theoretical Physics in 1892. His particular research interest was thermodynamics, the science that studies the way that heat is generated and transferred, and he developed his quantum theory to explain a problem concerning the radiation of heat from a black object – technically, 'black-body radiation'. Something black is the best possible radiator for heat, but according to classical physics any hot object should become violet in colour and send off heat mainly at high frequency. This is not what actually happens, as anyone can see: a hot body grows first red, then orange, and eventually white hot. What Planck

Max Planck

Jackson Pollock (1912–56) American
Painter

Pollock, one of the pioneers of the New York School, was born in Wyoming and grew up in southern California. In 1930 he moved to New York City to study at the Art Students League, and in 1935 signed up as a painter with the Federal Art Project of the Works Progress Administration.

By the early 1940s, with the emigration to the United States of such major figures as Mondrian (*q.v.*), Duchamp (*q.v.*) and other European artists, the centre of avant-garde art had shifted from Paris to New York. At the Museum of Modern Art and at the Guggenheim Museum, young American artists could see important paintings in the modern tradition, and it was in this environment that Pollock developed in the late 1930s and early 1940s. During these years he was greatly influenced by the work of Miró (*q.v.*) and Picasso (*q.v.*) and was liberated by the ideas of the Surrealists, who were concerned with expressing the subconscious in their paintings.

In 1943 Pollock had his first one-man show in New York. His paintings of the early 1940s include ritual themes based on Indian masks and totems, revealing his interest in the art of the native Americans. As the decade progressed, Pollock's work became more spontaneous and less tied to the subject-matter he was depicting. With the first 'drip paintings' of 1947, 'Pollock broke the ice', as it was phrased. Gone are the totem images painted with brush and palette knife, and soon the easel-painting tradition disappeared altogether from his work; now Pollock would tack an unstretched canvas to the floor and use sticks, knives and trowels to drip, splash and pour the paint on to the canvas beneath. 'I feel nearer, more a part of the painting, since this way I can walk around it, work from the four sides and literally be *in* the painting,' he said. This method came to be known as Action Painting or Abstract Expressionism, and Pollock likened it to the

In 1925 he was appointed Archbishop of Areopoli and began a career as a papal diplomat, serving as Vatican representative to Bulgaria, Greece and Turkey in turn. In 1944 he was made papal nuncio, or ambassador, to France. In 1953 he was created a cardinal and appointed Patriarch of Venice, and on the death of Pope Pius XII in 1958 he was elected pope as John XXIII at the age of seventy-seven.

Pope John's kindliness, cheerful good humour and vigorous directness and simplicity made a remarkable impact, and his popularity was by no means confined to Roman Catholics. He forbade the faithful to vote Communist, but called for a living wage for all workers and for assistance to underdeveloped countries. He gave a powerful impetus to the ecumenical movement, looking to the eventual reunification of all Christians in one Church. His principal role, however, was to encourage the modernizing and liberal tendencies within the Roman Catholic Church. The high-water mark of his period as pope came when he convened the Second Vatican Council, which met from 1962 to 1964. The Council embarked on a programme of modernization which tended to devolve responsibility from the pope to the bishops, and from the clergy to the laity, encouraged friendly relations with Christians of other denominations, allowed greater intellectual freedom in theology and largely did away with Latin in church services. The Council was still in session when Pope John died. His diary was published in 1965 as *The Journal of a Soul.*

method used by the Indian sand-painters of the western United States. He used sand himself, and broken glass and other materials, in his work. He painted directly; there were no studies, no preconceived ideas or subject matter. His great, large-scale canvases like *Autumn Rhythm* (1950) record the physical act of painting, the violent bodily gestures of the artist in the act of creating.

In 1956 Pollock was killed in a car crash, ending prematurely the life of one of the founders of Abstract Expressionism and one of the greatest American artists.

Pope John XXIII (1881–1963) Italian
Religious leader

One of the best-loved and most widely admired of all popes, the future John XXIII was born Angelo Giuseppe Roncalli, of peasant stock, at Sotto il Monte, near Bergamo. Educated for the priesthood in Rome, he was ordained in 1904. For ten years he was secretary to the Bishop of Bergamo and began to write a massive five-volume life of St Charles Borromeo, the sixteenth-century reformer, which was finally completed in 1952. During the First World War he served in the Italian army, first in the medical corps and later as a chaplain. He afterwards held various posts in Rome.

Pope John XXIII

Cole Porter (1891–1964) American
Composer and lyricist

Born into a rich environment in Peru, Indiana, Cole Porter flirted with a legal education before drifting into a dilettante life in the fleshpots of the Twenties, having developed a flair for songwriting which had flowered in infancy and been nurtured at Harvard. After an abortive assault on Broadway in 1919, he retired to Europe, living in some splendour in Paris and Venice. He finally shed the taint of amateurism in 1929 with a Broadway show called *Fifty Million Frenchmen*, after which he was recognized until his death as one of the most gifted songwriters of the century, matched only by Irving Berlin (*q.v.*) and Noël Coward (*q.v.*) in his ability to put his own words to his own music.

After writing several hit shows and intermittently contributing songs for Hollywood movies, he achieved his masterpiece in 1948 with *Kiss Me Kate*, a musical adaptation of *The Taming of the Shrew*.

Cole Porter's best work is characterized by brilliantly sophisticated verbal ideas synthesized in ingenious light verse, and, in the musical sense, considerably daring technical innovations, especially in the length of his songs. Among them is 'Begin the Beguine', the longest in the standard repertoire. He is equally revered for the passion of love songs like 'Night and Day' and 'I've Got You Under My Skin', and the wit of inspired squibs like 'Let's Do It', 'You're the Top' and 'Where is the Life that Late I Led?'

Ezra Pound (1885–1972) American
Poet

Pound was born in Idaho, and after studying at the University of Pennsylvania he left America to live in Europe, mainly in England and Italy, where his first volume of poems, *A Lume Spento* (1908), was published. In England Pound became the guiding spirit of the poetic movement known as imagism, which avoided unnecessary language in an attempt to give an absolutely clear image. He founded and edited the magazine

Cole Porter: a drawing by Soss Melik, 1953

Blast and was responsible for encouraging a number of major literary talents, among them T.S. Eliot (*q.v.*) and James Joyce (*q.v.*).

He developed an interest in Chinese poetry and published his own adaptations of the poems of Li Po in *Cathay* (1915). After he settled in Italy Pound turned his attention to economics and its influence on politics, and this led him to a firm belief in Fascism. These and other concerns are expressed in his epic work the *Cantos*, which he began in 1917 and continued to write and publish for the rest of his life. During the Second World War he not only continued to live in Italy but also broadcast Fascist propaganda to the United States. Arrested at the end of the war, he was tried in America and indicted for treason before being judged insane and committed to a hospital in Washington DC. He remained there until his release in 1958 when he was allowed to return to Italy.

His erratic political and economic theories notwithstanding, Pound was undoubtedly a brilliant literary innovator and a profound influence on an entire generation of poets. Informed opinion has remained divided on the question of his own value as a poet, but there can be no doubt of his importance as editor, critic and promoter of new literary talent. T.S. Eliot, in dedicating his masterpiece *The Waste Land* to Pound, referred to him as 'il miglior fabbro' ('the better craftsman'), and the *Cantos* are certainly the work of a master craftsman, a long epic poem in which all the most notable poetic cultures of the past are unified by Pound and expressed through his own modern mind and feelings.

LEFT *Ezra Pound*

Elvis Presley (1935–77) American
Pop singer and film actor

The safe, flabby world of the United States in the mid-1950s was a time ripe for change, with Dwight Eisenhower in the White House, the country in a seemingly unstoppable rising prosperity curve, automobiles getting longer and more chromium-laden, and suburbia on the instalment plan following the expressways across the country. The change came in the cinema – first with Marlon Brando's (*q.v.*) leather-clad anti-hero in *The Wild One*, then with the doomed

Elvis Presley in Jailhouse Rock, *1957*

youth James Dean, who played *Rebel Without a Cause* – focusing an increasing resentment among the young at the indifference of their parents' generation.

The change in popular music arrived with Elvis Presley, who overnight swept away the bland ballads and harmonic clichés from the charts. A wild boy of Memphis, Elvis strutted on to the stage in garishly mismatched clothes, his long black hair insolently greased down, holding his guitar like a phallic weapon. His sound was a synthesis of black rhythm and blues and the near hillbilly country music of his roots, put across with a frenzied, energetic feeling that electrified audiences. He began recording in his home state of Tennessee for the local market, but in 1955 an RCA contract resulted in instantaneous national sensation, with such singles as 'Heartbreak Hotel' and 'Blue Suede Shoes'. He was nicknamed 'Elvis the Pelvis' by his screaming girl fans on account of his gyratory hip motions in performance, and network television insisted on shooting him only above the waist after vigorous protests from shocked viewers. His disc career developing, he was also signed for films, of which he was to make thirty-three, most of them high-grossing vehicles for a string of songs, but with the possible exception of *Flaming Star* (1960) of little artistic merit. His much publicized induction into the United States army in 1958 brought with it a drastic change of image – the old rebellious, amoral, hip-swivelling Elvis, who gave apoplexy to morality groups, was replaced by a clean-cut, upright son of Uncle Sam

determined to do his duty for his country.

During the 1960s the Presley formula of record-making and turning out movies started to wilt, and the idol had begun to be puffy-faced and tired, semi-eclipsed by the emergence of new rock groups from England, such as the Beatles (*q.v.*) and the Rolling Stones. Then in the early 1970s he returned triumphantly to live performing, first at Las Vegas then on the road in such arenas as the Houston Astrodome and Madison Square Garden. But by the time Elvis was forty his day was done. He died of a heart attack in his bizarre Memphis mansion, Graceland, the corpulent victim of junk food and drugs.

Sergei Prokofiev (1891–1953) Russian Composer

The son of well-to-do, middle-class parents, Sergei Prokofiev was born in Sontzovka in the Ukraine. He had proved his musical ability by the age of five, when he first began to compose, and by the age of nine he had written an opera; he was also an accomplished pianist as a child. At the St Petersburg Conservatorium he was taught composition by the composer Rimsky-Korsakov, and also studied the piano. He was twenty-one when his first piano concerto outraged Russian audiences with its aggressively modern harmonies and its jagged rhythms and melodies. The concerto nevertheless attracted the attention of the impresario Diaghilev (*q.v.*), who commissioned ballet scores from the young composer. More acceptable to concert audiences was the 'Classical' Symphony (1917), still one of Prokofiev's most popular and accessible works.

In 1917 Prokofiev embarked upon a tour of the United States, and in fact did not live in Russia again until 1934, although he visited his homeland briefly in 1927. During this cosmopolitan period Prokofiev produced such works as the opera *The Love of Three Oranges*, commissioned by the Chicago Opera in 1921, a number of symphonies and piano concertos and smaller piano pieces, all much too *avant garde* for a Russia which, since the composer's departure, had undergone its communist Revolution of 1917. When Prokofiev returned to Russia he appeared to be able to turn himself into an acceptable Soviet composer, writing music that was much more conventional both in its melody and harmony than were his compositions of the 1920s. However, this is not necessarily to suggest that the music of Prokofiev's Soviet period is less valuable. In fact he probably came to grips with the real nature of his own talent only after his early experimental period. His scores for the Soviet films *Lieutenant Kije* (1934), *Alexander Nevsky* (1939) and *Ivan the Terrible* (1945) are justly famous, and his ballets *Romeo and Juliet* (1936) and *Cinderella* (1944) are considered classics of ballet music.

Sergei Prokofiev, 1910

Marcel Proust (1871–1922) French
Novelist

Marcel Proust is one of the indisputably great novelists of the twentieth century. The son of a Catholic father and a Jewish mother, he was born in Auteuil, Paris, a city in which he was always to live. His childhood in a middle-class environment was comfortable and secure, but it was not happy, for Proust suffered from asthma from the age of nine and was more or less a semi-invalid for the rest of his life. At the age of eighteen he went into the army for a year, and then studied both law and political science at the Sorbonne. Despite a snobbish fascination with titled society and a desire to advance himself socially, the young Proust was also a dedicated writer who contributed elegantly written sketches and

articles to literary magazines and newspapers. A collection of these short pieces was published in 1896 under the title *Les Plaisirs et les Jours* (*Pleasures and Days*).

For some years in the 1890s Proust worked on a long novel, *Jean Santeuil*, which he abandoned, and which was published posthumously in its incomplete state in 1952, revealing itself to be a kind of foreshadow of his master work, *A la Recherche du Temps Perdu*, the huge novel in many volumes to which Proust devoted most of his life. When his parents died in the early years of the twentieth century, he withdrew from society, retired to his sound-proofed apartment in the Boulevard Haussmann, Paris, and between frequent attacks of asthma concentrated on *A la*

Recherche. In this work he used a semi-autobiographical form to explore not only the society of his time but also the larger subjects of time itself, of love and the powers of memory. Proust himself was a homosexual, though the narrator in *A la Recherche* does not admit to being one, and in the novel there are portraits both flattering and unflattering of homosexuals. Most of the characters were based upon real people of Proust's acquaintance. The work, successfully translated into English as *Remembrance of Things Past*, consists of seven separate novels which, in the original French, ran to sixteen volumes. Vast in its scope, elegant in its style, *Remembrance of Things Past* is one of the great literary masterpieces of the century.

Q

Mary Quant (b. 1934) British
Fashion designer

Towards the end of the 1950s post-war austerity gave way to a certain prosperity. There was a new generation of consumers who were earning and who had more spare time than their parents; they wanted to spend their money on records, clothes, coffee bars and jazz clubs. Teenagers no longer wanted to dress like their elders, and under the influence of a new generation of British designers leaving art schools, clothes became aggressively original, a kind of tribal identification for the young.

The fashion leader for these new consumers was Mary Quant, a product of art school although not fashion school. She began her fashion career at Erik, the milliner, and in

ABOVE LEFT *A portrait of Marcel Proust by Jacques Emile Blanche, 1897*

LEFT *Mary Quant, who had the right ideas at the right time and caused a fashion revolution*

November 1955 opened Bazaar, a shop in the King's Road. As she began to buy stock, she found that she couldn't get the kind of clothes she wanted to wear herself. Although totally ignorant of how to go about it, she began to design her own clothes, buying fabrics over the counter at Harrods because she didn't know that they could be obtained wholesale. Soon, her shop was always packed with customers – a 'nonstop cocktail party' – and her bedsit was occupied until late every night by sewing women who were trying to produce enough clothes to fill the racks the next day. Stark striped pinafores, knickerbockers, brilliant orange crêpes, dungarees with buttons as big as golf balls – whatever Mary Quant designed sold out immediately. International buyers began to get interested, and in the wake of Bazaar hundreds of London boutiques cropped up overnight to become the most popular shopping-places for the young.

Within seven years of its opening, the Mary Quant business had a turnover of over a million pounds and the clothes she designed were available in 150 British shops and 320 American stores. The Mary Quant label eventually came to cover a business empire that marketed almost everything from underclothes and sheets to cosmetics and tights. Mary Quant was awarded the Order of the British Empire for her services to industry. She had led the revolution that gave the young their own fashion, and was the first designer who succeeded in turning the eyes of the fashion world from Paris to London.

R

Maurice Ravel (1875–1937) French Composer

Maurice Ravel studied the piano as a child and wrote his first compositions at the age of twelve, enrolling two years later at the Paris Conservatoire where the composer Fauré was one of his teachers. He remained a student for the next ten years, perfecting his technique but failing to win the one prize he wanted most, the Prix de Rome. He never married, living with his parents until they died and later with his brother. Ravel's emotional life, if he had one, remains an unbroken code: his music, it seems, was all that mattered to him. In the years leading up to 1914 he wrote a number of remarkable songs and some highly original piano music. Into this period fall the song cycle *Shéhérazade*, dating from 1903, and the *Valses Nobles et Sentimentales*, from 1911.

During the First World War Ravel volunteered for service but his slight stature (he was just over five feet tall) and his frail physique (he weighed only seven stone) disqualified him. After the war his fame as a composer spread abroad and he began to travel. His orchestral piece *Bolero* (1927) was phenomenally successful and he frequently conducted it at concerts as well as performing it as a solo pianist. Among his other most popular orchestral works are his music for the ballet *Daphnis et Chloé* (1912) and the choreographic poem, *La Valse* (1920). He composed two operas, both short, one-act works of great charm and warmth: *L'Heure Espagnole* (*The Spanish Hour*, 1911) and *L'Enfant et les Sortilèges* (*The Bewitched Child*, 1925), the latter to a delightful libretto by the novelist Colette.

From 1929 onwards Ravel's health began to deteriorate. He completed two piano concertos, one of them for the left hand only, and three *Don Quichotte* songs intended for a film of

Maurice Ravel: a portrait by Ludwig Nauer

the Cervantes novel. These were his last compositions. His condition grew worse and an operation proved unsuccessful. Though over sixty when he died, his powers as a composer were undiminished.

Jean Renoir (1894–1979) French
Film director

Son of the great painter, Jean Renoir reached as great a pinnacle as his father in another medium. His childhood was spent in a creative and artistic household, and a sense of that time, with sunshine, groaning tables and high spirits is felt in many of Renoir's films, particularly the early comedies. Originally he had intended to be a potter, but began making films in the mid-1920s in order to promote his actress wife, Catherine Hessling. Her performance in *Nana* (1926) drew comparisons with the young Garbo (*q.v.*), but this expensive film was a box-office disaster and a setback to Renoir's career. They continued to make films together until the partnership was dissolved with the coming of sound.

Renoir then embarked on the path that was to make him France's greatest director. By the time he made *La Chienne* (1932) he had achieved full creative control, and its star, who played a victim who becomes a murderer, was also the great star of his comedy *Boudu Saved from Drowning*, in which a tramp happily debunks bourgeois aspirations. There followed a series of brilliant films, broad in range – from social realism (*Toni, The Crime of Monsieur Lange, La Vie est à nous*), pastoral lyricism (*Une Partie de Campagne*), and literary adaptation (*Madame Bovary, Les Bas Fonds*) to a trio of masterpieces which closed the 1930s – *La Grande Illusion*, an anti-war film that examines the loyalties of class as well as nationality, *La Bête Humaine*, a study of the power of fate, and *La Règle du Jeu*, a classical comedy of manners, poorly received in its day but now regarded as one of the greatest films ever to emerge from France.

During the Second World War Renoir went to Hollywood and made films there, with less success, although *The Southerner* (1945), with its gentle, poetic affinity to the land, and *The Diary of a Chambermaid* (1946), an effective combination of sunlight and malevolence in a French period setting, are among his best films. After the war he made *The River* in India, his first in colour, and in Italy *The Golden Coach*. His first French film for fifteen years was *French Cancan* (1955), a colourful homage to *La Belle Epoque*. His last major work was *Le Caporal Epinglé*, in which he returned to the prisoner-of-war theme of *La Grande Illusion*. There is in all his films a deep regard for humanity with no bogus sentimentality. Renoir was as acute an observer of the rules of the game as there has ever been.

ABOVE *Film director Jean Renoir in exuberant mood*

Rainer Maria Rilke (1875–1926)
Austrian
Poet

Born in Prague – then in the Austro-Hungarian Empire – Rilke was to become the leading German-language poet of his time and is perhaps the most important German-language poet of the twentieth century. A sensitive child, his early years were frequently unhappy, plagued as he was by a mother who brought him up as a girl and gave him the nickname Sophie, and by a

Austrian poet Rainer Maria Rilke

father who sought to toughen him up by enlisting him in the military academy near Vienna. In adult life his friendship with a succession of aristocratic women who adored him, put their castles at his disposal, and generally mothered him, allowed him to concentrate on his poetry, which was much more real to him than the external world.

Rilke travelled widely – in Russia, Scandinavia, Italy, Egypt and Spain – though for many years Paris was his headquarters. He became the friend and secretary of the sculptor Rodin, about whom he wrote two monographs. Art, to Rilke, was a substitute for religion, and an almost religious ecstasy pervades much of his poetry. His early volume, *Das Stundenbuch* (*The Book of Hours*, 1905) is in fact written in the person of a monk, and subjectively shows, through the narrator's religious fervour, Rilke's strong tendency to escape from the world of reality. The best of his early work is to be found in *Neue Gedichte* (*New Poems*, 1907). During the First World War Rilke worked as a clerk in Vienna, writing little, but his later and best-known works, especially the *Duineser Elegien* (*Duino Elegies*, 1923), written at a princess's castle at Duino, near Trieste, show that he had continued to develop during his period of silence. The Duino poems are highly personal fore-runners of what would later be known as the existentialist school.

The prose work *Die Aufzeichnungen des Malte Laurids Brigge* (*The Notebooks of Malte Laurids Brigge*, 1910) is a curious creation, written as though it were a collection of journal entries into which the poet had poured some of his most morbid fears and neuroses. Rilke's last volume of verse, a death-haunted cycle of sonnets, was *Die Sonette an Orpheus* (*The Sonnets to Orpheus*, 1923).

John D. Rockefeller, who made a massive fortune with Standard Oil and gave away $446 million in shares

John D. Rockefeller (1839–1937)
American
Oil tycoon

The son of a quack medicine hawker in Richford, New York, Rockefeller controlled the entire American oil business by the age of thirty-nine. Three years later, in 1901, his massive Standard Oil Company had built his personal fortune to $200 million.

After an early struggle to get a job as an office boy in Cleveland, Ohio, Rockefeller's shrewdness and thrift soon pushed him ahead in the wholesale and produce business. Noting down in his accounts even the dimes given to charity, he prospered sufficiently to write out a cheque for $75,000 at the age of twenty-five, which bought his stake in a Pennsylvania oil refinery a few years after the first American oil strike at Titusville. He bought up more oil refineries, and

after forming Standard Oil in 1870 Rockefeller convinced the refinery sellers to take shares in his company instead of cash, ultimately making many of them millionaires. His operations were characterized by ruthless efficiency. His refineries were well run and used the best available equipment, but despite his claim to market 'the best oil at the lowest cost' public opinion was outraged when it was discovered that secretly negotiated rail discounts allowed him to undercut competition, either forcing competitors to sell or go out of business.

For the next thirty years, clergy, politicians and press were united in hostility against Rockefeller and his evil oil trust. But his lavish philanthropy soon out-distanced even his most strident critics. The University of Chicago, the Rockefeller Institute for Medical Research and the famous Rockefeller Foundation, as well as Oxford, Cambridge, London and Bristol universities, were all beneficiaries of the $446 million in shares which he gave away. Neither monopoly-breaking Teddy Roosevelt nor 'muck-raking' investigations into Rockefeller's business methods could dent the growth of his fortune as the demand for petrol grew. When the supreme court in 1911 finally ordered Standard Oil's break-up into individual parts like Esso (Eastern Standard Oil), the value of Rockefeller's shares almost doubled to $900 million. John D. Rockefeller, who died on his Florida estate, wizened and frail at the age of ninety-seven, had accrued a vast personal fortune in his lifetime and founded a remarkable family of businessmen and public administrators, but he will perhaps best be remembered for his infinite generosity, which has benefited people all over the world.

Franklin D. Roosevelt (1882–1945)
American
Political leader

Franklin D. Roosevelt, 'FDR', was born an American aristocrat, of a family that came to New York State from Holland in the 1640s. His mother's family were the equally distinguished Delanos.

From an early age he saw his future as being in public life. He went to Groton school, the Eton of America, and entered Harvard University when his uncle, Theodore (Teddy) Roosevelt, was Governor of New York State. While FDR was at Harvard, Teddy became President.

After some time in a New York law firm, FDR became a state senator as a Democrat (Teddy was a Republican) and then, in 1912, went to Washington as assistant secretary of the navy. He supported America's entry into the First World War. In 1920 he was the Democratic nominee for vice-president; however, the Democrats lost the election.

In 1921 disaster struck this golden boy of politics. While on holiday on Campobello Island in Maine he contracted polio, which paralyzed him from the waist down. But his will to live normally overcame his handicap. He went back to law and business, making money at that time of boom prosperity, and in 1927 he became campaign manager for the Democratic presidential candidate. At Warm Springs, Georgia, he found he could obtain relief for his paralysis and returned there every year, making it a centre for polio victims.

He became Governor of New York in 1928, and in 1932, in the midst of the Depression, was elected President. 'We have nothing to fear but fear itself', he said: he brought hope to America, sweeping into action with his Hundred Days of relief legislation and his New Deal for national recovery. He had trouble with Congress and the Supreme Court (FDR was stubbornly self-willed), but the many different groups of voters – city dwellers, ethnic groups, labour unions and Southerners – continued to support him for an unprecedented third term of office in 1940 and a fourth in 1944. Meanwhile, the Second World War had broken out in Europe, but the American people clung to isolationism. FDR was reluctant to join the war but helped the Allies as much as he was able with a 'lend-lease' agreement, which meant that war supplies could be lent, leased or sold to any country whose defence was thought to be of importance to the United States. On 7 December 1941 the Japanese attacked Pearl Harbor and the United States entered the war.

Roosevelt was a war leader who recognized the importance of scientific weapons and strongly supported the atomic programme. He was also a wonderful propagandist for the allied cause. But in international relations the traditional American Navy Department's suspicions of the British Empire must have influenced FDR's judgement, and he thought he could put some trust in 'Uncle Joe' Stalin (*q.v.*) at the meetings of the Big Three (Churchill [*q.v.*], Stalin and FDR himself) at Tehran and Yalta. Having worked himself into a very frail state, he died at Warm Springs while still in office, a matter of weeks before Germany's surrender.

Mark Rothko (1903–70) American, ex-Russian
Painter

Rothko began life in Dvinsk, Russia, and emigrated to the United States in 1913. It was not until he left Yale University in 1923 that he decided to become an artist. Although in 1925, when he settled in New York, he studied drawing at the Art Students League, he was largely self taught. Rothko had his first one-man show in 1933.

At Peggy Guggenheim's New York gallery, Art of this Century, Rothko had an important one-man show in 1945: his paintings represented the culmination of the Surrealist phase of his work – mythological and ritualistic subjects suggestive of human and animal forms, and subconscious imagery. At this time he was attracted by the work of Dali (*q.v.*), Miró (*q.v.*) and Ernst. In the transitional work of the late 1940s Rothko gradually began to formulate his mature, totally abstract style. His canvases were composed of large oblong or rectangular units of colour floating in space. Within this format he experimented with variations for the rest of his

LEFT *Franklin Delano Roosevelt by Douglas Chandor*

Black on Maroon *by Mark Rothko*

life, with two or three blocks of colour suspended one above the other. Although devoid of explicit subject matter, the diffuse shapes, blurred edges and above all the glow of the colours create extraordinary moods and atmospheric effects, sometimes evoking landscape, sky, sea and sunsets, or the brooding, tragic aspects of life.

In 1958 Rothko was commissioned to paint a series of murals for a New York restaurant. He completed three sets, each darker than its predecessor, the solid colour of his earlier work giving way to rectangles with open centres. But, dissatisfied with the restaurant space, he refused to deliver the work, and the second set of these sombre, tragic paintings he gave to the Tate Gallery, London.

His last major commission was a group of large murals for a chapel in Houston, Texas, which he worked on from 1964 to 1967. The subject was the Passion of Christ, but tragically Rothko committed suicide a year before the chapel was dedicated. In these late masterpieces the simple shapes, the deep reds and blacks evoke a mood of death, as if questioning the meaning of Christ's Passion. Rothko's remarkable achievement was his ability to create an abstract language in which form and colour are capable of suggesting vast spaces and inspiring in the viewer feelings of awe and wonder about the nature of human existence.

Artur Rubinstein (b. 1886) American, ex-Polish
Pianist

Artur Rubinstein revealed his talent for music at a very young age, and was sent from Lódź, the town of his birth, to Berlin to study piano and composition. At twelve years old he played a concerto at a public concert in Berlin with such success that he immediately began to receive engagements from abroad. His early successes came easily to him, and Rubinstein himself in his

Pianist Artur Rubinstein, superb interpreter of the romantic repertoire, especially of the music of Chopin

Memoirs has confessed that as a young man he was more concerned with enjoying himself socially than with practising. An extrovert who placed his love for music and for the piano in the context of his love for life and for people, Rubinstein nevertheless took stock of himself after he had been performing publicly for some years. He decided that he needed to act more responsibly towards his great gifts as a pianist and proceeded to become the finest performer of romantic music of his time.

Rubinstein lost most of his family in the Nazi concentration camps, and this stiffened him in his resolve never again to perform in Germany. His repertoire, in any case, was always geared less to the German classics than to the great romantic of the keyboard, Chopin, and to later romantic composers such as Brahms. He has always been the romantic pianist *par excellence*, his sheer love of the instrument leading him to find more in the piano music of Chopin than many another pianist has succeeded in doing.

For many years Rubinstein lived in America, but he returned to Europe after the Second World War to live in Paris. When he gave his last recital at the Wigmore Hall, London, Rubinstein was over ninety years of age, but had lost none of his vigorous exuberance: his performance of Chopin's A-flat major Polonaise was both stirring and immensely moving, despite some of the inaccuracies of old age. Rubinstein was a superb interpreter not only of Chopin but also of the modern Spanish school of the composers Albeniz, Granados and de Falla, whose *Ritual Fire Dance* he delighted to play as an encore.

Helena Rubinstein (1872–1965)
American, ex-Polish
Cosmetics tycoon

Having set out to study medicine at Cracow and Zurich, Rubinstein's anxious parents chased her off to Australia to end an unsuitable love affair. There, friends were impressed that the four-foot-ten-inch Polish beauty managed to keep her skin smooth and white against the ravages of the Australian sun. The secret was the Crème Valaze balm, made by a Hungarian cosmetician friend, that Helena had brought with her. When a popular actress told a journalist how good it was, Helena started to make it. She imported the cosmetician to help with the manufacture and in the first year netted £20,000. With more advertising to boost sales and with a beauty salon in Melbourne, the foundations of her massive fortune were already well and truly laid by 1904. Not content, she returned to Europe to spend three years studying dermatology with scientists in Berlin, Zurich and Vienna before moving to London to open what was to become the first of a world-wide chain of Maisons de Beauté.

Up to this point the Rubinstein products had been devoted to scientific care of the skin, but the clown-like spectacle of Manhattan ladies, white powder clashing horribly with skin chilled purple by the cold, now gave her the simple but stunningly original idea of colouring face powder to match skin tones. Unlike her rival, Elizabeth Arden, Helena Rubinstein saw her salons as just part of the marketing effort and built up mass sales of all her products, becoming the first cosmetics manufacturer to sell through department stores. As her business expanded, she recruited her relatives as executives. Perhaps her shrewdest coup was selling her American business to the investment bankers Lehmann Brothers for $2.8 million in the 1920s and buying it back for $800,000 after the 1929 crash. Hard working and innovative, Rubinstein had enormous influence in enabling ordinary women to buy cosmetics. She retained an active interest in her business empire until she died, when it was claimed that she was the richest self-made woman in the world.

Bertrand Russell (1872–1970) British
Philosopher, mathematician, political activist and educational reformer

A brilliant and controversial figure, Russell has been arguably the most influential philosopher of the twentieth century. His prodigious literary output was combined with an active engagement in politics which twice landed him in jail (in 1918 for pacifism, and in 1961 for acts of civil disobedience in the cause of nuclear disarmament); with running an experimental free school; and with an extensive network of friendships, romances and correspondence. He received the Order of Merit in 1949, was made Fellow of the Royal Society for his work on mathematics and was awarded the Nobel Prize for literature (there being none for philosophy) in 1950.

Russell was born in Trelleck, Monmouthshire, the second son of Viscount Amberly. Orphaned at three, he was brought up by his grandmother and educated at home until he went to Cambridge University. He was fascinated by the certainty and beauty of mathematics, and at Cambridge he drifted into philosophy on the track of clarifying that certainty. Only two constants characterized his changing philosophical ideas from then on: logical investigation of the language of philosophy, and making connections between philosophy and science. He pursued his changing thought through *The Principles of Mathematics* (1903), and the immensely ambitious three-volume *Principia Mathematica* (1910–13). This work is now regarded as a classic of modern mathematical logic, though it was understood by only a small

handful of intellectuals when it first appeared.

While teaching at Cambridge before the First World War Russell published immensely influential papers in professional journals. He both influenced and was influenced by his contemporary philosopher G.E. Moore and by his student Ludwig Wittgenstein (*q.v.*). He lived to see himself eclipsed by the latter in the minds of many philosophers, a development he deplored. Russell worked in the tradition that saw philosophy attempting to interpret and examine the

Graham Sutherland's famous portrait of Helena Rubinstein, 1957

The brilliant and distinguished Bertrand Russell at the age of ninety-six

foundations of the world picture of science and mathematics. He expressed this clearly in his introductory book *The Problems of Philosophy* (1912), and in his Harvard lectures *Our Knowledge of the External World* (1914).

After losing his Cambridge Fellowship in 1916 as a result of his pacificism, Russell lived by writing and lecturing and occasional academic appointments. He spent much of the Second World War in the United States, where he was, he boasted, 'judicially pronounced unworthy to be Professor of Philosophy at the College of the City of New York' (1940) and his lectureship was terminated after protests about his morality and lack of religion.

In his last decades Russell became a well-known voice on British radio, particularly through his appearances on 'The Brains Trust' and his Reith Lectures *Authority and the Individual* (1949). His *Autobiography*, published in three volumes between 1967 and 1969, was a bestseller: to a public accustomed to his logic, wit and rationality, it was a revelation to find a life so turbulent and emotionally full.

Babe Ruth (1895–1948) American
Baseball player

Sports – particularly spectator sports – need heroes if they are to capture the public imagination, to pull in the crowds and to prosper. This was even more true in the days before television,

RIGHT Baseball hero of the 1920s and 30s, Babe Ruth

in the days when deeds and deeds alone had the power to create legends.

No sport has created a bigger hero than Babe Ruth, whose name and unforgettable frame dominated the baseball pages of America's newspapers between the wars. He was a gift to the popular press and the radio stations of his day. They garlanded him with nicknames – The Bambino, The Home-Run King, The Sultan of Swat. They larded their pages with stories about his rags-to-riches rise to fame, about his incongruous appearance (fifteen-stone-plus body balanced on spindly legs and topped by a fat, potato-like face), about his vast capacity for food and drink (limited somewhat by the need for fitness in later years), about his love of roistering parties, and so on.

But Ruth was much more than just a huge personality. His supreme ball sense was such that his early mark on the baseball game was made not as a batter but as a left-handed pitcher at Baltimore and subsequently with Boston Red Sox. Indeed, it was as one of the country's most successful pitchers that he was bought in 1920 by the New York Yankees. There his batting potential was recognized, and the rest of his long career was spent in making life a misery for his former pitching colleagues.

Records tumbled before the onslaught of his left-handed slugging. In eleven seasons he hit more than forty home runs (a respectable *career*

tally for some good players), and in four of these more than fifty. His career accumulation of 714 home runs stood as a record for almost forty years, and his magnetism as the game's number one hitter brought the crowds flocking to see the Yankees. Their new-found wealth was invested in a new 70,000-seat Yankee Stadium, known to baseball fans everywhere as The House That Babe Built.

Much of the publicity about his later years centred, as so many sports stories do, around money – around the huge salaries Ruth demanded (and received) from the Yankees; the fact that in 1930 he was earning just $2,000 a year more than the president of the United States; and around the endorsements and public appearances after his retirement that made him a cool million dollars.

But his name remains inseparable from the game. Outside the United States the names of only two baseball players are familiar. One is that of Joe DiMaggio, because he married Marilyn Monroe. The other is Babe Ruth, because that vast figure hitting balls high and mightily into the crowd simply *is* baseball.

Ernest Rutherford (1871–1937) British
Physicist

Before Rutherford's research, the atom was thought to be solid, like a tiny billiard ball. He showed that it is mainly empty, with a small central nucleus, and his studies of this nucleus made him the father of nuclear physics.

Ernest Rutherford was born near Nelson, New Zealand, on 30 August 1871. He was the son of a wheelwright and farmer, and was educated at Canterbury College, Christchurch. Then, in 1895, he won a scholarship to Cambridge University to work with J.J. Thomson (*q.v.*), the physicist who had discovered the electron.

His main work in England, first at Cambridge and then, after 1907, at Manchester University, concerned radioactivity. Radioactive chemical elements were first recognized because they give off rays that penetrate solids to affect photographic film. Rutherford discovered that some of the rays had a positive electrical charge – these he called alpha rays – and others – called beta rays – had a negative charge. Later, uncharged rays were found and called gamma rays.

Then Rutherford studied the changes that happened to the radioactive elements and, in conjuction with the chemist Frederick Soddy, he discovered that a radioactive element changed to another element as it gave off rays, and that this in turn might give off rays and change again. He soon realized that the alpha and beta 'rays' were streams of tiny charged particles. Alpha particles were in fact charged atoms of helium, and beta particles were electrons.

When he sent a beam of alpha particles at a thin piece of gold foil, Rutherford found that most of them came straight through, a few were bent in their paths, and some bounced back. He saw that this meant that most of the alpha particles were going through the space in the atoms, and those that bounced off had been deflected by the tiny central nucleus of the atom.

Then he looked at the collisions of alpha particles with atoms of gas. He found that hydrogen atoms were stimulated to produce a bright spot on a screen. This he expected. But he also found a knock-on effect with nitrogen atoms, which are much heavier than hydrogen atoms. He realized that he had split the nucleus of the nitrogen atom, forming hydrogen, which was knocked out of the atom, leaving oxygen. He was the first person to split the atom, though he did not foresee the consequences. He returned to Cambridge to make, and inspire, a stream of brilliant discoveries in nuclear physics, and he received a number of awards and commendations for his work, including the Nobel Prize for Chemistry in 1908 and a peerage in 1931.

Martin Ryle (b. 1918) British
Astronomer

Science asks a few major questions, and one of the most fundamental is: how did the universe start? Martin Ryle has given what seems to be an answer: it started with a big bang.

Ryle was educated at Bradfield College and Christ Church, Oxford. After research at the

LEFT Ernest Rutherford (Lord Rutherford of Nelson), President of the Royal Society 1925–30

The world's largest radio telescope – the Very Large Array – with a dish 82 feet in diameter, in the plains of San Augustin, New Mexico (see Martin Ryle)

famous Telecommunications Research Establishment he returned to academic life and in 1959 was appointed Cambridge University's first Professor of Radio-Astronomy. His discoveries have been in this field.

Radio-astronomers' telescopes 'see' not light but radio waves from space, and as radio waves are far more penetrating than light rays, a radio telescope can see a great distance. Ryle devised a technique for his radio telescope that gave it astonishingly sharp definition – the equivalent of being able to see the details of a postage stamp on the Moon. His method was to spread a number of small telescopes along a railway line, and then

fit the signals from all these telescopes together so that they acted as one giant telescope. It was with this arrangement that he established the Big Bang theory of the origin of the universe.

Since early in this century it has been known that the universe is expanding. But towards the end of the 1940s, a new theory was proposed. This said that although the universe was expanding so that galaxies eventually were so far away and travelling so quickly that their light never reached us, new galaxies were steadily being formed near the centre of the universe to move out and take their place. This theory of 'continuous creation' led to what was called a 'steady state' universe. Because each disappearing galaxy was replaced by a new one, the universe always looked the same.

Ryle effectively demolished this theory. He made a meticulous map of the stars in the universe which showed that as one looked deeper and deeper into space one saw more and more stars. These must be the relics of the original Big Bang. It was for the delicate mapping and his confirmation of the theory that Martin Ryle was awarded a Nobel Prize in 1974.

S

Jonas Salk (b. 1914) American
Virologist

As a general rule, diseases that are caused by viruses – smallpox and measles, for example – cannot be cured by drugs. They can, however, be prevented by vaccination or some similar treatment. The threat of polio – 'infantile paralysis' – another virus disease, has in the last two decades been enormously reduced. It was Salk who produced the first vaccine that successfully prevents it.

When we are infected by a virus disease, we react by manufacturing antibodies that circulate in the blood and attack the virus. This is why we rarely twice catch measles, German measles or smallpox. Unfortunately, one attack of smallpox and polio is enough to cause serious harm, paralysis or death. But if we could arrange to be infected with a harmless virus that nonetheless caused us to manufacture antibodies, we would be protected against the disease. This is the principle of vaccination. The difficulty is to produce harmless but effective strains of virus. Salk solved this problem for polio.

Jonas Salk was born in New York and qualified in medicine there. Eventually he went to the University of Pittsburgh to carry out his research. He had to find a way of making the polio virus safe but effective. His method was to kill the virus but leave it in a state that would produce antibodies. The disease is so dangerous

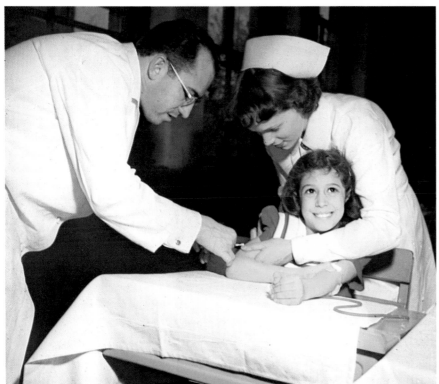

Jonas Salk injects a child with polio vaccine

that his first tests were carried out on children who had recovered from polio and who could not therefore catch it. His vaccine produced antibodies. Then he tried the vaccine on children who had not had polio, and it produced antibodies without infecting them. In 1954 Salk was ready to make the vaccine on a large scale, and in 1955 the vaccines were in enormous demand.

This led to a disaster. Some of the vaccines contained live virus – they had been produced hurriedly – and in a very small fraction of the injections the vaccine infected children with polio instead of protecting them. The vaccine became unpopular as a result, even though future batches were made with great care. As it happened, another New York researcher, Albert Sabin, was producing live virus that had been so damaged that it could not produce polio, even though it could encourage antibodies; it can be taken on a lump of sugar instead of being injected, it provides more effective long-term immunity, and is cheaper to produce; it has, therefore, largely replaced Salk vaccine. But it was Jonas Salk who took the first crucial steps towards combating this appalling disease.

Frederick Sanger (b. 1918) British
Chemist

Only two people have been awarded two Nobel Prizes for their scientific work, Marie Curie (*q.v.*) and Frederick – now Sir Frederick – Sanger. His research was concerned with the structure of proteins.

He was born in Rendcombe, Gloucestershire, on 13 August 1918, studied at Cambridge University and stayed there to carry out his research. Proteins are composed of a large number of compounds called amino acids, linked in chains, and Sanger's problem was to decide which amino acids were present in a particular protein and what their order was along the chain. It was a lengthy business.

He studied insulin, the chemical that the body produces to help it absorb sugar. A molecule of insulin contains about fifty amino acids arranged along two linked chains. He used chemicals to break up the protein into shorter chains and then locate the amino acids in them. And he found out how these short chains were linked into longer ones, and eventually how the longer chains were linked to form the insulin molecule. It took him eight years to work out the structure, but once the structure was known, it was possible for chemists to manufacture insulin. So far this has been done only on a laboratory scale, but once it can be done commercially it will make the treatment of diabetes much easier. At present diabetics have to rely on insulin from animals.

This research won Sanger the Nobel Prize for Chemistry in 1958. His second Nobel Prize came in 1980 for working out the structure of one form of DNA, the chemical that genes are made of. The example he studied was the complete chromosome from a virus. It contains 5,375 chemical groups in its molecule and Sanger identified and located every one of them.

Jean-Paul Sartre (1905–80) French
Philosopher and novelist

When Sartre died it can be said that the philosophy so long associated with his name, existentialism, died also. Born in Paris, Sartre's brilliance moved him rapidly through the French educational system, and after graduating from the Sorbonne he taught in Le Havre and Paris, resigning from teaching in 1944 to found and edit the journal *Les Temps Modernes*.

Sartre put much of his early thinking into short stories, novels and plays, some of which were filmed. He was always interested in German philosophy, an influence shown clearly in his important work *Being and Nothingness* (1943). This massive tome is full of brilliant ideas, psychological insights and commentaries on other writers – as well as passages that are almost unintelligible. He was later to sum up his philosophy by the slogan 'existence precedes essence'; translated this means that what a human being makes him or herself into, what mankind in total amounts to, is not predetermined. Men and women emerge as a species unformed, uniquely able to grasp their situation and to make of themselves what they will, and hence free and jointly responsible for what they amount to.

Frederick Sanger, winner of the Nobel Prize for Chemistry in 1958 and again in 1980

Jean-Paul Sartre

This philosophy appeals to those who look for freedom and responsibility; that it should be expounded and developed in literary work as well as in philosophical prose only adds to its attraction. Sartre's philosophy is a philosophy of life, and as such appealed to ordinary people in some ways more than it did to academic philosophers.

After serving in the Resistance during the Second World War, Sartre became more and more politically active, finally declaring himself a Marxist and claiming that existentialism and Marxism were compatible. When De Gaulle (*q.v.*) returned to power in 1958 Sartre allied himself with the opposition in French politics for the rest of his life, in 1968 identifying both with the workers and with the struggles within the French left-wing.

The dignity and brilliance of Sartre's works cushioned his reputation from the loss of prestige that could have accompanied the never-ending protests of the sad and rather clownish figure he became in the last years of his life.

Artur Schnabel (1882–1951) American, ex-Austrian
Pianist and composer

Schnabel studied the piano with the famous teacher Leschetizky and general musical culture with Mandyczewski in Vienna, making his first appearance as a concert pianist at the age of eight. In 1905 he married the singer Therese Behr, and for many years combined the life of a travelling solo pianist with that of a teacher. Schnabel was in fact a distinguished teacher of the piano and for a time was attached to the High

Artur Schnabel

School for Music in Berlin, until racial intolerance (he was Jewish) drove him from Germany in 1933. He then set up a series of master classes every summer at Tremezzo on Lake Como in Italy, which was visited by pianists from all over the world. From 1939 Schnabel lived in the United States, becoming an American citizen in 1945.

Although in his younger days he played some of the nineteenth-century romantic composers, Schnabel was primarily a classical player and above all a Beethoven pianist. He was the first to record all the Beethoven sonatas for the gramophone, which he did between 1931 and 1935, and by the late 1930s he was to many people the only Beethoven pianist. There were, of course, other distinguished interpreters of Beethoven's piano music, but for an entire generation Schnabel was the high priest of Beethoven, revered for the integrity and objectivity of his performances. Schnabel was the least showy of pianists, and the least interested in the techniques of other leading pianists of his day, though his technical accomplishment was certainly equal to the demands placed upon it by the composers he served.

In odd contrast to the music Schnabel played was that which he himself composed, for he considered himself a serious composer and produced a number of compositions in the style of his contemporary Arnold Schoenberg (*q.v.*), among them a piano concerto, several sonatas and a symphony.

Arnold Schoenberg (1874–1951) American, ex-Austrian
Composer

Arnold Schoenberg is generally regarded as being the father of twentieth-century music. He learned to play several stringed instruments as a child in Vienna, and began to compose while he was working in a bank in his teens. From the age of twenty-one he made his living as a musician, first obtaining a post as chorus-master with various workers' choral societies; later, with a friend, the composer Alexander von Zemlinsky, he formed an orchestral society where their own compositions, and those of other young composers, were performed. Schoenberg's earliest compositions were strongly influenced by Brahms. His first important work, still under the shadow of both Brahms and Wagner, is *Verklärte Nacht* (*Transfigured Night*, 1899). It was at this time that he left both the Jewish faith into which he was born and the city of his birth, becoming a Protestant, marrying Zemlinsky's sister, and moving to Berlin. However, Schoenberg and his wife soon returned to Vienna, where the composer began his long and distinguished career as a teacher, his pupils including Alban Berg (*q.v.*) and Anton von

Webern who, together with Schoenberg, were to constitute the 'Second Viennese school' of musical composition.

It was in 1908 that Schoenberg wrote the first pieces in which he moved away from traditional tonality, and in the years that followed he perfected his technique of composing with twelve notes instead of the conventional eight-note tonal octave. This was the beginning of 'atonal' or, as Schoenberg preferred to call it, twelve-tone music, the most significant musical development of the twentieth century.

Schoenberg's wife died in 1923 and in the following year he married the sister of the violinist Rudolf Kolisch, one of his earliest and most faithful interpreters. The rise of the Nazis led him to re-embrace the Jewish faith and to emigrate to the United States, taking up residence in Hollywood and becoming Professor of Music at the University of California.

Charles Schulz (b. 1922) American
Strip cartoonist

The originator of the world's most successful comic strip began life as the son of a barber in St Paul, Minnesota. Charles Schulz, who to this day retains the childhood nickname 'Sparky' from a horse in a comic strip, decided to become a full-time cartoonist after military service in the Second World War and a spell as a commercial artist. In 1950 he submitted a comic strip idea to the United Feature Syndicate in New York, based on a group of children, and in October of that year it was tentatively tried out in a number of newspapers. In spite of its title, *Peanuts*, which Schulz disliked, it quickly became popular, and eventually was to appear in more than 1,700 newspapers and magazines throughout the world. The spin-offs from the strip have included Broadway musicals, feature films, a long-running series on television, many best-selling books which have been translated into other languages, pop song hits, an ice extravaganza, and merchandise ranging from dolls to bottle openers.

The *Peanuts* empire has made Schulz one of the richest men in America. The appeal and the strength of the strip lies in its universal philosophy of children seeking life's answers. The central child character, Charlie Brown, is a sort of Everyman figure, except that he is a born loser whose perpetual efforts inevitably fail. He is, however, possessed of superhuman staying power and will always get up and try again.

Composer Arnold Schoenberg

Charles Schulz and Peanuts

Dr Albert Schweitzer

yellow bird, Woodstock, is touching evidence of the innocence which lurks beneath Snoopy's sophisticated hide. Schulz is a strongly-committed Christian, and does not hesitate to use the strip to impart a message of brotherhood to his enormous public. That he can manage to do so without becoming unbearingly didactic is a measure of the skill with which he conducts the strip. The visual style is extremely simple – no fancy angles, everything viewed four-square and on the same level as the little people and animals forming the subject matter. 'I'm probably the only cartoonist in America', he says, 'who even draws grass from the side view.'

Albert Schweitzer (1875–1965) German
Theologian, missionary and musician

Schweitzer's birthplace was Kaysersberg near Strasbourg in Alsace, now in France. The son of a Lutheran minister, he studied philosophy and theology at Strasbourg University and in 1902 became Principal of the St Thomas Theological College, Strasbourg. A highly accomplished organist and an expert on organ-building, he wrote a classic biography of Johann Sebastian Bach (1905). In 1906 he published *The Quest of the Historical Jesus*, which emphasized the importance in Jesus's teaching of the belief that the world would soon come to an end. The book influenced the later rise of 'crisis theology' in reaction to the horrors of the First World War and its aftermath, when mankind seemed to be living in a time of troubles comparable to that expected by the Gospel writers.

Deciding to give up his glittering career in Europe, Schweitzer trained in medicine and surgery at Strasbourg University, while his brilliant wife, Hélène Bresslow, trained as a nurse. In 1913 they went to Lambaréné in French Equatorial Africa (now Gabon). Starting with a chicken coop as a consulting room, they and their African helpers built a hospital and medical centre in the jungle on the banks of the Ogowe River. Schweitzer designed all the buildings himself.

During the First World War Schweitzer was held in France as a prisoner of war and wrote his *Philosophy of Civilization* (1923), in which he maintained that civilization would not survive without 'reverence for life', a principle he applied to all living things. In 1924 he returned to Lambaréné and rebuilt the abandoned hospital. He later added a leper colony and ruled as a benevolent autocrat over a team of European doctors and nurses and African workers. The hospital at Lambaréné became world famous as an inspiring example of practical Christianity in action. Schweitzer won the Nobel Prize for Peace in 1952 and in 1955 was awarded the Order of Merit. His autobiographical books include *Out of My Life and Thought* (1939).

His friends are all child embodiments of adult weaknesses: the aggressive, domineering Lucy; the sensitive Beethoven fanatic, Schroeder; the outspoken Peppermint Patty; the soft-bellied Linus, lost without his security blanket; the sweetly dim Sally, Charlie's sister, and so on. But the character who dominates the strip is not human at all but a dumb animal, the black and white beagle, Snoopy, who together with Mickey Mouse and Donald Duck must count as one of the greatest anthropomorphic creations of the twentieth century. Snoopy doesn't talk, but his thoughts are more eloquent than anyone else's. He is a daydreamer and a romantic, the possessor of several alter egos, the most famous of which is the celebrated First World War aviator locked in endless struggle with the dreaded Red Baron. His devotion to a tiny,

Andrés Segovia (b. 1893) Spanish
Guitarist

Born in Linares, a small Andalusian village, Segovia was first taught to play the guitar when he was six by a local flamenco guitarist. As a result, when Segovia appeared in public for the first time at the age of sixteen, it was to play flamenco music. However, he quickly became dissatisfied with such music and the technique which it required, and began to invent his own guitar technique. At the same time Segovia began to acquaint himself with composers of the past who had written for the guitar, for instance the early nineteenth-century Fernando Sor, called in his day the 'Beethoven of the guitar'.

Segovia was soon in demand for concerts not only in Spain but also abroad, and he embarked upon the life of a travelling soloist, visiting virtually every part of the world. He has continued to do so, even though he is now in his late eighties. For many years he has been accepted as a classical concert artist, winning an acceptance for the guitar as a concert instrument which formerly it had never achieved, and persuading a number of contemporary composers to write pieces for him to add to his ever-expanding repertoire. One of the most important and familiar of these works is the Guitar Concerto by Castelnuovo-Tedesco. Others are by Falla, Ponce, Roussel and Villa-Lobos. Segovia's great achievement has been not only to widen the repertoire available to the guitar but also to bring a wider audience into the concert halls and to classical music generally. Often he has done this through his own editions and arrangements of works originally written by great composers of the past for instruments other than the guitar.

During the Spanish Civil War Segovia settled in Uruguay. Later he lived in the United States, and he now divides his time between Spain and Switzerland. He has taught a number of pupils, many of whom, in their turn, have become admired concert artists and popularizers of the guitar: the best-known of them is John Williams.

Harlow Shapley (1885–1972) American
Astronomer

The history of astronomy has continuously reduced the cosmic significance of our Earth in particular and of the solar system in general, and we now know that there are innumerable other universes – galaxies really – in space, all much like our Sun and the stars of the Milky Way. Harlow Shapley's contribution to astronomy was to show that the Sun, far from being at the centre of the universe, is not even at the centre of our own galaxy.

Harlow Shapley was born in Nashville, Missouri, on 2 November 1885. He graduated

from the University of Missouri in 1910 and then went to Princeton. From 1914 to 1921 he worked at the Mount Wilson Observatory, using the giant 100-inch telescope, and from there he went as director to the Harvard Observatory.

At Mount Wilson, Shapley's particular study was of groups of stars known as globular clusters. About a hundred of these were known at the time, and each is an enormous, densely packed spherical accumulation of stars. There may be more than a million stars in one cluster. These strange objects, or rather collections of objects, are not evenly scattered throughout the sky around us; most of them are near, or within, the constellation Sagittarius. Shapley set out to measure their distances (they contain stars called Cepheid Variables whose distance can be calculated) and found that the stars appeared to be grouped in a spherical pattern around a point in the Sagittarius constellation.

It is logical, therefore, that this central point is also the centre of our galaxy, a surprising revelation because astronomers previously had assumed that the Sun was at or near its centre. Shapley showed that the error had arisen because dark clouds in the Milky Way hid some bright stars and gave us a false impression of our importance. The Earth, it turned out, was one planet of a minor star, far from the centre of the only galaxy then known, though we now know that it is by no means the only galaxy in the universe.

George Bernard Shaw (1856–1950) Irish
Playwright, novelist and philosopher

Shaw's birthplace was Dublin, where he was raised among shabby-genteel Irish Protestants, a 'downstart son', as he later described himself. In his teens he worked as an office clerk, and in 1876 he left for London, where his mother was living in exile from her marriage. For several years he attempted without success to establish himself as a writer, producing five novels between 1879 and 1883. Concurrently, he became a convert to socialism, and a powerful self-taught public speaker; by the 1890s he was a brilliant essayist and critic, on painting, on music, and finally, from 1895 to 1898, on the London theatre in the pages of *The Saturday Review*. He had begun writing plays in the 1880s, and despite problems with censorship, gradually succeeded in establishing himself as a dramatist, attacking slum landlordism in *Widowers' Houses*, the wages of sin in *Mrs Warren's Profession*, military posturing in *Arms and the Man*, and the anomalies of Anglo-Irish politics in *John Bull's Other Island*. By the First World War he was acknowledged a master of humorous paradox which masked a deeply religious passion for mankind, whose future he saw imperilled by its own stupidity and failure to meet changing reality, in which regard he was at one with his fellow socialist and writer, H.G. Wells (*q.v.*).

Shaw became a world celebrity, known for his vegetarianism, his anti-imperialism, and his preaching of the cause of 'creative evolution', by which a species might change by willing itself to change. His greatest plays include *Heartbreak House* (1917), an allegorical study of the dispersal of British power, and a chronicle play, *Saint Joan* (1923). He was awarded the Nobel Prize for Literature in 1925, after which he continued writing and pronouncing on public issues until his death on 2 November 1950. A literary stylist of genius, the humorous lightness of his style misled his contemporaries into taking him for an intellectual clown, but the passing of time has disclosed the fervour of his beliefs, which are so wittily expressed that even those who remain opposed to them cannot fail to be stimulated and diverted by them.

Charles Sherrington (1857–1952) British
Physiologist

Charles Sherrington was born in London on 27 November 1857, qualified as a doctor at Cambridge and then travelled abroad to extend his studies. He became a lecturer in physiology at St Thomas's Hospital, London, and later Professor of Physiology at Liverpool University. In 1913 he was appointed Professor of Physiology at Oxford.

He was particularly interested in mapping the

FAR LEFT *Sir Charles Sherrington, 1927: a portrait by G. Eves*

LEFT *William Shockley, inventor of the transistor*

nerves in the brain and body and in demonstrating how they work, and he showed that particular parts of the brain control particular muscles. A message sent along a set of 'motor' nerves makes a muscle act. Before Sherrington's research, however, it was thought that the nerves connected to muscles were there only to tell the muscles to act; he showed that at least a third of these nerves actually carried a signal away from the muscle, so that the brain knew how much the muscle had contracted and what position the limb, say, had reached. This is the secret of our delicate control of our movements.

Sherrington also studied reflex actions. If a finger is pricked we draw it away automatically; but Sherrington showed that reflexes have a much wider function than that. We can stand upright, for example, because a constant stream of messages is being relayed from the muscles to the brain, informing the brain of the position of the limbs and the tension of the muscles, and automatically producing the adjustments to keep us upright. We don't have to think about it, though we cannot normally stand upright while we are asleep. (Birds and some animals, on the other hand, have a reflex system that enables them to sleep standing up.)

Sherrington is most famous for his research into the nervous system, but he was also interested in medicine and he studied the prevention and cure of cholera, diphtheria and tetanus. He was awarded a Nobel Prize for Medicine in 1937.

William Shockley (b. 1910) American, ex-British
Inventor

We are used to the idea of radios that can be put into a pocket, but radios in the 1940s would barely go into a suitcase. Similarly, the first computer occupied an entire office, but now the same capacity can be fitted into a desk-top machine – soon into a hand-held one. The device that made this miniaturization possible is the transistor, invented by William Shockley in 1948, for which he and his two colleagues were awarded the 1956 Nobel Prize for Physics.

William Shockley was born in London on 15 February 1910, and gained a degree from the California Institute of Technology and a research degree from the Massachusetts Institute of Technology before joining the Bell Telephone Company. His particular research project was to find a replacement for the radio valve. Radio waves arrive at a radio receiver as tiny alternating currents – the current flows first one way and then the other, changing direction very rapidly. The radio receiver must contain devices to 'rectify' the current to make it flow in one direction only. Early rectifying devices were valves. The current must also be amplified to be powerful enough to drive a loudspeaker, and this was done in early radios by another kind of valve.

Shockley's great invention, the transistor, came to replace the valve. By joining a piece of silicon doped with one impurity to a piece doped with another (the impurities actually conduct the electricity), Shockley found that he could amplify currents with a transistor. The first transistors were small, reliable, and very economical in electricity, but they are now much smaller still. The electrical connections can be diffused on to a tiny piece of silicon, now called a chip. The impurities form microscopic individual units on the chip, and it is now possible for tens of thousands of transistors to be put on to a square chip with quarter-inch sides.

Dmitri Shostakovich (1906–75) Russian Composer

Shostakovich is one of the twentieth century's most popular and distinguished composers. He was born in Leningrad (then St Petersburg) into a musical family, began to study the piano when he was nine, and wrote his first compositions a year or so later. He studied both piano and composition at the St Petersburg Conservatorium, graduating at the age of seventeen. He was by then a brilliant pianist and at first thought of earning a living as a performer, but after a few years decided to concentrate on composing. His

RIGHT *Dmitri Shostakovich*

FAR RIGHT *Finnish composer Jean Sibelius at the age of twenty-nine, painted by A. Gallén-Kalella*

First Symphony was performed in Leningrad in 1926 when Shostakovich was still in his twentieth year. This work revealed the voice of a new composer of originality and stature, and it was soon being performed abroad and taken up by conductors such as Stokowski and Toscanini (*q.v.*).

Many of Shostakovich's compositions of the 1920s and early 1930s were influenced not only by the great symphonists of the past, notably Mahler, but also by the modern movement in Paris and Vienna, and this was to bring him into conflict with Soviet officialdom. His opera *Lady Macbeth of Mtsensk* (1934), at first popular, was

later attacked in the press and its composer accused of adopting the worst aspects of decadent western composers. Shostakovich weathered this and other storms by appearing to submit to official pressure. The score of his Fifth Symphony (1937) is headed with the words 'A Soviet artist's response to just criticism'. Nevertheless, he followed his own musical paths. His Seventh Symphony (the 'Leningrad' 1941), composed in the Second World War, became almost a national hymn of defiance.

After the war Shostakovich found himself in difficulties again with the Composers' Union. He reacted by producing work with mass appeal while continuing to compose string quartets, symphonies and piano music which satisfied his musical conscience. He composed fifteen symphonies in all, and has proved a worthy successor to Tchaikovsky and Mahler.

Jean Sibelius (1865–1957) Finnish Composer

Jean Sibelius is one of the most important of the later romantic composers (astonishingly he lived on into the second half of this century) and the only Finnish composer of international renown. His earliest compositions, the first of which was

written when he was ten, were in the genre of chamber music, jointly influenced by the Viennese classics and by Tchaikovsky. As a teenager Sibelius thought of himself primarily as a violinist, and later, when he was twenty-six, he actually auditioned for the Vienna Philharmonic Orchestra. At Helsinki University he studied law, but soon turned to music and after graduating made his way first to Berlin and then to Vienna, where he became a pupil of the Hungarian composer Carl Goldmark. It was after his return to Finland that he produced his first major orchestral composition, a huge symphony in five movements, influenced by Mahler, whose performance in 1892 immediately established Sibelius as Finland's leading composer.

During the 1890s he became increasingly identified with the Finnish nationalist movement that aimed to remove the country from the control of Tsarist Russia. His tone poems extolling the beauty of his native land, works such as *En Saga*, *Finlandia* and the *Lemminkäinen Suite*, consolidated his reputation as the voice of his country. But it was in the next phase of his development, when he left nationalism behind and embarked upon his first five symphonies and a violin concerto, that Sibelius's international fame developed. Much of his music has a haunting beauty and a sadness which was intensified to the point of desolation in his later symphonic and orchestral works, no doubt reflecting his own increasing melancholy after an illness in 1908.

Apart from some light music, the final two symphonies and the symphonic poem *Tapiola*, Sibelius wrote little of consequence after 1918. He slowly grew into the role of an elder statesman of music, living quietly in Finland until his death in his ninety-second year.

Frank Sinatra (b. 1917) American
Singer and actor

Francis Albert Sinatra was born in New Jersey on 12 December 1917. After winning a talent contest in 1933, his rise through the professional ranks was at first slow but then freakishly fast. His first major engagement was with the Harry James Orchestra in 1939. From 1940–2 he worked in the Tommy Dorsey Orchestra, after which he turned solo to become one of the world's most famous men, idolized by millions, a vocalist of such smoothness that he caused hysteria among the young. At the same time he became a Hollywood star, graduating from the comic unsophisticate of *Higher and Higher* (1943) to the virtuoso of the 1950s, in which decade, after recovering from a dip in his professional fortunes by winning an Academy Award for his role in *From Here to Eternity*, he rose to an eminence unprecedented in this century by any popular entertainer since Charlie Chaplin (*q.v.*). After semi-retirement in the 1960s, he resumed his concert career, travelling all over the world and singing his repertoire in bold defiance of his advancing years.

Sinatra's public image has been bedevilled by a combination of circumstances to which he has not always reacted with tact. Open warfare between him and the world's press has often been the press's fault; constant accusations of his criminal connections have been investigated by Government commissions without any definite conclusions being published, but in recent years even more damaging than any of these accusations has been his habit of travelling with an entourage of bodyguards who have had little

Frank Sinatra, 1965

diplomatic training.

Whatever the storms that have threatened his life away from the microphone, Sinatra has without any question established himself as the greatest interpreter of popular song of this century, by virtue of a natural voice, a sense of timing picked up from the jazz musicians of his early touring days, certain whimsicalities in his vowel sounds, and an ability to transform a lyric into a dramatic performance.

Jan Christiaan Smuts (1870–1950) South African

Military and political leader

Smuts was to wield a significant influence on the world stage for more than five decades, though he was unable to inspire unity among his own people.

Cambridge University fired his admiration for British institutions, but the Jameson Raid on the South African Republic doused it. When the Anglo-Boer War broke out in 1899, Smuts, though frail physically and without military training, became a general and excelled in daring commando raids deep behind enemy lines. He accepted peace at Vereeniging, fearing what he believed to be the only alternative – destruction of the Afrikaner nation.

Embittered by the harsh peace terms, he abandoned politics, but in 1906 his belief that Britain would ultimately prove generous was vindicated when the Liberal Government 'gave us back our country'. The Union of South Africa was the result, with Smuts holding three portfolios in the first Union Cabinet and striving for conciliation between English- and Afrikaans-speaking South Africans.

On the outbreak of the First World War, Smuts sided with Britain and attacked the German colonies in Africa. But by crushing a rebellion against this policy in South Africa, he aroused the anger of many Afrikaners, a schismatic event which dogged his political career for the rest of his life.

Smuts entered a wider field when he came to the Imperial Conference in 1917. His brilliant intellect was immediately recognized; he appreciated the new scope. Lloyd George made him a member of the War Cabinet, in which capacity he settled strikes in Wales, planned Middle East campaigns, and even supervised the creation of the Royal Air Force.

He became Prime Minister of South Africa in 1919 and, at the Versailles Peace Conference the same year, he promoted the League of Nations in a voice second only in importance to that of President Wilson, demonstrating foresight by opposing strongly the punitive treatment of Germany.

Returning to the much smaller platform of his

RIGHT General Smuts in London, October 1942

own country, he concerned himself with the ceaseless internal political struggles there. He was to admit: 'Unlike Louis Botha [under whom he served in the first Union Government], I have neither tact nor patience.' He commanded rather than consulted Cabinet colleagues.

He served a second term as Prime Minister when his United Party again won control in Parliament in 1939, on a vote to join Britain in the Second World War. He organized the guarding of the Cape sea route and sent a South African volunteer army to fight for the Allies in Ethiopia, North Africa and Italy. Smuts shared in many important decisions taken by the Allies during the war, and in 1941 became a field marshal of the British army.

In spite of misgivings about its future role, he took part in the formation of the United Nations organization after the war.

In South Africa he tried to make 'trusteeship' the main pillar of his policy towards blacks, but both blacks and the Nationalist Party Opposition (with their apartheid policy) were ranged against him. In 1948 he lost both the general election and his own seat.

Smuts turned in his final years to the solace of other abiding interests: botany and philosophy, especially the philosophy known as 'Holism' – essentially that the whole is greater than the sum of its parts, that progress in the world consists in the fusion of units into wider unities. He saw this achieved in a few world organizations, but very little in his own country.

Georg Solti (b. 1912) British,
ex-Hungarian
Conductor

Georg Solti was born in Budapest, and studied
piano, composition and conducting there with
some very distinguished teachers. His first
professional appearances were as a pianist, but
he soon turned primarily to conducting and was
engaged by the Budapest Opera. He remained
there until 1939 when the outbreak of the Second
World War forced him to take up residence in
Switzerland. After the war, on the recommendation of Bruno Walter (*q.v.*), Solti became General
Music Director of the State Opera in Munich,
and in 1952 took up a similar position in
Frankfurt. He first appeared in London at the
Royal Opera House, Covent Garden, in 1959 to
conduct Strauss's *Der Rosenkavalier*, and his
performances were so successful that he was
invited to become Musical Director of the Royal
Opera. He remained there until 1971, building
the company up to a high musical and artistic
level, and has since returned on numerous
occasions as a guest conductor.

Solti has been a prolific recording artist, one of
his most enduring achievements for the gramophone being the first complete recording of
Wagner's *Ring* with the Vienna Philharmonic
Orchestra. In 1953 he made his American debut
as conductor of the San Francisco Opera. He
subsequently became a frequent visitor to the
United States and eventually resident conductor
of the Chicago Symphony Orchestra.

One of the finest and most exciting conductors
of the operas of Wagner and of Richard Strauss,
Solti has been almost equally successful in those
Verdi operas which he has chosen to conduct,
namely *Don Carlos*, *Otello* and *Falstaff*. In 1971
he was knighted for his services to music in Great
Britain.

Alexander Solzhenitsyn (b. 1918) Swiss, ex-Russian
Novelist

Alexander Solzhenitsyn was born in Rostov,
Russia, and educated at the university there,
where he took degrees in mathematics and
physics. He joined the Soviet army in 1941, and
during the war was in command of an artillery
battery. However, this patriotism did not save
him from Stalin's (*q.v.*) prison camps and in 1945
he was arrested on charges of anti-socialist
behaviour and sentenced to eight years' imprisonment, followed by a further three years'
exile in Siberia. He was rehabilitated in 1956, but
the publication of his novel *One Day in the Life of
Ivan Denisovich* (1962), which described conditions in the prison camps, brought him into
trouble with the authorities again. For a time
Solzhenitsyn supported himself by teaching in
Ryazan and Moscow and continuing to write,
but he was expelled from the Union of Soviet
Writers in 1969 and forbidden to publish his
work either in the Soviet Union or abroad.

Solzhenitsyn produced more documentary
novels that exposed the evils in the Soviet system,
among them *The First Circle* (1968) and *Cancer
Ward* (part one, 1968; part two, 1969). In 1970 he
was awarded the Nobel Prize for Literature but
was unable to travel to Sweden to receive it, nor
was the secretary of the Swedish Academy
allowed to present the prize to the author at a
private ceremony in Moscow. When the first
instalment of *The Gulag Archipelago*, Solzhenitsyn's indictment of the Stalinist murders,

ABOVE LEFT *Georg Solti*

BELOW *Alexander Solzhenitsyn,
outspoken critic of Soviet
repression in such novels as* The
Gulag Archipelago *and* Cancer
Ward

was published in Paris in 1973, it was fiercely denounced by the Soviet authorities as 'unfounded slander' and its author was expelled from the Soviet Union in February the following year.

The Gulag Archipelago aroused enormous interest in the western world, selling more than half a million copies in Great Britain alone during 1974. Solzhenitsyn took up residence in Switzerland, and has continued to act as a stern critic of the Soviet Government in lectures and essays. In 1975 he published his autobiography, *A Calf Banged its Head against an Oak*.

Stephen Sondheim

Stephen Sondheim (b. 1930) American Composer and lyricist

Sondheim, the leading American theatrical composer and lyricist of the 1960s and 1970s, was taught his musical craft by the famous lyricist Oscar Hammerstein. After his parents were divorced Sondheim was all but adopted by the Hammersteins and went to live near them in Bucks County, Pennsylvania. After graduating in music he won a two-year scholarship to study with the composer Milton Babbitt, and his first real success in the theatre came in 1957 with the lyrics he wrote for *West Side Story* (music by Leonard Bernstein).

Though keen not to be known solely as a lyricist, Sondheim also worked in that capacity on *Gypsy* (1959, music by Jule Styne), last and among the best of the old-style Broadway musicals about backstage life. But it was with *A Funny Thing Happened On The Way To The Forum* in 1962 that Sondheim first came into his own as composer and lyricist and began to indicate the changes he was hoping to make in the shape of the conventional Broadway musical. Since then, no two shows of his have been alike; nor have they resembled in any way the more

RIGHT *Dr Spock*

traditional musicals of Rodgers and Hammerstein, though Sondheim did agree, after Hammerstein's death, to partner Rodgers in an unsuccessful throwback to those earlier shows, *Do I Hear A Waltz?* (1965).

The major Sondheim shows since *Forum* have been *Anyone Can Whistle* (1964), *Company* (1970), *Follies* (1971), *A Little Night Music* (1972), *Pacific Overtures* (1976) and *Sweeney Todd* (1979). On all of these he has been both composer and lyricist, and on almost all Hal Prince has been producer and director, thereby establishing a partnership between creator and stager which has been as important and influential as any of the more usual partnerships of composer and lyricist.

Though Sondheim has only ever had one song in the international hit parades ('Send in the Clowns' from *A Little Night Music*), and though his shows have by no means all proved profitable during their initial Broadway runs, in the long term there seems little doubt that he and Prince will be seen to have been the two men who dragged the stage musical, often with difficulty, into the second half of the twentieth century.

Benjamin Spock (b. 1903) American Paediatrician

Born in New Haven, Connecticut, and educated at Yale and Columbia Universities, Spock took his medical degree in 1929. A paediatrician in New York for many years, he served in the United States navy as a psychiatrist during the

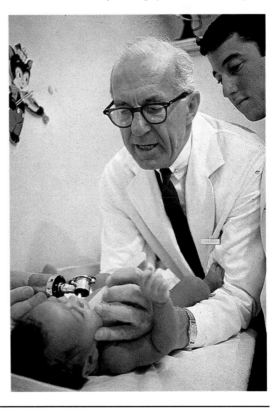

Second World War. He was Professor of Child Development at Pittsburgh University from 1951 to 1955 and at Western Reserve University in Cleveland, Ohio, from 1955 until his retirement in 1967. He had emerged as a leader of the opposition to American involvement in the Vietnam War and had taken part in many protest marches and demonstrations. In a trial which made headlines in 1968 he was found guilty of encouraging young men to resist being drafted into the armed forces, but the conviction was overturned on appeal the following year. In 1972 he was nominated as the People's Party's candidate for president.

Dr Spock's principal contribution to the twentieth century, however, has been as an important influence on the upbringing of children, especially middle-class children, in America and the rest of the English-speaking world since the Second World War. His first and best-known book, *Baby and Child Care* (1946), is a practical handbook, based on experience, broad-minded common sense and a dislike of narrow, dogmatic psychological systems. It has been frequently reprinted and revised, and has sold millions of copies in English and other languages. His other books include *Dr Spock Talks with Mothers* (1961) and *Problems of Parents* (1963).

Although he reacted at first against the old-fashioned principle of a strict upbringing for children, he later came to feel that too many parents had swung too far in the other direction and brought up their families in a permissive, undisciplined way which failed to train the young for the obligations and responsibilities of adult life.

Joseph Vissarionovich Stalin
(1879–1952) Russian
Dictator

Mediocre in intellectual ability, Stalin had cunning, ruthlessness, and a lust for absolute power that some have seen as madness. In 1922 he took over the infant Soviet Union from the brilliant Lenin (*q.v.*), who had suffered a series of strokes, and, using the general secretaryship of the Communist Party as his power base, soon became a ruler more feared and more absolute than any Tsar.

Born in Georgia of a peasant family, Stalin was at first trained as a priest. However, he was expelled from the seminary for revolutionary activity, and by 1905 he was rising within the Bolshevik Party. To raise funds, he organized bank raids in Georgia. At this time Stalin suffered the revolutionary's usual round of imprisonment and exile. With the 1917 Revolution that overthrew the Tsar, he became Commissar (the equivalent of Minister) for Nationalities, where he was responsible for the

non-Russians within what was to become the Soviet Union. Stalin's main policy was to suppress those nationalities he was supposed to protect.

Unlike other cleverer and more articulate Bolsheviks, Stalin seemed quiet and sensible, puffing on his pipe. Never did stiller waters run so treacherously and dangerously deep. Once in charge of the party, his grip tightened. Lenin in a last testament had warned of the danger of Stalin, but his prophetic words were suppressed. In 1926 Stalin's first purge saw many Old Bolsheviks, who might contend with Stalin for the leadership, expelled from office, including Leon Trotsky. Then, in 1935, began the first of the blood-lettings: Stalin arranged the murder of Kirov, the city boss of Leningrad, and, by means of extorted confessions, Old Bolsheviks were implicated. The same method was used systematically to destroy all the first-rank leadership from the days of the Revolution, the army generals, and millions of other party members and ordinary Russians and communists living in the Soviet Union. Trotsky himself was murdered by a Russian agent in Mexico in 1940. Stalin now had all possible opposition crushed and had

Joseph Vissarionovich Djugashvili, who became a lethal and fanatical tyrant known to the world as Stalin – 'man of steel'

achieved the absolute power he wanted. He demanded obedience, and more: love and worship – what the Russians were later to denounce as the 'cult of the personality'.

He made a peace pact with Hitler (*q.v.*) in 1939, and they divided Poland between them. Stalin was stunned when Hitler broke the pact and invaded Russia. He did, however, fight back tenaciously, and invoked the great national patriotism of the Russian people, who heroically repelled the invaders.

As the Second World War ended, Stalin was laying plans for the occupation and control of eastern Europe, which he mostly accomplished. He was about to launch another great purge on the Russian people when he died. At first buried alongside Lenin in a mausoleum in Red Square, Moscow, he was removed in 1961 and buried by the walls of the Kremlin.

Edward Steichen (1879–1973) American
Photographer

Steichen began his professional life as a lithographic artist in Milwaukee, Wisconsin, and exhibited his photographs for the first time in 1899. Two years later he held his first one-man show in Paris, where the broad range of his work attracted international attention. He decided to settle in Paris and gained the friendship of the sculptor Rodin, who allowed the youthful American to make a series of pictures of him and his sculptures. They were published in the influential magazine *Camera Work* and Steichen was hailed as the most promising member of the

An Edward Steichen fashion photograph of 1907

Photo-Secessionist movement, whose aim was to equate photography in importance with fine art. He quickly became renowned as a portrait photographer, and major figures of the day were happy to sit for him.

Steichen was a remarkably gifted photographer who was able to master many different branches of his art, from portraiture to reportage, from nature study to high fashion. He served in both the First and Second World Wars, pioneering photographic aerial reconnaissance in the First. Until then he had pursued a joint career as a painter, but after 1920 he concentrated purely on photography, applying himself to the task of understanding all the major processes and setting them to use. He was particularly concerned with raising the standard of magazine illustration, and during the 1920s worked for Condé Nast, not merely photographing *Vogue* fashion models but making portraits of the most eminent statesmen, actors, writers, artists and musicians of his time. He became the first curator of photography at the Museum of Modern Art in New York and established it as the pre-eminent centre in the United States for the cause of photography. During his curatorship he was responsible for more than forty exhibitions, of which the most important, to be shown throughout the world for several years, was a world-wide anthology of pictures representing 273 photographs from sixty-eight countries linked under the title *The Family of Man*. It has never been equalled in size or scope.

Steichen was more than a great photographer. He was a proponent, with Stieglitz (*q.v.*), for the cause of photography in general and American photography in particular. That the United States has produced so many of the greatest photographers is due to these two men conditioning the public into expecting and receiving the best quality.

John Steinbeck (1902–68) American
Novelist

John Steinbeck was born in Salinas, California, the state that was to figure prominently in his novels, and was educated at Stanford University. He worked at a variety of unskilled jobs before embarking upon a literary career, and his first published book, *Cup of Gold* (1929), was not a work of fiction but a biography of the buccaneer Sir Henry Morgan. Steinbeck's working-class sympathies led him to write about the poorer classes of the United States, especially the itinerant farm labourers of California. *Pastures of Heaven* (1932) is a collection of short stories set in a farming community, but it was with a novel, *Tortilla Flat* (1935), that Steinbeck's growing literary reputation was backed up by a popular success. *Tortilla Flat* examines with sympathy the plight of a group of simple labourers

Alfred Stieglitz (1864–1946) American
Photographer

Stieglitz fervently believed in photography as an art form at a time when such a view was unfashionable, but he also supported the simplest of approaches to the medium, preferring to use available light whenever possible, with the lens stopped down to provide rich detail. One of his most famous photographs, and his personal favourite, was *The Steerage*, a shot made during an Atlantic voyage in 1907, in which he leaned over the rail from the first class deck and photographed the untidy melée below, a gangplank diagonally bisecting the resulting image.

Stieglitz was a photographer for sixty years, usually working with simple equipment. There is an extraordinary directness about his work and a powerful aesthetic sense. He had begun as an engineering student in Berlin, and during that time won a contest in the London magazine *Amateur Photographer*, his first recognition. On

FAR LEFT *John Steinbeck*

BELOW The Steerage, *1907: an atmospheric and beautifully structured photograph by Alfred Stieglitz*

confronted with the complexities of modern civilization. Even more successful was *Of Mice and Men* (1937), a tragic story of two migrant workers in California, one of them a simpleton of tremendous strength who is looked after and protected by his more intelligent friend. Dramatized for the stage in the year of its publication and filmed in 1939, *Of Mice and Men* proved highly popular in these two media as well, and in 1970 it was made into an opera by the American composer Carlisle Floyd.

Steinbeck's masterpiece is generally agreed to be *The Grapes of Wrath* (1939), one of the finest examples of realistic working-class fiction to emerge from the years of the Depression, a moving account of the hardships of a family forced from their home in the Oklahoma dustbowl who drive to California in search of work. It won its author the Pulitzer Prize, the major American annual literary award.

In *The Moon is Down* (1942) Steinbeck moved away from the area he knew best to write of life in a European country occupied by the Nazis. His next three books were reportage, based on his work as a war correspondent, and it was not until *Cannery Row* (1954) that he returned to fiction and the workers of southern California. *Travels with Charley* (1962) is a highly engaging account of a trip across the United States with an elderly poodle, but the real Steinbeck is to be found in his compassionate, powerful if occasionally sentimental novels that celebrate the simple life simply lived.

returning to the United States he soon became involved in photography, and edited the equivalent American magazine. He set out to show that actuality photographs could have artistic quality, and some of his early work, such as a Harlem horse-drawn streetcar in a snowstorm, is remarkable in the context of the period.

Stieglitz was instrumental in founding the Photo-Secessionists, a select group of American photographers whose aim was to advance the cause of pictorial photography and whose first exhibition was held in New York in 1902. They published an influential journal, *Camera Work*, with Stieglitz as editor, which attempted to reproduce the Photo-Secessionists' pictures with the best printing methods available, and demonstrate to the world that the new medium could be considered a fine art. Stieglitz, usually using a 4 × 5 inch Graflex, spent many patient hours photographing clouds, raindrops and sunlight as well as carefully composed cityscapes, mostly of his beloved New York. In his declining years he merely photographed the view from his window, either in Manhattan or the old family home in the country. He still ran a gallery which exhibited photographs and paintings, and was responsible in his lifetime for encouraging many of America's most successful artists.

Karlheinz Stockhausen (b. 1928)
German
Composer

Stockhausen, a pioneer of electronic music, is the most prominent German composer of the post-war years. He was born in Cologne, where, from 1946, he spent three years at the High School for Music, and later made his way to Paris for lessons in composition with the composers Milhaud and Messiaen. His earliest compositions are much influenced by Messiaen, but Stockhausen soon became greatly intrigued with the work of Pierre Schaeffer, the inventor of *musique concrète*. The raw material of *musique concrète* is sound produced not by instruments or voices but by a variety of noises, which can be modified by using tape recordings; from the use of tape recordings during performances it is a short step to electronic music. Stockhausen undertook a study of these techniques in which virtually anything goes, and was soon employing them in composition. In 1953 he helped to found the electronic studio of West German Radio in Cologne, becoming its artistic director in 1962.

Stockhausen not only initiated the use of electronics in live performances but also introduced related techniques into music for conventional instruments, most notably in his *Gruppen* (1957) for three orchestras. He also experimented with aleatoric or chance techniques. These make improvisation on the part of the performer an increasingly important element in Stockhausen's music. In *Aus den sieben Tagen* (1968) this process of improvisation from Stockhausen's basic score had developed to such an extent that the score itself consisted only of short verbal texts, leaving the performer to invent the music himself.

Though many of Stockhausen's more recent works have moved still further away from conventional concepts of music, he has continued to produce substantial scores, often with texts influenced by eastern religions. Among such works are *Stimmung* (1957) and *Mantra* (1970).

A musical score by Karlheinz Stockhausen, as unconventional as the sounds it represents; INSET *the composer*

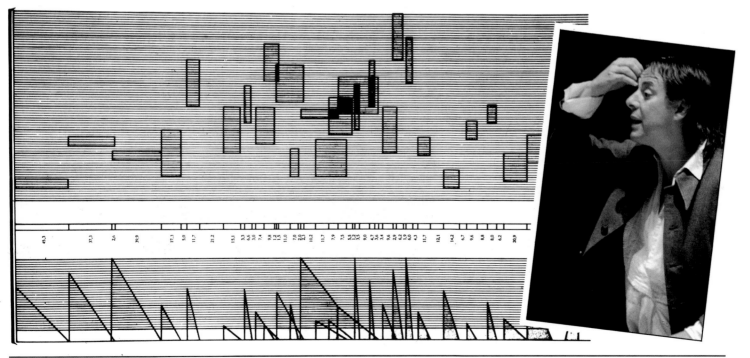

Marie Stopes (1880–1958) British
Pioneer of birth control

An advocate of birth control and sexual fulfilment, Marie Stopes did an enormous amount to free women from sexual ignorance and continual childbearing. She graduated in botany and geology at University College, London, in 1903, and took a doctorate in botany at the University of Munich the following year – the youngest Doctor of Science in Britain. She became the first female science lecturer at Manchester University, a specialist on fossil plants and coalmining, subjects she continued to study throughout her life. She already had a considerable academic reputation when the failure of her first marriage brought her attention to matrimonial and sexual problems.

In the preface to her book *Married Love*, published in 1918, she wrote: 'In my own marriage I paid such a terrible price for sex-ignorance that I feel knowledge gained at such a cost should be placed at the service of humanity.' Her marriage had been annulled in 1916, and two years later, a virgin of thirty-seven, she married the aircraft pioneer Humphrey Verdon Roe. *Wise Parenthood*, also published in 1918, put forward the idea of contraception – by no means respectable in itself, even into the 1920s – relying not on the 'safe period' but on the cervical cap. She wrote: 'I advocate the restrained and sacramental rhythmic performance of the marriage rite of physical union ... as an act of supreme value in itself, separate and distinct from its value as a basis for the procreation of children.'

In 1921 Marie Stopes founded Britain's first birth control clinic, and completed her comprehensive book on contraception in 1923. Despite vociferous opposition, she nevertheless laid the foundations for the Church and society gradually to change their attitude to birth control. She helped to give women control over their own bodies, and like the later liberationists urged that women's upbringing should not repress their instinctive delight in sex.

LEFT *Dr Marie Stopes, 1953*

Richard Strauss (1864–1949) German
Composer

Richard Strauss was the last of the great German romantic composers. The son of a horn player, he was musically precocious, beginning his study of the piano at the age of four and writing his first composition at six. At the University of Munich, his home town, he studied philosophy and aesthetics, but by the time of his graduation in 1883 he had already composed a large number of works, among them two of his most famous songs, much favoured by concert artists today: 'Zueignung' ('Dedication') and 'Allerseelen' ('All Souls' Day'). Soon afterwards he began a career as conductor, and composed the first of his tone poems for orchestra, *Aus Italien* (*From Italy*, 1886). As conductor, Strauss took up engagements in Munich and Weimar before being appointed conductor of the Court Opera and Orchestra in Berlin. Later he became General Music Director in Berlin, a post he held until 1924.

Though he continued for a time to write romantic tone poems for orchestra, such as *Don Juan* (1889) and *Tod und Verklärung* (*Death and Transfiguration*, 1890), Strauss eventually realized that his real career was as a composer of opera. Undeterred by the fact that his first opera,

Richard Strauss's Der Rosenkavalier: *a scene from Visconti's production at the Royal Opera House, Covent Garden, 1966*

Strauss elected to stay in Germany during the Nazi period, though his attitude to the regime remained ambivalent. His final opera, *Capriccio* (1942), provides a fitting elegiac close to his work for the stage, and his *Four Last Songs*, written in the last year of his life, are among his most beautiful tributes to the soprano voice.

Igor Stravinsky (1882–1971) American, ex-Russian
Composer

Igor Stravinsky, born in Oranienbaum on the Gulf of Finland, was one of the most important composers of this century. His father was a leading singer with the Imperial Opera in St Petersburg, and Stravinsky was taught piano and composition while still a child. At St Petersburg University, he dutifully read law to comply with the wishes of his parents, but consulted the composer and teacher Rimsky-Korsakov for musical guidance; he was strongly advised to continue his musical studies and Rimsky-Korsakov himself undertook to teach the young composer for some years.

Stravinsky's music came to the attention of the impresario Sergei Diaghilev (*q.v.*), who commissioned from him the music for a ballet, *The Firebird*, which was a huge success during the Russian season of opera and ballet in Paris in 1910, immediately establishing Stravinsky as a composer of international stature. For some years he continued to compose ballet music for Diaghilev: *Petrouchka* (1911) was followed in 1913 by *The Rite of Spring* which provoked a riot in the theatre when it was first performed because of the uncompromising harshness and violence of the music. But it was with this work that Stravinsky broke away from his Russian past and virtually invented modernism in music. He also began to move away from the world of ballet, though he never completely lost touch with it.

Stravinsky and his family lived in Switzerland from 1913 to 1920, and in France from 1920 to 1939. His neo-classical masterpieces *Oedipus Rex* (1927) and the *Symphony of Psalms* (1930) were completed during this French period. At the outbreak of the Second World War in 1939 Stravinsky emigrated to the United States, settling in Hollywood and becoming an American citizen. The major works of his American years include the Symphony in C (1940), Symphony in Three Movements (1945) and, in 1951, the opera *The Rake's Progress*, whose libretto was written by W.H. Auden (*q.v.*) and Chester Kallman. He continued to compose in his later years, his compositions becoming shorter and shorter until some lasted no more than a minute or so.

Sometimes enigmatic, often harsh in its

TOP *Igor Stravinsky;* INSET *Picasso's design for the cover of Stravinsky's* Ragtime, *1918*

Guntram, was not a success when it was first performed at Weimar in 1894, and was disastrously received in his home city of Munich, he persevered until his third opera, *Salome*, based on Oscar Wilde's play, caused a furore in Dresden in 1905. Though the more conservative minded were scandalized both by the subject matter and by Strauss's score, *Salome* made him an international celebrity. A long line of operas followed, many of which are a central part of any opera company's repertory today. Among them are *Elektra* (1909), *Der Rosenkavalier* (1911), *Die Frau ohne Schatten* (*The Woman without a Shadow*, 1919) and *Arabella* (1933), all with libretti by the Austrian poet Hugo von Hofmannsthal. Strauss's genius as a composer lay in areas which had been largely ignored for half a century: while contemporaries in almost every field were seeking uncluttered realism, Strauss's search was for beauty, for lyrical poetry and mellifluous textures. If this has led to his being called anachronistic, it has also made his music enormously popular.

dissonance and unorthodox rhythms, Stravinsky's music, springing from an immense creative energy, has an excitement, vitality and colour that have made it universally popular and accessible.

Joan Sutherland (b. 1926) Australian
Opera singer

Joan Sutherland received her first singing lessons from her mother, herself an excellent amateur singer. When she left school in Sydney she supported herself by working as a typist while studying not only singing but also speech and movement. In Australia at the end of the Second World War there were no professional opera companies, but there were nationwide singing-competitions which Joan Sutherland proceeded to enter and to win. With the prize money she was able to make her way to London where she continued her studies at the Royal College of Music. In due course she auditioned for the Royal Opera at Covent Garden and became a member of the company, singing a number of small roles and understudying leading dramatic sopranos. Her first leading role was Amelia in Verdi's *Un Ballo in Maschera*, and this was followed by Agatha in Weber's *Der Freischütz*, Pamina in Mozart's *Die Zauberflöte* and Eva in Wagner's *Die Meistersinger*, as well as other leading Verdi roles.

Joan Sutherland had by this time married Richard Bonynge, a pianist and fellow-student from Australia, and it was Bonynge who persuaded her to venture into the repertory of more dramatic and colourful roles. He maintained that her voice, a rich and extremely beautiful dramatic soprano, was potentially of greater range and flexibility than she or her former teachers had imagined. He was proved right when, in 1959, Sutherland triumphed in the title-role of Donizetti's *Lucia di Lammermoor* at Covent Garden. This immediately launched her upon an international career as a rival to the reigning queen of sopranos, Maria Callas (*q.v.*). At La Scala, Milan, they called Sutherland 'La Stupenda' and began to debate whether or not she was greater than Callas, 'La Divina'. The general view was that Sutherland sang more beautifully while Callas acted more convincingly.

Joan Sutherland's career has taken her to all the world's leading opera houses in the operas of Bellini, Donizetti and Verdi, and in recent years she has extended her repertoire to include French romantic opera, and even Viennese operetta. In addition to her superb technique and remarkable voice, she possesses a natural warmth of personality which communicates itself through her singing. She was made a Dame of the British Empire in 1979.

Joan Sutherland in the title role of Donizetti's Lucrezia Borgia, *a Royal Opera House production of 1980*

T

Dylan Thomas (1914–53) Welsh
Poet

Dylan Thomas, born and brought up in Swansea, South Wales, published his first volume of poetry, *Eighteen Poems* (1934), when he was twenty, though many of the poems had been written much earlier. In London, he was fortunate in being taken up and publicized widely by Edith Sitwell, then at the height of her literary fame. Thomas's early work was both derivative and obscure, but by the time his second and third volumes, *Twenty-Five Poems* (1936) and *The Map of Love* (1939), were published, the latter also containing prose, he had developed considerably.

Deaths and Entrances (1946), his best known and probably his finest volume of poems, did much to strengthen Thomas's reputation. The rhetoric is finally under control, the command of words and of rhythm now quite masterly, and the range of sympathies remarkable. Thomas was a superb reader in public of his own and other people's verse, and towards the end of his life he tended to write poems as much for their immediate aural effect as for any more lasting qualities. His autobiographical prose sketches in *Portrait of the Artist as a Young Dog* (1940) were greatly admired. He wrote a good deal for broadcasting: his most popular work, and one that brought his name to a much wider public

Dylan Thomas, poet and self-styled enfant terrible*: a portrait by Rupert Shephard (1940)*

J.J. Thomson (1856–1940) British
Physicist

Nowadays we accept that an atom is complex, containing a number of different particles. But the first indication of this came only when J.J. Thomson discovered the electron, a tiny particle with a negative electrical charge, that is contained in every atom.

Joseph John Thomson – he is frequently referred to simply as J.J. – was born in Manchester on 18 December 1856. He originally wanted to be an engineer, but in 1876 won a scholarship to Trinity College, Cambridge, as a mathematician. He conducted research in a number of fields of physics before he turned to the problems of electrical discharges through gases.

His major interest was in the rays that produce X-rays. If a positive and a negative electrode are separated by air, no current can flow between them (unless the voltage is high enough to produce small-scale lightning). But a current can flow if there is a near vacuum between the electrodes. Rays will travel from the negative terminal to the positive one.

These are called cathode rays, and if they strike a piece of metal they produce X-rays. Cathode rays were thought to be rays rather than a stream of particles, but J.J. Thomson showed that they could be bent by an electrical field, which meant that the rays were really particles. Thomson measured the mass of these particles and discovered that it was less than a thousandth of that of an atom of hydrogen, the lightest element known.

He found that the charge and the mass were the same whatever the electrode was made of, so he decided that the atoms of every element contained the new, negatively charged particles, which were eventually called electrons. At the time it was (wrongly) thought that the electrons were embedded in the atom like currants in a bun.

In a gas discharge, the electrons stream towards the positive terminal; the atoms of the negative terminal that have lost their electrons travel in the opposite direction. Thomson realized that the positive particles from the gas neon had two different weights – in other words that the atoms of neon were not all the same. These atoms of one element with different weights are called isotopes.

During most of his research J.J. Thomson worked at the Cavendish Laboratory in Cambridge, making it the greatest centre in the world for research into physics. In 1906 he won the Nobel Prize for Physics, and later seven of his research colleagues also achieved this distinction. He was an inspired director of research into nuclear physics, and a pioneer in his field.

than he reached with his poetry, was the play for voices *Under Milk Wood*, a whimsical fantasy about life in a Welsh village. But the best of Thomas is to be found in the simplicity and directness of much of his poetry.

Thomas's disorderly and drunken way of life, which he thought to be bohemian, was a major contributary cause of his death in New York at the age of thirty-nine while on one of his poetry-reading tours.

Physicist Sir Joseph John Thomson

James Thurber (1894–1961) American
Humorist and cartoonist

The inspired humorist James Grover Thurber was born in Ohio, into a family of such temperament that for the rest of his life he never tired of writing about it. After attending Ohio State University from 1913 to 1918, he drifted into journalism. He lived for a short time in Paris, but returned to New York and in 1927 joined *The New Yorker*, the magazine with which he remains the most closely associated. His sketches and essays reveal a mild misogyny and a preoccupation with the failure of modern urban man to meet the challenge of the highly mechanized twentieth century. His heroes fail to repair things, forget their obligations, bump into things, are constantly henpecked, and take refuge in dreams of romantic heroism. His story *The Secret Life of Walter Mitty* is the most famous of these ironic fantasies.

His technique as a cartoonist is primitive and even childish, but his cartoons have a peculiar pathos which often renders captions unnecessary, even though some of these one-liners are now world famous, including 'Touché' and 'All right, have it your way. You heard a seal bark.' It seems likely that the insubstantiality of his drawn world has as much to do with his poor eyesight as with any theories about art.

Thurber excelled in several forms, and his play *The Male Animal* (1941) is a plea of surprising passion for freedom of speech. He published a series of slapstick homilies called *Fables For Our Time* (1940) and two fantasies for children, *The 13 Clocks* (1950) and *The Wonderful O* (1957). His most popular collection is *My Life and Hard Times* (1933), but perhaps the most revealing of his books is *The Thurber Album* (1952), an affectionate celebration of his various family connections.

A meticulous, neatly organized stylist, James Thurber gained his comic effects by the classical method of recounting hysterical events with the deadpan expression of an ironist.

Josip Tito (1892–1980) Yugoslav, ex-Austro-Hungarian
Political leader

Tito, born Josip Broz of a peasant family (Tito was just one of many aliases he adopted), trained as a mechanic, became a factory worker, and then, in the 1930s, a full-time Communist Party official.

The world remembers Tito principally as the elegantly uniformed, independent-minded and outspoken leader of modern Yugoslavia. But perhaps the most remarkable period in Tito's life was when he was a Comintern trainee in Russia in the 1930s. (The Comintern – its full name was

LEFT *James Thurber during a visit to London;* BELOW *a Thurber dog*

the Third International – was the co-ordinating body for world communist revolutionary activity. By the time Tito reached Moscow, it was completely dominated by Stalin [*q.v.*].) The notorious purges began at this time, and millions of Stalin's opponents and many dissidents were shot, including foreign communists. Tito himself had nerves of steel. He kept a low profile, held his tongue, and seemed a nonentity whom Stalin could rely upon. He was therefore appointed General Secretary of the Yugoslav Communist Party in 1939, and was in Yugoslavia during the

Tito, a courageous and independent leader of modern Yugoslavia

Second World War when the Germans bombed Belgrade on 6 April 1941. Just over two months later, they also invaded Russia. The Nazi-Soviet alliance was at an end.

As General Secretary, Tito could now organize Yugoslav communist resistance to the Germans. He was a brilliant guerilla commander and the partisans – men and women – were highly disciplined: looting was punished by death, and sexual relations were forbidden.

By 1945 the partisans controlled Yugoslavia, the only Communist Party to have liberated its country without Russian military help. Until 1947 Tito was loyal to Moscow. Then Stalin began to think him too independent and decided to teach him a lesson: 'I will shake my finger, and there will be no more Tito', he said. Agents were sent to kill Tito but were foiled. Yugoslavia rallied around him. This challenge to Soviet authority worked and Tito took an independent, 'non-aligned' policy, and indeed became the leader of the non-aligned communist bloc in world affairs. At home, he liberalized his regime. Foreign newspapers were permitted into the country and the citizens were allowed passports and trips abroad. The economic and government structures were decentralized, and something close to a market economy developed. Occasionally, Tito reined back those states that wished to gain even more autonomy for themselves (Yugoslavia was now a federation of states) or those who were too outspoken as critics of the system. But though he was dominant and authoritarian in manner, Tito liked to work with colleagues, not sycophants. He was very human, but with the real politician's ability both to be coolly calculating and, when the time was right, to go for the high stakes; and he had the courage to carry through policies that would most benefit his country, whether Moscow agreed to them or not.

Arturo Toscanini (1867–1957) Italian Conductor

Toscanini studied at the Conservatorium in Parma, where he was born, and began his career as a cellist. At the age of eighteen, while he was playing the cello in the orchestra of the opera house in Rio de Janeiro, he was given his first opportunity to conduct, as the public booed at the conductor already engaged for the opera *Aida*. Toscanini's success in stepping on to the rostrum and triumphantly conducting the entire opera from memory was such that he immediately began to receive engagements at home in Italy as a conductor. In 1892 he conducted the premiere of Leoncavallo's *Pagliacci* in Milan; in 1896 he introduced Wagner's *Götterdämmerung* to Italy and some weeks later conducted the first performances of Puccini's *La Bohème* in Turin. Before he was thirty he had become principal conductor at La Scala, Milan.

From his earliest days Toscanini expected absolute control over the compositions he conducted. He left La Scala in 1902 after four years because he refused to allow a tenor to perform an encore in the middle of an opera, and the audience had expressed its disapproval in no uncertain terms. He made his way to New York; there he conducted a series of performances at the Metropolitan Opera which earned him a reputation as the leading conductor of Italian opera of his time. La Scala, Milan, and the Met, New York, remained Toscanini's two main centres of influence for the rest of his life. He also became renowned as a conductor of classical symphonies, but though he had a devoted following in the concert halls his interpretations of the symphonies of Beethoven and Schubert had in general a stiffness that made them less appealing than the warmer and more humane approach of great Austro-German conductors such as Walter (*q.v.*) and Klemperer (*q.v.*).

Sternly opposed to Fascism, Toscanini remained in America after Mussolini rose to power in Italy, returning to La Scala after the Second World War to conduct a re-opening concert

Toscanini at a recording session of Debussy's La Mer, *March 1947*

there in 1946. As a youth he had played the cello at the first performance of Verdi's *Otello*, and all his life remained a devoted enthusiast and distinguished interpreter of the operas of Italy's greatest composer.

Alan Turing (1912–54) British
Computer designer

While the idea of a computer has existed for around two hundred years, the modern electronic computer was thought out only in 1936 by Alan Turing, who went on to organize the building of one of the first.

Turing was born in London and educated at King's College, Cambridge, and at Princeton University. It was there that he defined a 'universal' computer, as opposed to one that was limited to solving particular problems. He returned to Britain in 1938 and spent the Second World War with the British Department of Communication. His particular interest was in code-breaking, for which a computer is well suited: it can rapidly test an enormous number of possible codes to see which one works, then produce a decoded message. However, even a computer cannot test every possibility in a reasonable amount of time, and Turing devised ways of limiting the task. These were effective, and part of the success of British Intelligence in the Second World War was due to its ability to break enemy codes.

After the war Turing went to Britain's National Physical Laboratory to work on the design and building of a giant national computer, but he left in 1949, irritated by lack of progress, and went to Manchester University to work on the construction of what was then the computer with the largest memory in the world (its memory storage would now be thought very modest).

Turing was particularly interested in using computers in 'artificial intelligence' – as a machine that could 'think' in a way that was indistinguishable from human thought. He saw no limits to a computer's ability to think, and envisaged games-playing computers and the modern computers that can make complex decisions intelligently. He saw that there was a special sense in which a computer could actually do better than the person who made or pro-grammed it.

Writing a program for a computer is a subtle, logical process that nowadays has been made easier, in many cases, by the 'ability' of the computer itself. It was Turing who demonstrated the mathematical logic behind programming in the days when writing even a simple business program was a major intellectual task. Most of the current ideas on 'machine intelligence' – 'thinking' computers that can translate or plan safety measures for a spacecraft in trouble, for example – are based on his work.

V

Laurens van der Post (b.1906)
South African
Writer and explorer

'Modern man has more to learn from primitive man than from any scientist', Van der Post has said. It is a message he has diligently and passionately tried to instil in the western world through his writing and documentary films, pointing up people's estrangement from their natural environment and their denial of their instinctive, natural selves.

The genesis for this outlook could well be two old Bushmen, survivors of near-genocide, on his grandfather's South African farm. But his beliefs were first forged in the fires of the Second World War. He helped to organize the revolt against the Italians in Ethiopia, and later served in the Middle East, the Western Desert and Burma. In Java he was captured by the Japanese, but knowledge of their language saved him from execution as many other prisoners of war perished around him.

After the war he undertook several missions for the British Government in Africa, bringing to each not only leadership but also his unique blend of European and African philosophy and culture. He is a man who regards every stage of his life as a journey both to reach and to define a goal, a man unafraid to acknowledge a mystic element in life, and one with a supremely balanced view of the dilemma of Africa: 'If we expect the white man in Africa to renounce the

Alan Turing, computer designer; he saw no limits to a computer's potential

LEFT *Laurens van der Post in 1973;* BELOW *three of his remarkable studies of the people of Africa, combining exploration and anthropology with a compassionate understanding of Africa's current dilemma*

corruption of power, we must also expect the black man to hold out against the bitterness provoked by his lack of power.' His defence of the Bushman and his heritage – in books, films and lectures – has been unremitting and fiercely protective. Able to talk to both sides of the cultural divide in Zimbabwe, his discreet good offices were used extensively in the moves towards independence there in 1980.

Van der Post attacks 'the narrowing of consciousness down to a purely cerebral activity' as he promotes actively the precepts of Jung (*q.v.*) in his biography and a film of the psychiatrist's life, *The Story of Carl Gustav Jung*, made in 1971. Among his many other publications are *Venture to the Interior* (1952), *Creative Pattern in*

The Seagram Building, New York, designed by Mies van der Rohe and completed in 1958

Primitive Man (1956), *The Heart of the Hunter* (1961), *The Seed and the Sower* (1963), *The Hunter and the Whale* (1967) and *A Far Off Place* (1974), several of which have won literary prizes both in Europe and South Africa. The widely acclaimed *Lost World of the Kalahari* (1958) appeared as a film in 1956.

Van der Post was knighted in 1981.

Ludwig Mies van der Rohe (1886–1969)
American, ex-German
Architect

The most profound single influence upon the architecture of this century was Ludwig Mies van der Rohe. Le Corbusier (*q.v.*) probably had more influence on architects; but it is the work of Mies, the master of the International Style, which emphasizes that the design of a building must be influenced by its function, that is still echoed in the architecture of the 1980s.

His professional career falls into two stages: before and after 1937. Although he had no formal architectural training, he came to the attention in 1909 of the foremost German architect of the period, Peter Behrens, for whom he worked for three years. By the time he left to set up his own practice, Mies had become thoroughly steeped in Behrens' neo-classical influences.

In 1919 Mies suddenly turned from neo-classicism to a revolutionary modernism, with his extraordinarily prophetic designs for glass skyscrapers (1919, 1920 and 1921) and for a reinforced concrete office building (1922). These projects never became reality, but the few designs from the period before 1937 which *were* built show the same total, and totally successful, commitment to modernism. The exquisite German Pavilion at the Barcelona International Exhibition (1929) – little more than a reinforced concrete slab supported by chrome-plated steel columns – and the Tugendhat House at Brno (1930) are both milestones in modern architecture.

The Nazi regime made life impossible for Mies in Germany, and in 1937 he emigrated to the United States, becoming an American citizen in 1944. In this second period of his life he broadened his reputation, which came to be based on actual structures rather than on ideas. Those buildings – notably the Farnsworth House (1950) in Illinois, the Chicago Lake Shore Apartments (1951), the Seagram Building (1958) in New York and his buildings for the Illinois Institute of Technology – are no less than the archetypes for modern steel-and-glass architecture. Very simple, dominated by vertical and horizontal lines and beautifully finished, these almost mechanically pure buildings begin to explain Mies's enigmatic statement that 'less is more'.

Madeleine Vionnet (1875–1974) French
Fashion designer

The least remembered of the great fashion designers of this century, Vionnet was responsible for freeing women from corsets and for cutting fabric on the bias so that, for the first time, dresses could flow over the body like water.

A small woman with a deep, strong voice out of all proportion to her size, Vionnet was a provincial from the Jura, the mountainous region that joins France to Switzerland. In her heyday her salon in the Avenue Montaigne in Paris employed 1,200 workers who turned out 600 models a year and dressed the queens of Spain, Belgium and Romania, the Duchess of Marlborough, Marchesa Casati and Pavlova.

Vionnet began her training at the age of

eleven, when she worked as a seamstress for the local dressmaker. At eighteen she married, but divorced a year later, and soon afterwards her child from the marriage died. After this tragic series of events she left Paris for five years and went to London to work at the House of Kate Reilly, who dressed the late Victorian court in stiff voluminous clothes that must have been abhorrent to Vionnet. Back in Paris at twenty-four she began her real career at the famous House of Callot, working for Madame Gerber who exacted the highest standards of workmanship in Paris. In 1907 Vionnet moved on to the House of Doucet, where she began to make her own models – loose, fragile *deshabillés* for actresses and *demi-mondaines*. These dresses were bought by customers as peignoirs and négligées, but for Vionnet they were a finished statement about all clothes. She found the body beautiful in movement and hated any garments that hid that beauty. She always said that the body must show itself through the veil of a dress and must, in her own words, 'smile when the wearer smiles'. She loved to design one-piece dresses without stiffening that took their shape from the woman inside, and called the corset 'une chose orthopédique'.

When a client went to Vionnet her measurements and proportions would be worked out in three dimensions on a small wooden doll eighty centimetres high. At a time when Paris workrooms were sweatshops packed with women and children ruining their eyesight and on the breadline, Vionnet's were light, warm, airy and scrupulously tidy and clean. Both Balenciaga and Dior paid tribute to her unique place in the modern history of fashion, and in one of her last interviews, aged ninety-six, Vionnet was able to say, 'I am the best dressmaker in the world, and I *feel* it too'.

Wernher von Braun (b. 1912) American, ex-German
Rocket pioneer

Not even the aeroplane had been invented at the beginning of this century, but by the end of 1969 space travel was so advanced that men could go to the Moon. The man who developed the rockets that took them there was Wernher von Braun.

Von Braun was born in Wirsitz, Germany (now Poland), and educated in Zurich and Berlin. At the beginning of the century it had been shown that only rockets could reach a high enough speed to leave the Earth, and that to do this they would have to be multi-stage rockets, so that the final spacecraft was not burdened with the mass of the spent rocket that had been used to overcome the Earth's gravity. Research in the United States proved that only liquid-fuelled

LEFT *Madeleine Vionnet, photographed by Cecil Beaton*

Werner von Braun, rocket pioneer, who developed the Saturn v launcher for Apollo 11

Friedrich von Hayek (b. 1899) Austrian
Economist and philosopher

Born in Vienna, Hayek took doctorates in both law and economics before becoming director of the Austrian Institute for Economic Research. He accepted the Tooke Professorship of Economic Science and Statistics at the London School of Economics (1931–50), and thereafter taught in Chicago and Freiburg. He was joint recipient of the Nobel Prize for Economics in 1974.

On arrival in England Hayek entered a fierce controversy with Keynes (*q.v.*), arguing that, in a Depression, to stimulate consumption could make unemployment worse, and that with full employment increased consumption will reduce real investment. Apart from economics proper, Hayek is likely to be remembered as a (misleadingly labelled) neo-conservative thinker of the mid-century. This first became apparent when he published during the Second World War a critique of totalitarianism and socialism entitled *The Road to Serfdom*. This gauntlet was taken up by the left, who rapidly elevated him to their demonology.

However, while it is undoubtedly true that Hayek was highly critical of the attempt to centrally plan the economy, he could hardly be labelled as a conservative in the sense of one who wishes to conserve and not change. Hayek argued very vigorously for two principal kinds of change: more free market and less state control; and stronger reliance on entrenched laws guaranteeing the liberty of the subject against the state and the majority. He also made contributions to intellectual history. He was not unaware of the shock value of ideas like 'a planned economy is a contradiction in terms', or that the answer to inflation is to end government monopoly of the creation of money.

Professor Friedrich von Hayek

rockets could be controlled delicately enough for space travel and some experimental rockets had been built that flew a mile or two into the air.

In the 1930s, when he was a student, groups in the United States and Germany were interested in using rocket power for space travel. In Germany, one society, the VIR (Society for Spacetravel), coordinated the efforts of a number of researchers, and in 1930 von Braun joined it. The group built dozens of successful liquid-fuelled rockets, and in 1932 the programme was taken over by the German army. The research was centred at Peenemünde, on the Baltic, in 1936. While sporadic, the research led to the development in 1944 of a rocket missile, the V2, which the Germans used against Britain in the Second World War.

When the war ended, von Braun and a number of his colleagues fled westwards to avoid the invading Russians, and surrendered to the Americans. Becoming an American citizen, he designed a series of military rockets, but his plans for space rockets were obstructed until the Russians launched the Sputnik satellite in 1957. Almost certainly, von Braun would have been first had he not been held back by the American Government. But in January 1958 he used one of his military rockets to place a satellite in orbit.

In 1960, von Braun's group was appointed as civilians to the National Aeronautics and Space Administration (NASA) and given the task of putting a man on the Moon within the decade. It was he who developed the giant Saturn v rocket that launched Apollo 11 in 1969.

Herbert von Karajan (b. 1908) Austrian
Conductor

Herbert von Karajan is one of the most important musicians of our time. He was born in Salzburg, where he studied at the Mozarteum, before proceeding to Vienna, where he attended the University and the Music Academy. In 1929 he gave his first concert with the Mozarteum Orchestra in Salzburg, achieving a huge success with Tchaikovsky's Fifth Symphony. Within a few months he was engaged in Germany as a conductor at the Stadttheater in Ulm, Bavaria, where he stayed for six seasons, learning about opera in the most practical way by conducting a wide and varied choice of works. In 1935 he went to Aachen, where he became the youngest music director in Germany. Before he was thirty Karajan had conducted at the leading opera house in Germany, the Berlin State Opera, and during the War the German capital was his principal scene of action.

In 1947 Karajan began his career afresh in Salzburg and Vienna, and in 1955 the Berlin Philharmonic Orchestra chose him as their principal conductor for life. From 1957 until 1964 he was also the director of the Vienna State Opera, but since then his performances of opera have been mainly confined to Salzburg, where he is able to produce and stage the works himself as well as conduct them, often arranging for operas to be recorded and filmed after they have been staged. At his own financial risk Karajan founded the Salzburg Easter Festival, at which he has staged a number of Wagner operas. In the regular summer festivals at Salzburg he has conducted operas by Richard Strauss, Mozart and Verdi to great acclaim.

Karajan is a pioneer in that he represents a new class of musician and man of the theatre, one whose interests embrace the latest technological advances in recording, and who is concerned with scientific research into various aspects of music (such as pitch and acoustics). He aims for perfection in his performances and achieves it remarkably often. Somehow, he has also found time to indulge his other passions: skiing, fast cars, and flying his own jet plane.

ABOVE *A dynamic figure in music today, Herbert von Karajan, Principal Conductor of the Berlin Philharmonic Orchestra*

Bruno Walter (1876–1962) German Conductor

Bruno Walter, one of the leading conductors of the twentieth century, was born into a German-Jewish family (his real name was Bruno Schlesinger) in Berlin, where he studied music at the Stern Conservatorium. After experience of conducting in a number of provincial opera houses, he graduated to the Berlin State Opera and then became assistant to Gustav Mahler in Vienna, eventually succeeding Mahler as Director of the Vienna Opera in 1907. From then on, Walter was intimately associated with music-making in the city of Vienna, both at the opera and with the Vienna Philharmonic Orchestra, although he travelled widely and was often away from Vienna for long periods. From 1913 to 1922 he was, in fact, General Music Director in Munich, and in the 1920s and 1930s he conducted frequently in London. He was an early enthusiast for the symphonies of Mahler, which he did much to popularize through his own performances of them.

Walter's career in Germany came to an abrupt end with the rise to power of the Nazis in 1933, and from then until the outbreak of the Second

Bruno Walter, a peerless interpreter of much of the German classical repertoire

World War in 1939 he worked mainly in Vienna and Salzburg, his performances in Salzburg becoming a central part of the annual festival. In 1939 he made his home in the United States, where his outstanding performances of the Viennese classics were greatly appreciated. After the war he returned to Europe, conducting the Vienna Philharmonic in his beloved Mahler, as well as in Schubert and Beethoven, not only in Vienna but also on tour to the United Kingdom.

A man of wide literary culture, Walter wrote a fascinating volume of memoirs, *Theme and Variations*, and an extremely useful book on Mahler. The warmth and humanity of his interpretations not only of Mahler but also of the symphonies of Mozart, Schubert and Beethoven, and the operas of Mozart, have yet to be equalled. His performances of Beethoven's *Fidelio*, with his life-long friend Lotte Lehmann (*q.v.*) as Leonore, have acquired legendary status. Walter was also an accomplished pianist, and he can be heard in this role on gramophone records, in Mozart's D Minor Concerto, and also as accompanist to Lotte Lehmann.

Andy Warhol (b. 1928) American
Painter

Warhol is the most influential and celebrated proponent of the American 1960s Pop Art movement. Born in McKeesport, Pennsylvania, of immigrant Czech parents, he attended the Carnegie Institute of Technology and settled in New York in about 1949, where he worked as a commercial artist.

Pop Art was born in the United States in the

Pop artist Andy Warhol

early 1960s, its advocates claiming that any subject, however unlikely, is suitable for art and can be depicted by any method. In 1960 Warhol was doing paintings based on comic strip characters, as in *Dick Tracy*. Two years later he had his first commercial success and achieved instant fame when he exhibited his hand-painted Campbell's soup pictures, shown in Los Angeles in 1962. That same year he discovered the photo-mechanical silkscreen printing process and began a succession of portraits of Marilyn Monroe (*q.v.*), the first of a series which has included Elizabeth Taylor, Jackie Kennedy, Elvis Presley (*q.v.*) and Chairman Mao (*q.v.*). His mass-produced images were made at 'The Factory', as he called his studio, with an

indifference to the artist's traditional skill in working with his materials and to the idea of a single hand-worked masterpiece. As in the work of Duchamp (*q.v.*), which Warhol greatly admired, the creative act is not in depicting the subject but in choosing it – a soup can or a photograph – and the subject can then be reproduced mechanically. In the early 1960s he focused on everyday items: a Coca-Cola bottle, a matchbox, newspaper headlines, a dollar bill, often repeating the image many times in a single work.

In 1964 he had boxes made to order, then silkscreened them on all sides with the Brillo pads label. In the same year he produced silkscreens, based on photographs, which reflected the violence of American society: his subjects were race-riots, suicides, the electric chair, car accidents and, most poignant of all, Jacqueline Kennedy (in the series known as *Jackie*) at the time of Kennedy's (*q.v.*) assassination.

Warhol has also made films: he began by showing his friends acting out dramas and fantasies, and then in 1966 he made *Chelsea Girls*, a commercial success that was notorious for its sexual frankness. His many films have had a marked influence on commercial film-making. As an artist, film-maker and cult figure, Warhol's life, like Dali's (*q.v.*), has attracted publicity and controversy, while his art, like Duchamp's, remains enigmatic and is endlessly discussed.

Thomas J. Watson (1874–1956)
American
Computer tycoon

Anyone with the foresight to have invested $3,000 in the shares of Watson's creation, IBM, in its early days would have found that fifty years later, in 1967, their initial stake would be worth $18 million. By the 1930s Watson was the highest-paid man in the United States. Some of his employees invested their savings in IBM stock and retired millionaires, and IBM created the cult of the equity, of the growth stock bought by employees that could make a capitalist out of the small investor.

Apart from a short spell as a bored book-keeper in a butcher's, Watson was a salesman all his life. First it was organs, pianos and sewing-machines, and then at National Cash Register Watson really learned the techniques of selling. Under a suspended jail sentence in 1914 for what the court said were excessively cut-throat, unprincipled sales practices, Watson was fired from NCR and joined the newly created Computer-Tabulating-Recording Company. By the 1920s he had asserted his control, re-named it International Business Machines and was selling three billion punch cards a year. Driven by his fervour, selling became a religion. It was not

Tom Watson's invention, the IBM computer, in a streamlined modern form, the IBM 3081

sufficient for employees to appear in the regulation sober suit, tie and white shirt; IBM employees had to be abstemious, union-free and clean-living, and even today no alcohol is permitted on IBM's premises. Sales slogans exhorted employees to 'Think' and 'Do Good' and the company hymn, 'Ever Onward', urged them to 'pledge sincerest loyalty to the corporation that's best for all'. Successful sellers of the business machines joined the 100 Per Cent Club and were invited to the Homestead, IBM's own hotel; the less successful were eased out.

The company was white, Protestant and became its own corporate state in which Watson was the sovereign who laid down the code of behaviour and power structure. Watson always backed his salesmen with formidable investment in developing new products. In 1943 he gave Harvard University $1 million, which produced the first, stuttering electro-mechanical computer; it weighed two tons and was fifty-one feet long. Ever the salesman who knew what his customers would buy, Watson fought the scientists and insisted on enclosing the machine in curved glass and a stainless steel case. It was his most fruitful invention. After a faltering start, IBM's computer-based growth was unstoppable. Sales reached $5 billion in 1966 and by the end of the 1960s the corporation was making and selling four out of every five of the western world's computers.

Evelyn Waugh (1903–66) British
Novelist, diarist and biographer

At Oxford University, where he read Modern History, Evelyn Waugh paid little attention to his studies and instead enjoyed, to use his own words, an 'idle, dissolute and extravagant' life. After Oxford he studied for a time at an art school in London and then became a teacher until he was dismissed for drunkenness. In 1928 he published both a study of Rossetti, the Victorian painter and poet, and his first novel, *Decline and Fall*. It was with his second novel, *Vile Bodies* (1930), that he became popular, and there followed a series of comic satires on the fashionable London society of the 1920s and 1930s which gained him a huge following. Waugh's conversion to Catholicism in 1930 seemed to increase his feelings of melancholy and to bring occasional bitterness into his work, but *A Handful of Dust* (1934) and *Scoop* (1938) are both highly entertaining.

Put Out More Flags (1942), a satirical war novel, was followed by *Brideshead Revisited* (1945), in which the Catholic message tends to introduce an uneasy sentimentality into Waugh's formerly sharp style. He returned magnificently to form with *The Loved One* (1948), a satire on American, especially Californian, funeral customs, and with *Sword of Honour* (1965), a three-part novel about the Second World War that

Evelyn Waugh

many consider to be a masterpiece of modern English fiction.

The publication, after his death, of Waugh's letters and diaries reveal him to have been an essentially sad figure, very concerned to present himself as a 'gentleman', scornful of those he considered less well bred than himself, and decidedly limited in his sympathies. Yet it is from these characteristics that he found his great strength as a satirist of society in his novels of the 1930s. At his best, his comic ebullience was exhilarating. He may have lacked the charity of the great novelists, but he compensated instead by making superb use of malice in his satires.

Sidney (1857–1943) & Beatrice Webb (1858–1947) British
Social reformers and historians

Webb was a civil servant, a progressive member of the London County Council, President of the Board of Trade, 1924, Labour Member of Parliament (1922–9), and, as the First Baron Passfield, Secretary of State for Dominion Affairs, 1929–31. His public career is perhaps less significant for his influence than his scholarly and reformist endeavours entered into with his wife, Beatrice. Unlike the lower middle-class Sidney, Beatrice was born into a wealthy family but had

Sidney and Beatrice Webb, 1929, by William Nicholson

wearied of 'society', and turned her interests to research into the cooperative movement and the life and labour of the people of London. To assist her research on trade unionism she was put in touch with Webb and they married in 1892.

In 1884, together with H.G. Wells (*q.v.*), George Bernard Shaw (*q.v.*) and others, Webb was an early member of the Fabian Society, an organization of middle-class intellectuals advocating the gradual implementation of socialism, rather than revolution (the society still exists today). Perhaps the most impressive single achievement of the Fabians was the foundation of the London School of Economics and Political Science in 1895. They also founded the *New Statesman* weekly in 1914.

The Webbs ploughed through immense reports of nineteenth-century public inquiries to write their works on socialism, cooperatives, trade unions, industrial democracy and, above all, their ten-volume history of *English Local Government* (1906–29). These works and many others, including the pamphlets, official reports and draft reforms, have an air of fustiness about them which chimes well with Beatrice's self-characterization of Sidney and herself as bourgeois, bureaucratic and benevolent. Nevertheless, ideas generated in Beatrice's Minority Report for the Royal Commission on the Poor Laws anticipated much of the social legislation introduced after 1945.

The last decades of their life were coloured by their reactions to a trip to the Soviet Union in 1932, published in *Soviet Communism, A New Civilisation* (1935). Unlike many socialists, who saw through the rhetoric and showcases of Lenin's (*q.v.*) Russia to the cruelty and ruthlessness of the new regime, the Webbs seem to have been captivated by what they saw.

Max Weber (1864–1920) German
Social scientist

Weber's influence today is pervasive in the social sciences. A specialist in economics, he became famous as a sociologist, and this has had considerable bearing on his thoughts on economic history. Marxist thought reduces political and social history to economic history, an exciting prospect for economists. Weber, however, was unconvinced by it, and in his single reasonably accessible book, a study of the origins of capitalism (*The Protestant Ethic and the Spirit of Capitalism*) he attempts to show that the religious views that lead certain classes of men to work hard and accumulate wealth, to save that wealth and reinvest it in productive machinery, and to see in all this the fulfilment of their religious and moral duty, are factors that cannot be eliminated from an account of the growth of capitalism, which Marxism would do. This theory has had great impact on contemporary social science.

Weber believed economics and sociology to be unlike history and biography in that they concentrate on the patterns to be found in social behaviour and organization, on the typical rather than the individual. In order to make them amenable to study, subjects must first be simplified and idealized, and from these 'ideal types', representing entities such as types of action or religion, comparisons can be made and theoretical explanations developed. Weber applied this method of analysis particularly to patterns of authority in society and the effects they had on the way the world appeared.

Two of his analyses of authority have been especially influential: those concerning bureaucracy and charisma. It was Weber who first defined bureaucracy, outlining its rules, rationality and influence. He also coined the phrase 'charismatic authority' to describe personal qualities which could evoke immediate popular acceptance. His overall view was that the modern world was in the process of becoming rationalized by machinery and its resulting social organizations, such as bureaucracy, and was being emptied of enchantment and mystery.

Sociologist Max Weber

Chaim Weizmann (1874–1952) Israeli, ex-Russian
Political leader

From a remote Jewish rural community in Russia, where Jews were actively discriminated against by the Tsarist Government, Weizmann

Dr Chaim Weizmann addressing members of the Israeli State Council, of which he was president, in Tel Aviv. Behind him is a portrait of Theodore Hertzl, founder of the Jewish state, and, front left, Premier David Ben-Gurion

made his way to Germany to obtain the finest scientific education then available. He was a brilliant student, and sold his first patent as he graduated. From then on his concern for Zionism – the movement for an independent Jewish nation – and his researches marched hand in hand in an exceptionally busy life, during which he seemed to meet every international statesman of interest to the Zionist cause.

Dr Weizmann came to Manchester in 1904, and immediately galvanized the British Zionist movement into concentrating its efforts to obtain a national home for Jews in Palestine. He worked on the Jews themselves, the rich, the well established – including those assimilated into British upper-class life, some of whom opposed the Zionists – and the poor, who might become settlers in the new Zion. British politicians, scientists, financiers, all who could help were met by this man of immense intellectual ability and conviction, qualities formidably allied to charm and great persuasive power. The idea of a national home for the Jews was urged on the British, and Weizmann's efforts led to the Balfour Declaration (November 1917) which stated that Britain would do its best to make this a reality. International approval was reached at the peace treaty after the First World War and Britain began its troubled Palestine Mandate. Weizmann then campaigned for funds, especially in the USA, to raise the 'absorptive capacity' of Palestine for settlers. He believed at first that Jews and Arabs could live together in harmony, both profiting from prosperity.

Alas, this was not to be – violence broke out.

Then the evil Nazi holocaust forced up the demand from Jews to find refuge in Palestine. After 1945 the British found it impossible to continue to govern Palestine, and withdrew. To Weizmann's immense personal distress the British, whom he appreciated (even being called by his enemies a 'British agent'), showed considerable hostility to the idea of an independent Israel. But Weizmann obtained the ear of President Truman, and with this American support the United Nations agreed to a realistic partition of Palestine. On 15 May 1948 the independent state of Israel came into being. Weizmann on that day was telegrammed by Ben-Gurion (*q.v.*) and the provisional Government: 'You have done more than any living man towards [Israel's] creation.' Two days later Weizmann was elected the first President of Israel.

Orson Welles (b. 1915) American
Film director and actor

America's Halloween of 1938 was a night of sensation, as mass panic gripped thousands of people listening to a free adaptation of H.G. Wells' (*q.v.*) *The War of the Worlds*. Partly as a result of war hysteria, and partly through the verisimilitude of the broadcast, many listeners thought that Martians had actually landed in New Jersey. The young Welles, director of the Mercury Theatre, which produced the adaptation, became an overnight *enfant terrible*, acquiring a reputation he has never shaken off. Invited to Hollywood to do what he liked, he part-wrote,

Orson Welles in Claude Chabrol's La Décade Prodigieuse, *1971, released in Britain as* Ten Days' Wonder

directed and played the title role in *Citizen Kane* (1941), probably the greatest of all American films, although on first release it was a box-office failure. Its portrait of a grotesque newspaper tycoon of limitless wealth, bolstering his insecurity with a magpie-like acquisition of the world's art treasures, many of which remained in their packing cases in the basement of the vast Gothic castle he built for himself, was taken by the real-life newspaper owner William Randolph Hearst (*q.v.*) as a personal attack. He began a vendetta against Welles and RKO, the studio responsible. As a consequence, Welles' second film, *The Magnificent Ambersons* (1942), a gently paced evocation of a turn-of-the-century American family, was cut, as Welles alleges, 'by the studio janitor' and released in a double bill. Even in its mutilated eighty-eight-minute version it is a brilliant film.

Welles proved he could be a commercial director with *The Stranger* (1946), in which he played a Nazi gone to ground in a New England town, a workmanlike thriller of modest distinction. He then went off the rails again with *The Lady from Shanghai*, a bizarre thriller of monumental complexity and excitement, now recognized as a near masterpiece. Welles, an ardent Shakespearean, filmed *Macbeth*, with the actors muttering in a Scots brogue, and later made *Othello*, triumphing in the face of great production difficulties. His reputation as an international celebrity was enhanced by his performance in a semi-cameo role as Harry Lime in *The Third Man*. Welles has frequently lent his ever more corpulent presence to much lesser films, often as a means of financing his own projects which the industry regards with customary apathy. He directed the imaginative thriller *Touch of Evil* (1958), playing a corrupt Mexican policeman, a less-than-satisfactory version of Kafka's (*q.v.*) *The Trial* (1962), and a homage to Falstaff, *Chimes at Midnight* (1966). Regrettably, to the public at large he is known not as a genius of the American cinema but as a portly raconteur on television talk shows and the voice-over on beer and sherry commercials.

H.G. Wells (1866–1946) British
Novelist

Herbert George Wells was born in Bromley, Kent, on 21 September 1866. He was the author of over a hundred works varying between fiction and controversial discussion, between short stories and some of the longest tomes of his epoch, between the most fanciful make-believe and the most ruthless realism concerning the future of mankind. Born into the working class, son of an occasional gardener and a ladies' maid, he was largely self educated, and became one of the first beneficiaries of the then new guinea-a-

H.G. Wells

week scholarships at Kensington's Normal School of Science. His scientific studies were soon eclipsed by his literary work, and with *The Time Machine* (1895), *The Invisible Man* (1897) and *The War of the Worlds* (1898) Wells founded a new school of modern scientific romance. He steadily developed into a naturalistic novelist and his most triumphant works, *Kipps* (1905) and *The History of Mr Polly* (1910), earned him comparison with Charles Dickens and have confirmed their status as modern classics. Concurrently, he produced a series of social-conscience, semi-political novels, of which the best are *Tono Bungay* (1909) and *The New Machiavelli* (1911). These highlight a problem that was never far from the surface in his own life, the clash between public duty and private passion. When he died, on 10 August 1946, he had become resigned to a deep pessimism regarding the future prospects of survival for the human race.

Wells was unique among outstanding novelists in that he scorned the role of the artist, insisting that in times of crisis it was the thinking man's duty to apply himself to educating his fellows to the point where they would be able to save themselves. In this regard his massive *Outline of History* (1920), although rejected by the academic establishment, which perhaps could not understand it, became his most important book. 'I went to bed an educator', he later said, 'and awoke a best-seller.' He saw evolution as a desperate race between technological advance and moral growth, and in the end, living to see the dropping of the atomic bomb, was convinced that the race was lost. His earlier work abounds with scientific forecasts of extraordinary accuracy, including anticipations of atomic war, the submarine, the tank, aeroplanes and space travel.

Patrick White (b. 1912) Australian
Novelist

Although born in London, Patrick White came from a family that had settled in New South Wales in the 1820s, and most of his novels are set, at least in part, in Australia. Brought up in Sydney, he was sent to England for schooling when he was thirteen, and returned to work on farms in Australia until he came back to England as a student at King's College, Cambridge. After graduating in 1935, he lived for a time in London, writing poems, novels, plays, and sketches for revue. A volume of poems, *The Ploughman* (1935), was published in Sydney, and in 1939 a London publisher issued one of White's novels, *Happy Valley*. During the war White served in the Royal Air Force, mostly as an intelligence officer in North Africa and the Middle East. In 1946 he returned to Australia, where he has lived ever since.

Patrick White's distinctive style emerged clearly with his third novel, *The Aunt's Story* (1948), but it was with *The Tree of Man* (1956) that he became a best-seller, and with *Voss* (1957) that he achieved an enormous critical success both in England and the United States, critics comparing him to Dostoevsky, though reviewers in his own country remained suspicious and hostile. *Voss* is a remarkable exploration of outer and inner deserts, the arid Australian bush and the spiritual emptiness of the life lived there. *Riders in the Chariot* (1961) is an even more remarkable work, of great scope and stature, embracing a number of themes and a rich variety of acutely observed characters.

For a time in the early 1960s Patrick White began again to write plays, but it is as a novelist, combining in his style the elegant irony of a Jane Austen with the power of a Dostoevsky, that he is incomparable. Among the finest of his later novels are *The Vivisector* (1970), *The Eye of the Storm* (1973) and *A Fringe of Leaves* (1976). White was awarded the Nobel Prize for Literature in 1973.

Australian novelist Patrick White in 1979

Frank Whittle (b. 1907) British
Inventor

The jet engine was developed in England and Germany without any support from either the armed services or the manufacturers of aircraft engines. In Britain the inventor, struggling against indifference, was Frank Whittle.

Whittle was born in Coventry on 1 June 1907 and educated at Leamington College. He joined the RAF while still a youth, and quickly turned to the problems connected with fast aircraft. An aircraft engine driving a conventional propeller – an airscrew – is very limited in what it can achieve; it pulls its aircraft forwards rather inefficiently. A jet engine hurls air backwards rapidly and in large masses, and potentially, it was realized quite early in aircraft history, can propel an aircraft at very high speeds. A jet engine is very economical in fuel, and therefore doubly attractive. Frank Whittle quickly saw that a gas turbine could be used to propel the air backwards, and patented the idea in 1929. But he was unable to get any support, and allowed his patent to lapse in 1935.

However, the RAF sent him to Cambridge as an engineering student, and he eventually managed to find financial backers and set up a company, Power Jets Ltd, which produced the first jet engine in 1937. It wasn't very good, and finances again became very straitened. It wasn't until 1939 that Whittle received any Government funding.

When support came the Gloster Aircraft Company was able to collaborate in Whittle's development, and the first British jet plane, the Gloster jet fighter, had a test flight in May 1941. The development of a production version was amazingly slow, considering that the Second World War was by then being fought largely in the air. There were, however, some British jet planes available to attack the German VI aircraft, themselves crude, pilotless jet planes, in 1944.

Norbert Wiener (1894–1964) American Mathematician

Even among mathematicians, who often show their brilliance when young, Norbert Wiener stands out as a prodigy. He was born in Columbia, Missouri, on 26 November 1894 and took his first degree, from Tufts College, at the age of only fourteen, helped, his father has recorded, by a careful and efficient home education. He received a doctorate from Harvard at the very early age of eighteen.

Wiener was particularly interested in extending the uses of computers beyond pure calculation, and he worked with the American Government during the Second World War, first on the control of anti-aircraft guns and then on increasingly complex problems of electronic control. He saw that the ideas of 'information' and 'control' could be generalized to include extreme examples, from running a steam engine to the complexities of modern business management, in which computers, thinking more widely and more quickly than a human ever can, make major decisions.

In 1948 Wiener published a book, *Cybernetics*, dealing rather technically with information and control. He himself coined the word 'cybernetics' – it comes from a Greek word for the steersman of a ship (the word 'governor' has the same source). This book was vital in the development of the electronic control systems that characterize the end of the twentieth century and will become even more significant in the twenty-first, as robot factories, computerized education, and automatic government all become possible.

Wiener was a sensitive man, acutely and very early aware of the disturbance that the electronic revolution could bring with it. As he pointed out, the first industrial revolution dramatically reduced the value of those who had nothing to offer society but their muscle; the second one would

ABOVE *Sir Frank Whittle's jet engine and Gloster jet fighter of 1941*

LEFT *Norbert Wiener, an influential figure in a world of advanced electronics* have the same effect on those who had nothing to offer but their brain – accountants, junior managers, even designers could be replaced by machines. He voiced his disquiet in a book, *The Human Use of Human Beings*, which remains a tract for the future.

Tennessee Williams (b. 1914) American
Playwright

Born at Commons, Mississippi, Williams was christened Thomas Lanier Williams but took the name Tennessee because, he said, his father's family had fought Indians there and he knew that the life of a playwright was going to be like 'defending a stockade from savages'.

A literary prizewinner at school (from which he was withdrawn by his father for failing the Officers Training Course) Williams started out as a shipping clerk. He had his first nervous breakdown while still in his twenties, and many of the characters in his plays are neurotic and self-destructive. His first full-length play, *Battle of Angels*, was produced in Boston in 1940.

Five years later he made his name on Broadway with *The Glass Menagerie*, which characterized the main Williams dramatic theme – that, he said, of 'the need for understanding and tenderness and fortitude among individuals trapped by circumstance'. *The Glass Menagerie* also introduced some now-familiar Williams characters – the faded genteel older woman needing the kindness of strangers, the young innocent girl, the tough hero from a humble background – against a seedy deep-South background.

After *The Glass Menagerie* came *A Streetcar Named Desire* (1947), awarded the Pulitzer Prize, *Summer and Smoke* (1948), *The Rose Tattoo*

American playwright Tennessee Williams

(1951), *Cat on a Hot Tin Roof* (1955), also awarded the Pulitzer Prize, *Orpheus Descending* (a rewrite of his first play, 1957), *Sweet Bird of Youth* (1959), and *Night of the Iguana* (1962), so that across fifteen years Williams was rivalled only by Arthur Miller (*q.v.*) as America's leading and most prolific dramatist. In Hollywood, too, he was familiar for screenplays of some of his Broadway successes, as well as *Baby Doll* (1956) and *Suddenly Last Summer* (1958). Elizabeth Taylor and Paul Newman were among many stars who returned more than once to his work.

Sadly, his last twenty years have been marked more by periodic nervous breakdowns and Broadway and London flops than by a continuation of his earlier success and popularity. However, his ambition remains, as he once put it, 'to show how to get beyond despair and still live', and there is always the chance of another stage hit.

Woodrow Wilson (1856–1924) American
Political leader

Elected president of the United States in 1912 mainly on a pledge to oppose corruption, Wilson had been a great governor of New Jersey and a fine president of that state's most distinguished university, Princeton. He was an academic political scientist and an admirer of British constitutional practice, in which the head of Government is powerful within the legislature. He must often have thought of this at the end of his second presidential term, when he was locked in combat with the Senate, which refused to ratify America's membership of the newly formed League of Nations.

America saw the old world go to war in 1914 with a certain self-righteous disdain, and Wilson held aloof from the conflict. Germany was much admired in the United States not only by the large number of German immigrants but by many others, and there was suspicion of Britain. However, the beginning of submarine warfare meant that Americans were drowned in the U-boat sinkings; in 1915 the *Lusitania* sank and many of the richer east-coast Republicans wanted war. Wilson, however, was a Democrat, and he believed that eventually his role, and that of the United States, would be as arbitrator in the combat. Meanwhile, America grew richer, as gold went from France and the Bank of England to Fort Knox, and America became the world's creditor, making arms and equipment for the allied armies and feeding their peoples.

Germany eventually decided on unrestricted submarine warfare. This the German Government realized would bring America into the war, so attempts were made to persuade Mexico to attack the United States, promising them Texas, New Mexico and Arizona in return. This offer was disclosed by British intelligence to the

Americans, and Wilson declared war on 2 April 1917.

Wilson now became the prophet of the free world for which the Allies were fighting. The aim was 'to make the world safe for democracy'. He proclaimed his 'fourteen points', which included open diplomacy, reduced armaments, freedom of navigation and trade, and the triumph of the principle of nationality: the points also included the germ of the League of Nations. These were the basis for both the Armistice and the Treaty of Versailles, which ended the war. But Wilson, autocratic and 'bitterly partisan' in American politics, brought no Republicans with him on the American delegation to Versailles. He appealed to the American people to support him, but the Senate refused to approve either the Treaty of Versailles or American membership of the League of Nations. Defeated, Wilson's health gave way and his party lost the presidency in 1920 to the Republican Warren G. Harding.

Ludwig Wittgenstein (1889–1951) British, ex-Austrian
Philosopher

Wittgenstein began life in Vienna but trained as an engineer in Berlin and Manchester. Aeronautical interests led him to mathematics and its philosophical foundations, and in 1912 he began studying under Bertrand Russell (*q.v.*) at Cambridge. After the First World War he worked as a schoolteacher and architect before returning to Cambridge early in 1929; there he was made professor in 1939, a post he resigned in 1947.

Wittgenstein published only one short book and a single article in his lifetime, but in the last twenty years of his life he wrote and lectured constantly; much of this material is still being published. His book, a series of short paragraphs

and aphorisms on logical and philosophical topics, was published as *Tractatus Logico-Philosophicus* in 1922 with an introduction by Bertrand Russell.

He was moody, ascetic, intensely serious, given to dark sayings, and there collected around him at Cambridge a group of clever and intensely loyal students with whom he shared his thoughts. Two concerns dominated his thinking: criticism of his own earlier ideas in the *Tractatus* and, implicitly, those of Russell to which it is indebted; and attempts to find a legitimate role for philosophy. Both lines come together in close scrutiny of the use of language. In the *Tractatus* he had argued that the limits of language are the limits of the world, and that investigation of the world is done by science. Anything that is said that is not science is without meaning, and is perhaps just expression or exclamation. His later view was that this was much too narrow a view of language, which is diverse and complex, not reducible to description and exclamation.

Language is used in all sorts of ways for all sorts of social purposes, he argued, and it functions on the basis of rules. This led Wittgenstein to look to the connections between what we can say is the case and what the social make-up of language enables us to say. Our thought and our social life are connected.

P.G. Wodehouse (1881–1975) American, ex-English
Novelist and playwright

Pelham Grenville Wodehouse was the author of a hundred books, nearly four hundred song lyrics, and more than fifty plays and musical comedies. He was born in Guildford on 15 October 1881. After an education at Dulwich College, he entered the world of freelance journalism and began publishing, between 1902 and 1907, a series of novels about public school life. In 1905 his first songs were performed in the London theatre, soon after which he began commuting between London and New York, where he became established as a writer of comic short stories and light novels. In 1917 his partnership with composer Jerome Kern and librettist Guy Bolton brought about a new style of musical which discarded the chorus line and ponderous plots. Concurrently, he proved one of the most prolific novelists in the history of English literature, producing a long succession of novels in which the dizzying convolutions of plot were matched by an extraordinary use of language and a mastery of comic effect. His most famous characters include the archetypal manservant Jeeves and his foolish master Bertie Wooster, the man-about-town Psmith, the grubby opportunist Ukridge, and the dotty peer Clarence, ninth Earl of Emsworth.

LEFT *Woodrow Wilson: a portrait by Edmund C. Tarbell*

Ludwig Wittgenstein

ABOVE *P.G.Wodehouse, a master of comic effect*

ABOVE RIGHT *Virginia Woolf*

In 1940, while living at Le Touquet, Wodehouse was interned by the Germans, and later that year went to Berlin to deliver six Nazi-controlled broadcasts whose intent was woefully misinterpreted in Britain. It was later agreed that what some had taken for treason was merely foolishness worthy of one of Wodehouse's characters. Gradually his reputation was re-established, but although forgiveness was complete, with a knighthood a few weeks before his death in 1975, it is significant that he never again set foot in his native land. There are in his novels rather more re-workings of his private experience than was once thought likely, and if Blandings Castle, the retreat of the Emsworths, could hardly be said to exist, its more plebeian counterpart, the happy suburb of Valley Fields, which figures in so many of his novels, was certainly the Dulwich of his schooldays. By developing a mid-Atlantic approach, Wodehouse was one of few writers to be equally popular in Britain and America.

Virginia Woolf (1882–1941) British
Novelist and critic

Virginia Woolf was born in Kensington, London, the daughter of the eminent biographer and critic Sir Leslie Stephen. Literature and the arts were important in the family environment in which she grew up and she began to write at an early age. When her sister Vanessa married the art critic Clive Bell and moved from Kensington to unfashionable Bloomsbury, Virginia and her brother took a nearby house, and it was from the meetings of their various friends in these houses that what was later to be called the Bloomsbury Group sprang up. Its members, which included the essayist Lytton Strachey, the novelist E.M. Forster, and the economist Maynard Keynes (*q.v.*), shared liberal attitudes and a belief in the central importance in life of personal relationships.

In 1912 Virginia married Leonard Woolf, who was to become a political writer and publisher. Together they founded the publishing house The Hogarth Press in 1917, partly as a therapeutic outlet for Virginia who was a manic-depressive, and partly to encourage new young writers and poets. Virginia Woolf had written literary criticism, and 1915 marked the publication of her first novel, *The Voyage Out*. This and her second novel were fairly conventional, but her experiments with the 'stream of consciousness' technique in *Jacob's Room* (1922) led on to such works as *To the Lighthouse* (1927), a masterpiece and perhaps her greatest novel, and *Orlando* (1928), the latter of great liveliness and imagination whose hero-heroine undergoes not only a sex change but also a journey from Elizabethan times to the present.

The Waves (1931) is the most highly stylized of Virginia Woolf's novels, composed of interior monologues spoken by its six leading characters with poetic interludes between the monologues describing the sun, the waves and the seasons. She was a genuine innovator and a writer of great intelligence and sensibility – a genius in the eyes of many. In 1941, more than usually depressed by the war and by what she took to be the worsening state of her mental health, she committed suicide by drowning.

Wilbur (1867–1912) & Orville Wright
(1871–1948) American
Aviators

It is sometimes difficult to remember that there are people who have lived through the entire history of the aeroplane to date. The first ever powered flight was in the Wright brothers' *Flyer* in 1903, the first fully controlled flight in their *Flyer III* in 1905.

Wilbur Wright was born at Millville, Ohio, on 16 April 1867, Orville at Dayton, Ohio, on 19 August 1871. Both died at Dayton – Orville in 1948, by which time he had seen jet engines, supersonic flight and military aircraft used in two world wars.

They started as bicycle repairers – Orville was a racing cyclist – and they turned to flying after reading an account of successful gliding attempts. The Wright brothers aimed to make a gliding machine that was completely controllable and safe and they even built their own wind-tunnel for their research. Once they had achieved full control in gliding, which included inventing moveable wingtips to control banking, they turned to powered flight. They built an astonishingly lightweight petrol engine and eventually, on 17 December 1903, they made four short powered flights (two by Orville, two by Wilbur), the first in history. They continued to improve the plane until by 1905 they had built *Flyer III*, a biplane with two 'pusher' propellers, launched by catapults and landing on skids. This was a completely controllable plane that was flown in circuits and figures of eight.

The historic invention attracted much less attention than one might expect. They patented the plane and offered it to the American army, eventually getting a reply – an order – in 1908. Wilbur went to Europe and arranged for a French company to go into production and an American company was set up in 1909.

Y

W.B. Yeats (1865–1939) Irish
Poet and playwright

Dublin-born William Butler Yeats was the son of a well-known Irish painter, John Butler Yeats. Part of his childhood was spent in London, and when he returned to London in his twenties he helped to found the Rhymers' Club, a group of poets. His own earliest poetry was much pre-occupied with the melancholy world of 'the Celtic twilight', as he called it; his much-anthologized poem, 'The Lake Isle of Innisfree' dates from this early period. Yeats's love for the Irish nationalist leader Maud Gonne led to an

interest in politics and to the poetry that he wrote about the Irish 'troubles', and the need for independence from Britain that eventually led to the rising of 1916 and the establishment of Home Rule.

A man of wide intellectual curiosity, Yeats also interested himself in the revival of Irish theatre, and together with Lady Gregory, George Moore and others he founded the Abbey Theatre, encouraged new Irish playwrights, among them Synge, to write for it, and began himself to write plays. He was also interested in magic and the occult, and in the less orthodox religious beliefs such as theosophy. In 1917 he married a woman much younger than himself, a spiritualist-medium named Georgie Hyde-Lees, and under her influence wrote *A Vision* (1925), a curious work of occult philosophy and magic.

Obsession with the occult influenced Yeats's later poetry, and critical opinion has remained divided as to whether the influence was beneficial or not. Certainly, Yeats's mature and late poetry, with its metaphysical content and mystical sounds, is deeply fascinating and vastly different from the less complex poetry of his earlier years. For his *Collected Poems* (1933) Yeats rewrote many of his earlier poems in accordance with the stylistic and philosophical prejudices of his

ABOVE *Orville (left) and Wilbur Wright;* ABOVE LEFT *Wilbur Wright in a biplane of 1908*

Augustus John's portrait of W.B. Yeats in 1917, the year he married

maturity. Among the best known of the individual poems are 'Sailing to Byzantium', 'Easter: 1916' and 'Leda and the Swan'.

Though some people disliked his aristocratic, anti-democratic political stance, Yeats in his later years was very much the popular idea of the great poet: loaded with honours, among them the Nobel Prize for Literature, he was a member of the Irish senate, and was looked up to by many of the young as a sage.

Z

Babe Zaharias (1914–56) American
Athlete and golfer

In the 1920s and 1930s, despite the emancipation that had grown in the years of the First World War, women's sport was still at its 'dog walking on its hind legs' stage – a curiosity rather than a serious provider of excitement and entertainment. After 'The Babe' no one could take women's sport anything but seriously. She competed, it was said, 'like a man', and though not everyone would have taken that as a compliment, she herself would never have

dreamed of giving less than total dedication, drive and aggression to any game she played. As a result, almost inevitably, she excelled at all of them.

As a schoolgirl Babe Didrikson (nicknamed Babe because she could hit a baseball in the uncompromising manner of the legendary Babe Ruth [*q.v.*]) excelled at all track and field athletic events, at basketball and at golf. At the age of eighteen, in 1932, she won the team title at the United States Women's Athletic Championships *on her own*, winning five of the eight events. Later that year she was the outstanding woman performer at the Los Angeles Olympic Games: she won both the 80-metres hurdles and the javelin, and was demoted to second place in the high jump only on a technical objection to her style of jumping.

From athletics Babe Didrikson – later Babe Zaharias – turned to golf and took to it with a dedication and a power exemplified by her 315-yard drive from the tee. By the mid-1940s she was well-nigh unbeatable by any woman, and in 1947 her win in the British Women's Championship was the culmination of seventeen successive tournament victories.

Her drawing power on the young and hitherto humble women's professional golf circuit was such that she could make around $100,000 in a good year, despite fast failing health. By the time she died of cancer in 1956 much of the groundwork for the emancipation of women's sport was complete; her share had been incalculable.

RIGHT *Babe Zaharias: she competed, it was said, 'like a man'*

Acknowledgments

The publishers have taken all possible care to trace and acknowledge the ownership of all the illustrations. If we have made an incorrect attribution we apologise sincerely and will be happy to correct the entry in any reprint, provided that we receive notification.

Sources in roman type indicate the owners of paintings and photographs; those in italics refer to illustration sources only.

6 Camera Press, London (photo Karsh): 7 Fiat Auto (UK): 8 Colorific!, London: 9 ABOVE Illustrated London News Picture Library, London; BELOW Camera Press (photo Halsman): 10 ABOVE LEFT Space Frontiers, Havant; ABOVE RIGHT United States Information Service; BELOW *British Film Institute, London*: 11 Daily Telegraph Colour Library, London (photo Munzig): 12 ABOVE Tate Gallery, London; BELOW Zöe Dominic, London: 13 LEFT Camera Press (photo Mark Gerson); RIGHT Sotheby's, Belgravia: 14 ABOVE Wellcome Institute for the History of Medicine, London; BELOW Camera Press (photo Karsh): 15 IBA, Zurich: 16 Colorific! (photo Terence Spencer): 17 The Observer, London (photo Jane Bown): 18 ABOVE Camera Press (photo Werner Braun); BELOW LEFT Royal Opera House, Covent Garden (poster design by Tim O'Brien); BELOW RIGHT Universal Edition, London: 19 *British Film Institute*: 20 ABOVE BBC Hulton Picture Library, London; BELOW National Portrait Gallery, London: 21 Colorific! (photo Eliot Elisofan): 22 ABOVE LEFT Nobel Foundation, Sweden; ABOVE RIGHT Camera Press; BELOW IBA: 23 LEFT Camera Press (photo Kevin Dowling); RIGHT Central Press, London (*Hamlyn Group Picture Library, Feltham*): 24 ABOVE *Royal Institution, London (Cooper-Bridgeman Library, London)*; BELOW The Royal Society, London: 25 Philadelphia Museum of Art: Louise & Walter Arensberg Collection: 26 United Artists (*British Film Institute*): 27 LEFT Phillips Collection, Washington DC; RIGHT Mansell Collection, London: 28 National Portrait Gallery, London: 29 ABOVE *British Film Institute*; BELOW Africana Museum, Johannesburg: 30 Erich Auerbach, London: 31 ABOVE Camera Press (photo Karsh); BELOW BBC Hulton Picture Library: 32 Rank Xerox: 33 ABOVE The Observer (photo Jane Bown); RIGHT Mander & Mitchenson Theatre Collection, London: 34 Erich Auerbach: 35 ABOVE Colorific!; BELOW BBC Hulton Picture Library: 36 Colorific!: 37 ABOVE *British Film Institute*; BELOW John Hillelson Agency, London (photo Constantine Manos): 38 Imperial War Museum, London: 39 LEFT Collection Brisgand, France; RIGHT National Portrait Gallery, London: 40 James Austin, Cambridge: 41 Fondation Cousteau, Neuilly: 42 ABOVE Camera Press; BELOW BBC, London: 43 The Kobal Collection, London: 44 Snark International, Paris: 45 LEFT Museum of Modern Art, New York (Mrs Simon Guggenheim Fund); RIGHT Weidenfeld & Nicolson Archives, London (photo Jerry Bauer): 46 Archiv für Kunst und Geschichte, Berlin: 47 LEFT Popperfoto, London; RIGHT Private Collection, London: 48 *British Film Institute*: 49 Harper's Bazaar, London (*Weidenfeld & Nicolson Archives*): 50 Colorific! (photo Eliot Elisofan): 51 Philadelphia Museum of Art (*Cooper-Bridgeman Library*): 52 ABOVE Mander & Mitchenson Theatre Collection; BELOW By courtesy of the Kodak Museum, Harrow: 53 Wellcome Institute for the History of Medicine: 54 IBA: 55 ABOVE *British Film Institute*; BELOW Illustrated London News Picture Library: 56 ABOVE LEFT IBA; ABOVE RIGHT Weidenfeld & Nicolson Archives: 57 Colorific! (photo Eliot Elisofan): 58 BBC Hulton Picture Library: 59 Camera Press: 60 ABOVE John Hillelson Agency (photo Mary Ellen Mark); BELOW Godfrey Argent, London: 61 ABOVE Royal Opera House, Covent Garden; BELOW LEFT Department of Audio Visual Communication, St Mary's Hospital Medical School, London; BELOW RIGHT The Royal Society, London: 62 Mike Davis Studios (photo Jesse Davis): 63 ABOVE Ford Archives/Henry Ford Museum, Dearborn, Michigan, USA; BELOW National Motor Museum, Beaulieu: 64 *British Film Institute*: 65 ABOVE Library of Congress, Washington DC; BELOW Photri, Virginia: 66 ABOVE EMI; BELOW Colorific!: 67 *Weidenfeld & Nicolson Archives*: 68 *British Film Institute*: 69 Mansell Collection: 70 ABOVE Bern Schwartz, California; BELOW Erich Auerbach: 71 National Portrait Gallery, Smithsonian Institution, Washington DC: 72 ABOVE Amanda Todd (*The Bodley Head*, London); BELOW *British Film Institute*: 73 John Hillelson Agency (photo Elliot Erwitt): 74 ABOVE John Frost Historical Newspaper Service, New Barnet; BELOW John Hillelson Agency (photo Rene Burri): 75 Colorific! (photo Larry Burrows): 76 ABOVE *George Allen & Unwin, London*; BELOW Royal Geographical Society, London: 77 Camera Press (photo Halsman): 78 Colorific! (photo Jaeger/LIFE): 79 Camera Press (photo William Warbey): 80 The Royal Society, London: 81 Space Frontiers: 82 ABOVE LEFT Weidenfeld & Nicolson Archives; ABOVE RIGHT IBA; BELOW National Portrait Gallery, London: 83 Camera Press (photo Karsh): 84 ABOVE Mary Evans Picture Library, London; CENTRE *Weidenfeld & Nicolson Archives*; BELOW Courtesy of the Art Institute of Chicago: 85 MGM (*British Film Institute*): 86 Colorific!: 87 ABOVE W & N Archives; BELOW National Portrait Gallery, London: 88 Colorific! (photo Frances Miller): 89 ABOVE Erich Auerbach; BELOW National Portrait Gallery, Smithsonian Institution, Washington DC: 90 LEFT John Hillelson Agency (photo Gosset/Sygma); RIGHT Camera Press (photo Les Wilson): 91 BBC Hulton Picture Library: 93 Ronald Grant Archive, London: 94 LEFT National Portrait Gallery, London; RIGHT By kind permission of Penguin Books, London: 95 ABOVE IBA; BELOW Novosti Press Agency, London: 96 Courtesy of Unilever (photo Geoff Goode): 97 BOTH Camera Press: 98 BBC Hulton Picture Library: 99 ABOVE Colorific! (TIME Inc. Archives): 100 Illustrated London News Picture Library: 101 William Sewell (*Weidenfeld & Nicolson Archives*): 102 Illustrated London News Picture Library: 103 The Kobal Collection: 104 IBA: 105 Colorific! (photo Dmitri Kessel): 106 Camera Press (photo Bob Whitaker): 107 ABOVE Bern Schwartz; BELOW John Hillelson Agency (photo Inge Morath): 108 Albright-Knox Art Gallery, Buffalo (Room of Contemporary Art Fund): 109 Tate Gallery, London: 110 ABOVE Camera Press (photo Karsh); BELOW Colorific! (photo Eisenstaedt): 111 Maria Montessori Training Organization, London NW3: 112 Bern Schwartz: 113 ABOVE Sony (UK); BELOW Tim Graham, London: 114 Colorific! (photo Jaeger/LIFE): 115 ABOVE Weidenfeld & Nicolson Archives; BELOW Scala, Florence: 116 Camera Press (photo Jitendra Arya): 117 Collection Viollet, Paris: 118 Camera Press (photo John Bulmer): 119 ABOVE Mike Davis Studios (photo Jesse Davis); BELOW BBC Hulton Picture Library: 120 Bern Schwartz: 121 LEFT National Theatre, London; RIGHT Mansell Collection (photo Hoppé): 122 ABOVE Weidenfeld & Nicolson Archives; CENTRE Popperfoto, London; BELOW By kind permission of Penguin Books: 123 ABOVE Camera Press; BELOW BBC Hulton Picture Library: 124 BBC Hulton Picture Library: 125 Colorific!: 126 ABOVE Mick Alexander, London; BELOW IBA: 127 Museum of Modern Art, New York (Lillie P. Bliss Bequest) (*Giraudon, Paris*): 128 Ronald Grant Archive: 129 ABOVE Courtesy of Searle Pharmaceuticals, Bucks. (photo Geoff Goode); BELOW BBC Hulton Picture Library: 130 ABOVE Museum of Modern Art, New York (Cooper-Bridgeman Library); BELOW Camera Press (photo Karsh): 131 National Portrait Gallery, Smithsonian Institution, Washington DC: 132 ABOVE Daily Telegraph Colour Library (photo C. de Jaeger); BELOW MGM (*National Film Archives*): 133 Archiv für Kunst und Geschichte, Berlin: 134 LEFT Mme Mante Proust (*Snark International, Paris*); RIGHT Syndication International, London: 135 Archiv für Kunst und Geschichte: 136 *British Film Institute*: 137 ABOVE Mary Evans Picture Library; BELOW Mansell Collection: 138 ABOVE Photri, Virginia; BELOW Tate Gallery: 139 Bern Schwartz: 140 Beaverbrook Art Gallery, New Brunswick: 141 ABOVE Camera Press (photo Snowdon); BELOW BBC Hulton Picture Library: 142 The Royal Society: 143 ABOVE Space Frontiers; BELOW Popperfoto: 144 ABOVE John Hillelson Agency (photo Gisèle Freund); BELOW Nobel Foundation: 145 EMI: 146 ABOVE Archiv für Kunst und Geschichte; BELOW John Hillelson Agency (photo Jim McHugh): 147 Colorific! (photo George Silk/LIFE): 148 ABOVE Bern Schwartz; BELOW Space Frontiers: 149 National Trust, London: 150 LEFT The Royal Society, London; RIGHT Camera Press: 151 LEFT Erich Auerbach; RIGHT Archiv für Kunst und Geschichte: 152 Colorific! (photo John Dominis/LIFE): 153 Popperfoto: 154 ABOVE Erich Auerbach; BELOW Camera Press: 155 ABOVE Zöe Dominic; BELOW John Hillelson Agency (photo Wayne Miller): 156 Novosti Press Agency: 157 W & N Archives: 158 LEFT John Hillelson Agency (photo Gisèle Freund); RIGHT Sotheby's: 159 LEFT Universal Edition; RIGHT Erich Auerbach: 160 ABOVE BBC Hulton Picture Library; BELOW Reg Wilson Photography, London: 161 ABOVE Erich Auerbach; BELOW J. W. Chester/Wilhelm Hansen, London: 162 Zöe Dominic: 163 ABOVE National Portrait Gallery, London; BELOW IBA: 164 ABOVE BBC Hulton Picture Library; BELOW Colorific! (photo Paul Conkin): 165 Robert Hupka (*Weidenfeld & Nicolson Archives*): 166 ABOVE The Royal Society, London; BELOW Edward Morgan (*Chatto & Windus, London*): 167 Angelo Hornak, London: 168 Cecil Beaton (*Sotheby's*): 169 ABOVE Photri, Virginia; BELOW Camera Press (photo Jan Kopek): 170 BOTH EMI: 171 Camera Press (photo Halsman): 172 Weidenfeld & Nicolson Archives: 173 ABOVE Camera Press (photo Mark Gerson); BELOW London School of Economics (*Cooper-Bridgeman Library*): 174 ABOVE IBA; BELOW Associated Press, London (*BIPAC, London*): 175 Hemdale Films, London (*British Film Institute*): 176 John Hillelson Agency (photo Gisèle Freund): 177 John Stockdale (*Jonathan Cape, London*): 178 ABOVE Science Museum, London; BELOW John Hillelson Agency (photo Burt Glinn): 179 The Observer (photo Jane Bown): 180 ABOVE Photri, Virginia; BELOW IBA: 181 LEFT Camera Press (photo Tom Blau); RIGHT John Hillelson Agency (photo Gisèle Freund): 182 Illustrated London News Picture Library: 183 ABOVE Glasgow Art Gallery; BELOW Sport & General, London.

Illustrations on pages 25, 27 LEFT, 51, 84 BELOW, 108 and 140 are copyright © A.D.A.G.P., Paris, 1981; those on pages 46, 82 BELOW, 127 and 134 LEFT are copyright © S.P.A.D.E.M., Paris, 1981.